WORLD HISTORY
FOR
A GLOBAL AGE
BOOK 2

JACK ABRAMOWITZ

Globe Book Company, Inc.

New York • Cleveland • Toronto

Jack Abramowitz, Ph.D.

Dr. Abramowitz has had a distinguished career as a teacher of social studies. His work includes over twenty years of classroom experience at a variety of levels, and curriculum development and consulting for school districts in Oregon, Ohio, New York, Texas, California, Indiana, Georgia, and New Hampshire. Dr. Abramowitz is the author of numerous texts and journal articles in the social sciences, and speaks frequently to teacher and other professional groups. He was Visiting Professor at the University of London's Goldsmith's College.

Consultants:
Donald Schwartz, Ph.D.

Dr. Schwartz is Assistant Principal of Social Studies,
Sheepshead Bay High School, Brooklyn, New York.

Sara Moore, M.A.

Ms. Moore is a teacher of History and English,
Palo Duro High School, Amarillo, Texas.

Editorial Staff

Project Editor: Adriane R. Ruggiero
Map Editor: Patricia A. Rodriguez
Photo Editor: Adelaide Garvin Ungerland

Photo Acknowledgments begin on page 250

Cover Art and Design: Bass and Goldman Associates
Maps by: General Cartography, Mel Erikson

Second Edition 1987

ISBN: 0-87065-648-1

PRINTED IN THE UNITED STATES OF AMERICA   3 4 5 6 7 8 9

Contents

Maps, Charts, and Graphs

Enrichments

Unit 1
Imperialist Powers Seek Colonies

By the 1800s the leading industrial countries of the world were Great Britain, the United States, Germany, France, and Italy. They needed raw materials for their factories. They also needed places to sell their goods. Raw materials and markets for goods were to be found in Africa, the Middle East, Asia, and Latin America. In time, the industrial countries took control of these parts of the world. Such control is called imperialism.

In Unit 1, you will read about the causes and results of imperialism. You will learn how Great Britain took over India and made it a colony. You will also learn how European countries spread their influence in China. At first, they set up trading posts there. One such trading post is shown in the picture opposite. By the early 1900s, Japan had become an industrial ccuntry. It began to seek colonies, too. Imperialist countries were able to spread their rule to Africa and Southeast Asia. Finally, you will learn how the people in colonies felt about being ruled.

In Unit 1, you will read the following chapters:

Chapter 1

Imperialism and Racism

> **Understanding Global History**
>
> Think about the following statements as you read about imperialism.
> 1 The culture in which we live influences our view of other people.
> 2 The nations of the world depend upon each other economically.
> 3 Contact among peoples and nations can lead to cultural changes.

This cartoon shows Great Britain as an octopus grabbing colonies.

Learning New Words and Terms

The following words are used in this chapter. Think about the meaning of each one.

imperialism: the system in which one country takes over other countries and rules them as colonies

parent country: a country that takes over another country and rules it as a colony

Western: connected with the ideas, customs, and ways of life of Europe and America

racism: the belief held by people of one race that they are better than people of other races

Think As You Read

1. Which nations were the imperialist powers in the 1800s and 1900s?
2. Why did nations engage in imperialism?
3. What was the connection between imperialism and racism?

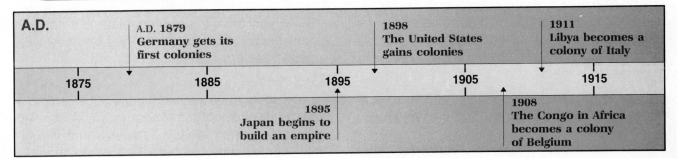

A.D.

A.D. **1879**
Germany gets its first colonies

1898
The United States gains colonies

1911
Libya becomes a colony of Italy

1875   1885   1895   1905   1915

1895
Japan begins to build an empire

1908
The Congo in Africa becomes a colony of Belgium

The Need for Raw Materials and Markets

Because of the Industrial Revolution, countries needed more and more raw materials for their factories. They did not always have enough in their own countries. Even when they did have enough, the raw materials were often costly. Some of these materials were much cheaper in other parts of the world.

Besides raw materials, industrial countries needed markets in which to sell their finished goods. Industrial countries began to look for raw materials and markets in other lands.

What Is Imperialism?

The industrial countries began to take over other countries. When one country takes over other countries to rule them, it is starting an empire. The whole idea of building an empire is called **imperialism**.

There has been imperialism since early times. The early Romans had an empire. The kind of imperialism that began in the 1800s was different from that of the Roman Empire. In the new kind of imperialism, the industrial countries began to take over and rule the less-developed countries.

The Industrial Countries Begin Their Empires

In the 1800s, most of the industrial countries were found in Europe. They included Great Britain, France, Germany, Italy, Belgium, and the Netherlands. Great Britain and France began building empires earlier than the others. They began during the 1600s and 1700s. Part of their empires was land in America. This land that they controlled gave them much money.

Germany did not get its first overseas colony until 1879. At that time it took land in Samoa. Samoa is the name of some islands in the Pacific. Germany also gained land in Africa. Italy got Libya, in North Africa, in 1911. Belgium began to take over the Congo in the 1870s and 1880s. The Congo became an official colony in 1908. The Congo, in Africa, is now mainly the country of Zaire.

Non-European Countries Gain Colonies

Two countries outside of Europe also began to gain colonies. The United States gained colonies from Spain after winning the Spanish-American War in 1898. These colonies were Puerto Rico, Guam, and the Philippine Islands. Cuba also belonged to Spain until the Spanish-American War. Cuba became an independent nation instead of a colony. Even though Cuba was independent, it was still under the influence of the United States.

Japan, in Asia, began its empire in 1895. Japan took control of Taiwan in 1895. In 1910, Japan took complete control of Korea. In 1931, it took over all of Manchuria.

"Have" and "Have Not" Countries

Great Britain was the strongest imperialist nation. The British and the French held most of the richest colonies. Because of this, the British and French were called the "have" countries. Germany, Italy, Belgium, and other European nations did not gain as much wealth from their colonies. They were thought of as the "have not" imperialist nations. After a while, problems began to come up between the "have" and the "have not" imperial powers.

How the Parent Countries Thought of Their Colonies

The imperialist, or **parent**, **countries** often thought of the people in their colonies as children. The parent countries thought that they had to teach the people in their colonies how to live and behave.

Because the countries they ruled were not industrial, the parent countries thought they were backward. The people in the parent countries did not understand the customs, traditions, and cultures of their colonies. Most of the parent countries were in lands west of their colonies. Their way of life became known as **Western**. Because the colonies had different customs, the parent countries thought that the colonies needed to learn how to live the "right way." This meant the Western way.

Great Britain—The Leading Imperialist Nation

By the 1800s, Great Britain was the leading imperialist nation. Most British people were proud that their country was a world power. To keep its empire, Great Britain kept a large army and a strong navy. In the late 1800s, the British people liked to claim that "the sun never sets on the British Empire." If you look at the map opposite, you could see that the claim was true. British colonies included Canada, India, Burma, South Africa, Rhodesia (now called Zimbabwe), and many other small and large lands. Somewhere in the world there was always daylight in the British Empire.

Reasons for Taking Colonies

There were three main reasons imperialist countries took over foreign colonies.

- They wanted to get raw materials and markets for their goods.
- They wanted places where their ships and merchants could stop safely to get food and supplies. This was important in case of war.
- Having colonies made a parent country important. It made the imperialist country feel powerful. Even though some countries did not gain much from their colonies, they felt they were world powers.

Ideas of Racism

The strong feelings of nationalism in Europe, in the 1800s, helped imperialism grow. Along with nationalism went ideas of **racism**—the thought that people of one race were better than people of another race.

Most of the people in the parent countries had white or light skin. Most of the people in the colonies had black, brown, or yellow skin. People in the parent countries thought that they were more advanced than the people of their colonies. They said that this proved that white people were a superior, or better race. All other people, they said, belonged to inferior, or less able, races. They even tried to prove their racist ideas scientifically.

What Is Wrong with Racism

Scientists today have studied the idea of racism. They have studied people of many races and colors. They have learned that skin color does not make a person better or worse. Scientists today say that there is no superior or inferior race. There are people of high intelligence and high ability in all races.

In addition, historians now know more about civilizations of the past. They know that the great early civilizations were not found in Europe. They were found in Asia, the Middle East, and Africa. During the Middle Ages, the people of Europe were backward compared with the people in many parts of Asia, the Middle East, and Africa.

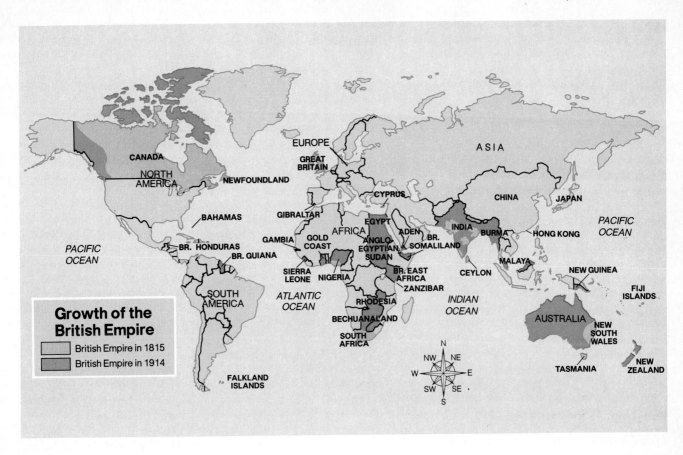

Growth of the British Empire

British Empire in 1815
British Empire in 1914

While art, science, mathematics, and literature were very advanced in Asia, the Middle East, and Africa, culture in the countries of Europe was growing far more slowly.

The people in Europe in the 1800s had little or no idea about the cultures of the countries they ruled. Their racist ideas got in their way. For the most part, Europeans were not interested in the history or culture of their colonies. They thought of the countries they ruled as backward. Because each parent country thought that their own culture was better, they tried to make their colonies follow that culture.

The "White Man's Burden"

People in the industrial countries thought that it was their duty to rule the countries they felt were backward. Most of the colonies were in Asia, Africa, and South America. The people in most of the colonies were not white. The people in the parent countries were mostly white. People in the parent countries started talking about the "white man's burden." They meant that it was the duty of

white people to bring civilization to the less-industrial countries and people.

People in industrial countries used the idea of the "white man's burden" as their reason for ruling other people. In some cases, imperialist countries did bring better health care, more centrally organized government, and more industry to their colonies. While they were bringing these good things, they also destroyed some of the good things that the colonies already had.

The Effects of Imperialism

Imperialism and racism caused some problems between peoples of different cultures in many parts of the world. Some of these problems are still with us today.

In spite of the problems, ideas were exchanged. The imperialist countries brought their Western ideas of trade, industry, transportation, health care, and government to their colonies. At the same time, non-Western ideas, customs, cultures, and religions became better known in Europe and the United States.

Exercises

A. Finding the Main Ideas:
Put a check next to the sentences that give the main ideas of what you have just read.

_____ **1.** Imperialism was found in early times.

_____ **2.** There were imperialist powers in Europe.

_____ **3.** There was racism in the world.

_____ **4.** Imperialist countries had reasons for their actions.

_____ **5.** There were links between racism, nationalism, and imperialism.

B. What Did You Read?
Choose the answer that best completes each sentence. Write the letter of your answer in the space provided.

_____ **1.** The major imperialist countries of the 1800s did *not* include
   a. France.
   b. China.
   c. Italy.
   d. Belgium.

_____ **2.** Because of the Spanish-American War, the United States took over
   a. Cuba and Puerto Rico.
   b. Cuba and the Philippines.
   c. Puerto Rico and the Philippines.
   d. Puerto Rico and Panama.

_____ **3.** Great Britain's colonies included
   a. India, Syria, and South Africa.
   b. Canada, Rhodesia, and Arabia.
   c. Burma, India, and Canada.
   d. Syria, Burma, and South Africa.

_____ **4.** The "have not" imperialist countries did *not* include
   a. France.
   b. Belgium.
   c. Italy.
   d. Germany.

6

C. Checking for Details:

Read each statement. Put an F in the space next to each statement if it is a fact. Put an O in that space if it is an opinion. Remember that facts can be proved, but opinions cannot.

_____ **1.** Cuba was under United States influence after the Spanish-American War.

_____ **2.** Having colonies is better than not having colonies.

_____ **3.** Industrialism was one cause of modern imperialism.

_____ **4.** Great Britain was the leading imperialist country of the world.

_____ **5.** Imperialism brought new ideas about trade, industry, and culture to colonial areas.

_____ **6.** Canada was Great Britain's most important colony.

_____ **7.** One reason nations wanted to be imperialist powers was that they wanted to be important in the world.

_____ **8.** Imperialists believed that one race was better than others.

D. Word Meanings:

Match each word in Column A with the correct meaning in Column B. Write the letter of each answer in the space provided.

Column A
_____ **1.** imperialism
_____ **2.** racism
_____ **3.** parent country
_____ **4.** Western

Column B
a. a country that has colonies
b. the system in which a country takes over other countries and rules them as colonies
c. having to do with the ideas of Europe and the United States
d. believing in one's country
e. the belief that one race is superior to another

E. Understanding Global History

On page 2 you read about three factors in global history. Which of these factors applies to each statement listed below? Fill in the number of the correct statement on page 2 in the space provided. If no factor applies, fill in the word NONE.

_____ **1.** Even though there were disagreements between cultures, parent countries and colonies exchanged ideas.

_____ **2.** The imperialist countries wanted the raw materials and the markets of faraway lands.

_____ **3.** The imperialist countries did not understand or want to understand the customs, traditions, and cultures of other peoples.

Chapter 2

India—From the Maurya Empire to the Rule of the Moguls

The Taj Mahal is one of the most famous buildings in the world. It was built by the Mogul ruler of India, Shah Jahan, as a tomb for his wife.

Learning New Words and Terms

The following words are used in this chapter. Think about the meaning of each one.

non-violence: dealing with problems in a peaceful way

suttee: a custom in which a wife must die when her husband dies; the wife throws herself on her husband's funeral pile.

Deccan: the southern part of India, especially the large plateau in the central part of the south of India

Mogul: one of the Muslim rulers of India in the 1500s and 1600s A.D.

regent: a person who rules in place of a ruler who is too young or not able to rule for other reasons

Think As You Read

1. How did Greek ideas reach India in early times?
2. What important contributions were made during the Gupta dynasty?
3. What were the relations between Hindus and Muslims in India?
4. How did Akbar and the Mogul dynasty influence India?

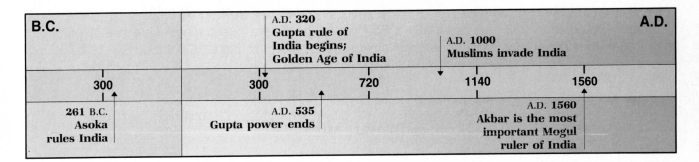

B.C.					A.D.
		A.D. **320** Gupta rule of India begins; Golden Age of India		A.D. **1000** Muslims invade India	
300		300	720	1140	1560
261 B.C. Asoka rules India		A.D. **535** Gupta power ends		A.D. **1560** Akbar is the most important Mogul ruler of India	

India's Early Civilizations

Before any Western countries came to rule India, there were great civilizations in India. India, in fact, had some of the world's great early cities. Along the Indus River, there were two great cultures. One was Harappa (hah-RAHP-uh). The other was Mohenjo-Daro (moh-HEN-joh-DAH-roh). Harappa had a system of writing. It also had ties with Mesopotamia. Both Harappa and Mohenjo-Daro lasted from about 2500 B.C. to 1500 B.C.

Around 1500 B.C., Indo-Aryans, or Aryans, from Persia started to move into the Indus Valley. They gained control of the valley. Unlike the people already there, the Aryans were not city people. They raised flocks of animals.

It was the Aryan people who wrote the first great religious books of India—the Vedas. It was also the Aryan people who started the caste system. The caste system was outlawed in the twen-

tieth century. However, aspects of the caste system still continue in some parts of India.

The Effect of Alexander's Armies

Alexander the Great's armies invaded India from 327 to 325 B.C. During that time, Greek ideas began to spread through the parts of India that were ruled by Alexander. Just after Alexander's army left, big changes began to take place.

The Maurya Empire

In the 300s B.C., after Alexander's army left India, the kingdom of the Maurya (MAWR-yah) family became an empire. The Maurya Empire covered most of India, except for the south. It also included most of what is now Afghanistan. Maurya rule lasted from 321 B.C. to 184 B.C. Maurya rulers had contacts with Syria, Egypt, and Sri Lanka. Their culture used ideas from Greece and Persia, but it was mainly a culture of India.

Asoka, A Great Maurya Ruler

The most famous of the Maurya rulers was Asoka (uh-SOH-kuh). He began his rule by going to war. Asoka wanted as much land as possible. After a bloody battle, in about 261 B.C., he changed completely.

Asoka gave up wars to gain land. He became a Buddhist and began to practice **non-violence.** Non-violence means dealing with problems in a peaceful way. He encouraged people to change to Buddhism. He also made Buddhism the empire's official religion. However, Asoka allowed all religions to exist in peace. Asoka sent missionaries to other countries to spread Buddhism.

Asoka was a great ruler. He made his government work well. He tried to help people live good lives. Asoka put up stone pillars with great sayings on them. Some of those pillars are still standing today.

The End of the Maurya Empire

After Asoka died in 232 B.C., the Maurya Empire began to fall apart. Instead of one great empire, there were many smaller kingdoms in northern India. These kingdoms kept up contact with empires in nearby central Asia.

Some of the central Asian peoples invaded parts of India. Once again, the invading armies brought Greek ideas with them.

Other parts of India kept up trade with other lands. They traded goods and shared ideas with people from central Asia, the Roman Empire, and China.

The Gupta Dynasty Begins

In the 300s and 400s A.D., a new dynasty, or ruling family, began to grow stronger. It was the Gupta dynasty. The Gupta dynasty gained control of about the same area that the Maurya dynasty held. The Gupta period lasted from A.D. 320 to A.D. 535. Gupta rulers brought a "Golden Age" to India.

The Gupta "Golden Age"

The Gupta rulers were interested in furthering education in India. Contact with Greeks and

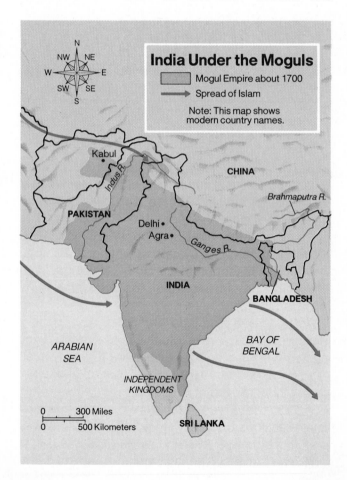

10

Arabs helped them see the need for education. During the Gupta period, India became known for its fine schools. Indians studied science, medicine, and mathematics. India was also a place of great works of art. The Gupta period was a "Golden Age" for India. Indian literature, art, and sculpture blossomed.

The culture of India became important in other countries as well. Both Burma and Thailand were affected by Indian culture. Indian art spread to Cambodia and parts of what is now Indonesia.

Indian mathematicians invented a new way of writing numbers. Arab traders liked the new number system and began to use it. They taught it to Europeans. The Europeans thought that the Arabs invented it. Europeans called it Arabic numerals. We still use the system today, and we still call it Arabic numerals.

Women in the Gupta Empire

During the Gupta dynasty, women held a high status in India. Some women served as village leaders and as governors of areas.

During this period, however, the custom of **suttee** began to spread through India. Suttee was a custom in which a wife was expected to die when her husband died. Usually, the man's body was burned on a pile of sticks and the wife threw herself into the fire. Suttee did not say that a husband was expected to die if his wife died. The custom seems to show that even though women held high positions, there were different standards for men and women. The custom of suttee continued even until the early 1900s. It has since been outlawed by the Indian government.

Buddhism During the Gupta Period

Hinduism was still the most important religion of India. Buddhism, however, still stayed strong. Buddhism spread out from India. It became an important religion in China and other Asian lands. This spreading of a religious belief shows how changes take place because of contacts between people and nations.

Gupta Power Comes to an End

After the early Gupta emperors died, Gupta power grew weaker. Tribes from central Asia began to invade India. The invasions helped to bring about the end of the Gupta dynasty.

A statue of Buddha.

Now, India was open to attack from other invaders. Muslim warriors, Huns, and other Asian invaders poured into northern India. Most of the invaders accepted the Hindu religion.

The Muslim invaders, however, kept their faith in Islam. They tried to convert Hindus to Islam, as well. Bad feelings came about between religious groups. These bad feelings remained a part of Indian life for the next 1,400 years.

The Southern Part of India

Neither the Maurya Empire nor the Gupta Empire reached all the way to southern India. The Islamic invaders did not reach southern India either. Southern India had its own kingdoms and rulers. Local dynasties ruled different parts of the **Deccan,** or southern, lands until the 1300s. The Dravidian peoples lived at the very southern part of India.

More Muslim Invasions

Greater numbers of Muslim invaders began to raid India. These raids started about A.D. 1000.

For more than 400 years, the invaders destroyed parts of India. The invasions added to the bad feelings between Hindus and Muslims.

The Mogul Emperors

In the early 1500s, a new group of Muslims defeated northern India. They were led by a man named Babur. The Indians thought that Babur was a Mongol. They used the word **Mogul** to describe Babur and his army. The Moguls really came from west of India. They came from Turkey and Afghanistan.

Babur started a new dynasty in India. He ruled until 1530. He was a very able ruler. Babur's grandson Akbar ruled India during the greatest time of the Moguls.

Akbar the Great

Akbar began his rule at the age of 14. At first, a **regent,** or guardian, did most of the ruling. In 1560, Akbar fired his regent. Akbar began to rule himself. He then took over more land for his empire.

Akbar believed that people of different religions should live in peace together. He tried to take ideas from Islam, Hinduism, other Indian religions, and Christianity and make one religion out of them. He felt that the most important thing was a belief in one God. After Akbar's death, in 1605, the religion he tried to start came to an end.

The End of the Mogul Empire

There were several more Mogul emperors after Akbar. Art, literature, and architecture stayed great during Mogul times.

Akbar had tried to make relations between Hindus and Muslims better. After he died, the bad feelings returned. Most of the Mogul emperors

This picture shows Akbar the Great.

that came after Akbar tried to make Islam the religion of India. Some of the emperors treated Hindus badly. India was again divided by religious beliefs.

The last strong Mogul emperor died in 1707. The empire became a group of kingdoms. Often the kingdoms fought with each other.

Exercises

A. Finding the Main Ideas:

Put a check next to the sentences that give the main ideas of what you have just read.

_____ **1.** Alexander the Great took over part of India.

_____ **2.** In India, bad feelings between Hindus and Muslims go back many centuries.

_____ **3.** The culture of India spread to Cambodia and Thailand.

_____ **4.** Many other areas of the world affected the culture of India.

_____ **5.** There were three great dynasties with empires that ruled India.

_____ **6.** The Dravidians lived in the southern part of India.

B. What Did You Read?

Choose the answer that best completes each sentence. Write the letter of your answer in the space provided.

_____ **1.** After the fall of the Maurya Empire, India traded with all the following *except*
   a. central Asia.
   b. China.
   c. Japan.
   d. Rome.

_____ **2.** During the Gupta period, India became known for its
   a. science.
   b. medicine.
   c. schools.
   d. ability in all of the above.

_____ **3.** The custom of suttee had the greatest effect on
   a. Muslims.
   b. Indian warriors.
   c. Buddhists.
   d. Indian women.

_____ **4.** The term Mogul is connected with all of the following *except*
   a. Babur.
   b. Buddhism.
   c. Akbar.
   d. Muslims.

C. Time Line Skills:
In which period of time did each of the following events occur? You may use the text and the time line on page 9 for help:

_____ **1.** Mogul rule of India

_____ **2.** Gupta Empire in India

_____ **3.** Maurya Empire in India

_____ **4.** Invasion of northwest India by peoples from central Asia

D. Understanding What You Have Read:
Tell whether each of the following involves (P) political, (E) economic, (R) religious aspects of Indian life. Place the correct answer in the space provided.

_____ **1.** Buddhism was spread by the Maurya dynasty.

_____ **2.** India traded with Rome and China.

_____ **3.** Hinduism kept on being popular in India.

_____ **4.** The Maurya dynasty ruled India.

_____ **5.** Muslim invaders brought Islam to India.

_____ **6.** Local kingdoms ruled the Deccan area.

_____ **7.** The Mogul Empire came to an end in 1707.

E. Checking for Details:
Read each statement. Put a T in the space next to each statement if it is true. Put an F in that space if it is false. Put an N if you cannot tell from the reading if it is true or false.

_____ **1.** Asoka was a great warrior and a wise king.

_____ **2.** The Gupta dynasty brought a higher status for women in India.

_____ **3.** Buddhism was the most important religion of India.

_____ **4.** The Chinese were more religious than the Indians.

_____ **5.** The "Golden Age" of India was during the time of the Guptas.

_____ **6.** Arabic numerals really came from India.

14

_____ 7. The Muslim invaders of India accepted the Hindu religion.

_____ 8. The Dravidians settled in the southern part of India.

_____ 9. Akbar was a well-educated ruler.

_____ 10. The culture of India spread to Burma and Thailand.

F. Understanding Global History:

On page 8 you read about three factors in global history. Which of these factors applies to each statement listed below? Fill in the number of the correct statement on page 8 in the space provided. If no factor applies, fill in the word NONE.

_____ 1. Buddhism began in India and moved to China and other Asian lands where it became very important.

_____ 2. Invasions by tribes from central Asia in the north of India helped put an end to the Gupta dynasty.

_____ 3. Peoples in central Asia helped to bring Greek culture to India.

Shiva is one of many gods in Hinduism.

Chapter 3

Imperialism Comes to India

Understanding Global History

Think about the following statements as you read this about imperialism in India.
1 Events occurring in one part of the world have influenced developments in other parts of the world.
2 People should learn to understand and appreciate cultures different from their own.
3 Nations borrow and adapt ideas and institutions from other nations.

A Muslim mosque in Delhi, India. The mosque was built by India's Mogul rulers. Mogul power began to weaken in the 1600s.

Learning New Words and Terms

The following words are used in this chapter. Think about the meaning of each one.

rajah: an Indian prince

tariff: a tax on goods coming into a country

sepoys: Indians who fought as soldiers for the British

indirect rule: rule of a land by taking charge of its leaders or institutions; the other land does not become a real colony of the imperialist country

mutiny: a rebellion against the people in charge

direct rule: rule of a colony by the imperialist country

viceroy: person who is in charge of a colony; the viceroy rules in the name of the imperialist country's ruler

segregated: to be kept apart; when people of different races are separated from one another

Think As You Read

1. How did the British gain control over India?
2. How did the Sepoy Mutiny change the way the British controlled India?
3. What benefits did the British claim they brought to India?
4. Why did the Indians dislike British rule?

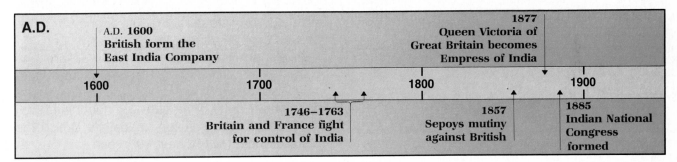

A.D.

A.D. **1600**
British form the East India Company

1877
Queen Victoria of Great Britain becomes Empress of India

1600 — 1700 — 1800 — 1900

1746–1763
Britain and France fight for control of India

1857
Sepoys mutiny against British

1885
Indian National Congress formed

The First Europeans in India

In the 1490s, India had been opened to European trade by an ocean route. Vasco da Gama had found a trade route to India by sailing around Africa. Da Gama sailed for Portugal. Therefore the Portuguese set up the first European trading posts in India.

In the early 1600s, other European nations began to set up trading posts in India. The French, the British, and the Dutch began to trade with India.

Most of the Europeans arrived as India came under the rule of the Mogul Empire. At first the Moguls were strong. After the death of Akbar, in 1605, Mogul power began to weaken. As the Indian government grew weaker, European traders tried to control some of the weaker **rajahs,** or rulers. After 1707, when the last Mogul emperor died, India was left with many small, weak rulers. There was a Mogul ruler until the middle 1800s, but he had no real power.

The British and French in India

British merchants formed the East India Company in 1600. The East India Company was a private trading company. It sold British goods in India and Indian goods in Britain.

A little later in the 1600s, the French East India Company began to trade. The British company wanted to be the only company to trade in India. But, so did the French company.

How British People Felt About Trade With India

At first the British people were happy to get cloth and other goods from India. After a while, British people who made cloth found they were losing business. People in Great Britain were buying less expensive Indian cloth instead of British cloth. British cloth manufacturers began to complain.

Soon, the British government made new laws. British companies could sell cloth and other manufactured goods in India without any **tariff,** or tax, on the goods. India could sell only raw materials to Great Britain. Manufactured goods from India had a tariff so high that they could not be sold in Great Britain.

Now Indian cloth weavers were finding they were out of business because of the British cloth and tariff laws.

Divide and Conquer

The British East India Company began a policy of divide and conquer to control India. The company knew that there were bad feelings between Hindus and Muslims. They knew that some rajahs wanted to take land from their neighbors. They knew that India had people speaking many different languages. The British took sides with different groups in India. This action divided the Indian people more. The French company did the same. By doing this, the British and French made the different Indian groups each feel that the Europeans were fighting on their side.

An Indian rajah.

Wars Between the British and French

By the middle 1700s, France and Great Britain were fighting for control of India. The two countries were also fighting in other places. Great Britain defeated France in a war fought on three continents. In Europe the war was known as the Seven Years' War. The same war was called the French and Indian War in North America. In India the war was called Clive's War.

At first, the British tried to put rulers who were friendly to Great Britain on the thrones of India. The French tried to put rulers who were friendly to the French on Indian thrones. From 1746 to 1763 India became a battlefield between the French and the British.

Clive's War

Robert Clive had come to India to work for the British East India Company. In 1757, he led British forces to victory against the French in India. He was only 25 years old.

Clive's army had 1,000 British soldiers and 2,000 Indian soldiers. The Indian soldiers were called **sepoys.** Clive's small army crushed a much larger army of a rajah who had joined with the French. Clive's victory made the British the rulers of India for the next 190 years.

Indirect Rule Through the East India Company

At first, Great Britain did not rule India directly. It had **indirect rule** over India. The East India Company controlled most of the Indian rulers. This privately owned company had agents in many parts of India. Because many of the local Indian rulers were weak, the company's agents could control them and also much of Indian life.

The East India Company brought a lot of money to the people who owned shares in the company. Company agents in India also grew rich. The agents made money by special trade deals or by taking bribes. Many young Englishmen working in India as agents made fortunes.

Great Britain ruled India through the East India Company for nearly 100 years. The company had its own military force of Indian soldiers, or sepoys. The sepoys were led and trained by British military officers.

Robert Clive was the founder of British India. He is shown on the left.

The Sepoy Mutiny

Many of the British officers knew little or nothing about Indian culture and customs. They did not understand that the sepoys might not like the ways the British treated some Indian rulers. The British did not understand some of the social and religious customs of the Indians. They did very little to learn about Indian beliefs.

Sometimes the British wanted the sepoys to go overseas. Many sepoys did not want to do this. According to Indian belief they would lose their caste in a voyage over the ocean. To lose one's caste was a terrible thing to the Indians.

Then the British brought a new kind of gun cartridge to India. The cartridges were greased with the fat from cows and pigs. Hindus do not eat meat from cows. Muslims do not eat meat from pigs. The sepoys were ordered to open the greased cartridges by biting them. This insult was too much for the sepoys.

In 1857, the sepoys began a **mutiny.** A mutiny is a rebellion against the people in charge. British soldiers finally put down the mutiny after much loss of life on both sides.

India Comes Under Direct British Rule

Because of the Sepoy Mutiny, British policy changed. The East India Company lost its power in India. The British government began to rule India directly as a colony. This is known as **direct rule.**

The colony of India was run by a **viceroy.** This was a person placed by the British government. The viceroy ruled in the name of the British ruler. In 1877, Queen Victoria of Great Britain was crowned Empress of India. British ownership of India was now complete.

Owning India brought both money and status to Great Britain. India was called the jewel of the British Empire. It was easy to see how the British

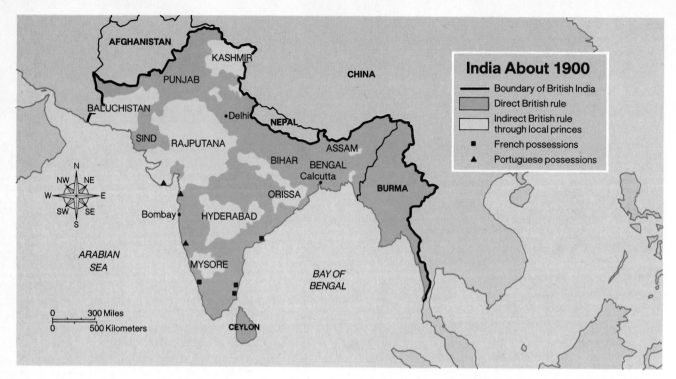

India About 1900

- — Boundary of British India
- Direct British rule
- Indirect British rule through local princes
- ■ French possessions
- ▲ Portuguese possessions

gained by ruling India. The British said, however, that India also gained under British imperialism.

How the British Believed They Helped India

The British said India gained from British rule. For example,

- Indians had better chances for an education. Most Indian people still could not read, but some young Indians did get an education. The English language was taught in the schools. Some Indian students were even sent to British schools for a higher education.
- Law and order was improved in India. The British organized the police to break up bands of robbers.
- The British made medical care and health conditions better in many Indian cities and some larger villages.
- The custom of suttee was ended. A wife no longer had to die when her husband did.
- India got new industries and a new railroad system. The railroad joined all parts of India.

What Indians Did Not Like About British Rule

The Indians said that there were also many bad things about British rule. They said that some of the things the British did hurt India.

- India's wealth and resources were used to help Great Britain, not India. All the manufactured

goods that the British were bringing in were ruining Indian industries.

- British rule was destroying the culture of India.
- The divide-and-conquer policy of the British helped add to the bad feelings between Indians. By making religious and political bad feelings stronger, the British were harming India.
- Educated Indians did not have much chance to move ahead in India. The highest government jobs were taken by British people.
- Many educated Indians felt like people without a country. Their educations at British universities gave them no understanding of their own country. Yet, they were not British, either.
- Many Indians did not like the way they were **segregated,** or kept apart, by the British. After the Sepoy Mutiny, the British kept Indians out of hotels, clubs, and restaurants used by the British. This caused a great deal of bad feelings among the Indians.

Indians Begin to Organize

Many Indians did not want to remain under British rule. In 1885, some Indians began to join together to help get more for Indians. They wanted to be included when the British made decisions about India. They called their group the Indian National Congress.

Exercises

A. Finding the Main Ideas:

Put a check next to the sentences that give the main ideas of what you have just read.

_____ **1.** The British and Indians did not agree about how British rule affected India.

_____ **2.** Educated Indians had little chance to get ahead.

_____ **3.** France and Great Britain each tried to get control of India.

_____ **4.** At first the British controlled India through the East India Company.

_____ **5.** After 1707, Mogul power in India grew weaker.

B. What Did You Read?

Choose the answer that best completes each sentence. Write the letter of your answer in the space provided.

_____ **1.** The sepoys fought for the
   a. Moguls.
   b. French.
   c. British.
   d. Portuguese.

_____ **2.** A viceroy ruled India in the name of the
   a. East India Company.
   b. Mogul emperor.
   c. Indian rajahs.
   d. British ruler.

_____ **3.** The first European trading posts in India were set up by the
   a. French.
   b. Portuguese.
   c. British.
   d. Dutch.

_____ **4.** British rule in India brought all of the following _except_
   a. better law and order.
   b. better medical care and sanitation.
   c. a railroad system joining all of India.
   d. peace among different Indian groups.

C. Checking for Details:

Read each statement. Put an F in the space next to each statement if it is a fact. Put an O in that space if it is an opinion. Remember that facts can be proved, but opinions cannot.

_____ **1.** India was called the jewel of the British Empire.

_____ **2.** The British sent manufactured goods to India.

_____ **3.** Indian students were better off not going to British schools.

_____ **4.** British people had all the highest government jobs in India.

_____ **5.** The Sepoy Mutiny brought a change in the way Great Britain ruled India.

_____ **6.** Vasco da Gama found an ocean route to India for Portugal.

_____ **7.** The European traders arrived when the Moguls ruled India.

_____ **8.** The British were the best traders in India.

_____ **9.** East India Company agents were bad for Indian life.

_____ **10.** Many British army officers knew nothing about Indian culture.

D. Chronology Skills:

In the space provided, write the letter of the event that took place first. You may use the text and the time line on page 17 for help.

_____ **1. a.** Clive's War
     b. Vasco da Gama's trip
     c. Mogul power grows weak

_____ **2. a.** Sepoy Mutiny
     b. a viceroy rules India
     c. Clive's War

_____ **3. a.** Mogul power grows weak
     b. direct rule of India by Great Britain
     c. Sepoy Mutiny

_____ **4. a.** India ruled by East India Company
     b. Vasco da Gama's trip
     c. Clive's War

_____ **5. a.** Queen Victoria crowned Empress of India
     b. Sepoy Mutiny
     c. indirect rule of India by Great Britain

E. Understanding What You Have Read:

Tell whether each of the following involves (M) military, (P) political, or (E) economic aspects of Indian life and history. Place the correct answer in the space provided.

_____ **1.** During the 1700s, India was run by many local rulers.

_____ **2.** The Portuguese, British, French, and Dutch set up trading posts in India.

_____ **3.** The British defeated the French in Clive's War.

_____ **4.** The East India Company had its own army in India.

_____ **5.** The British colony of India was ruled by a viceroy.

_____ **6.** The British set up new industries in India.

_____ **7.** The Indian cloth industry was ruined by British goods brought into India.

F. Word Meanings:

Match each word in Column A with the correct meaning in Column B. Write the letter of each answer in the space provided.

Column A

_____ **1.** mutiny
_____ **2.** viceroy
_____ **3.** segregate
_____ **4.** rajah
_____ **5.** direct rule
_____ **6.** indirect rule
_____ **7.** tariff

Column B

a. an Indian soldier who fought for the British
b. an Indian prince
c. a tax on goods brought into a country
d. a rebellion against the people in charge
e. to separate people of different races
f. person who is in charge of a colony
g. rule of a colony by the imperialist country
h. rule of a land by taking charge of its leaders

G. Understanding Global History:

On page 16 you read about three factors in global history. Which of these factors applies to each statement listed below? Fill in the number of the correct statement on page 16 in the space provided. If no factor applies, fill in the word NONE.

_____ **1.** New kinds of education, law, medical care, and industry were brought to India by the British.

_____ **2.** Able and educated Indians did not have a chance to get better jobs.

_____ **3.** By the middle 1700s, France and Great Britain were fighting wars for the control of India.

_____ **4.** Most of the British in India did not understand the Indian languages or culture.

Chapter 4

China—From the Hsia Dynasty to the T'ang and Sung Dynasties

Understanding Global History

Think about the following statements as you read about early China.
1 People use the environment to achieve economic goals.
2 Contact among people and nations can lead to cultural changes.
3 Nations borrow and adapt ideas and institutions from other nations.

Chinese women pounding silk. Silk was an important trade item in early China.

Learning New Words and Terms

The following words are used in this chapter. Think about the meaning of each one.

civil service: people who work for the government in most jobs except military jobs

protectorate: a country that is controlled by a stronger country but is not a colony of the stronger country

Think As You Read

1. What are three important features of Chinese history?
2. Why was the Great Wall built?
3. What were some contributions of the Han dynasty?
4. What were some contributions of the T'ang dynasty?

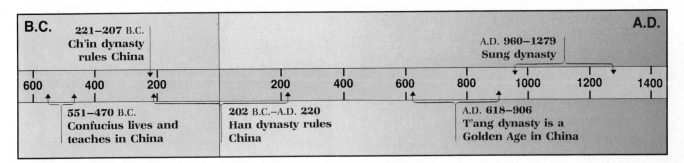

Some Important Facts About Chinese History

There are three important facts to keep in mind about Chinese history.

- Chinese civilization and history began in the Huang Ho valley. This river is found in northern China. China has grown over the centuries. Its borders have grown wider. Even so, the Huang Ho has always been important in China.
- From early times until 1911, the Chinese people were ruled by families. These families were called dynasties. The greatest dynasties ruled all of China. When no dynasty was strong enough to rule, different parts of China were ruled by local rulers. As each dynasty fell from power, another great dynasty took over. Or small local rulers took over. These rulers fought to gain power over the land.
- The many invaders and conquerors that came into China became part of China's culture. They brought some new ideas. They also became Chinese. Because of this, Chinese culture is made up of many cultures.

The Hsia and Shang Dynasties

The earliest dynasty that the Chinese talk about is the Hsia (SHYAH) dynasty. It is believed to have ruled from about 2000 B.C. to about 1700 B.C. Little is known about this dynasty. It ruled the land along the Huang Ho.

The Shang dynasty is the first Chinese dynasty for which we have any records. It too ruled the land along the Huang Ho. During the Shang dynasty, an early form of the Chinese system of writing came into use. People of that time used goods made of pottery and bronze. They also worshipped the spirits of their ancestors.

The Chou Dynasty—about 1027 B.C. to 256 B.C.

The Chou (JOH) rulers came from north of the Huang Ho. They invaded China and became a part of Chinese life. The Chou dynasty ruled China for about 800 years. Their land was mainly between two rivers—the Huang Ho and the Chang Jiang (see map, p. 27).

The Chou dynasty ruled over a feudal society. Canals, reservoirs, and irrigation systems were built. Walls were built in some parts to keep out tribes that might invade China. People began to use iron instead of bronze during the Chou dynasty.

One man who lived during the Chou dynasty had an important effect on the rest of China's history. This man's name was Confucius (kun-FYOO-shuss).

Confucius and His Teachings

Confucius lived from about 551 to 470 B.C. He was a great teacher. Obedience and order were two of the most important things he taught. Confucius taught that there were five important relationships:

- of a man to his ruler
- of a son to his father
- of a younger brother to his older brother
- of a wife to her husband
- of loyalty among friends

The older Chinese liked the ideas that Confucius taught. They liked the idea that children should honor their parents even after the parents died. Even a poor person knew his children would honor him after death.

The Importance of Right Behavior

Confucius taught the importance of the right way to behave. Right behavior set an example for others. This right kind of example was especially important for rulers. Confucius said, "The people are like grass, the ruler is like the wind. The blowing of the wind is what bends the grass."

While he lived, only a small group paid attention to Confucius. Some of them gathered his sayings into books. More than a hundred years later, a man named Mencius (MEN-shus) began to tell people to follow the ideas of Confucius. Because of Mencius, the ideas of Confucius became the basis of much of the later Chinese way of life.

The Chou Dynasty Grows Weak

There was a reason why Confucius began to teach obedience and order. The Chou dynasty was no longer able to keep the country at peace. People were not obedient to their emperor. They were not keeping order. The land that the Chou dynasty ruled was getting smaller. For the last 500 years of the Chou dynasty, there were wars in the land. Finally, the fighting among the local lords forced the Chou rulers to leave the throne. There were 35 years of civil war in China before the next dynasty took over.

The Ch'in Dynasty—221 to 207 B.C.

The name China comes from the Ch'in dynasty.

The Chinese philosopher Confucius.

The first Ch'in ruler, however, was an invader of China. The main aim of the Ch'in dynasty was to join together China and to make it stronger. Most of the things the Ch'in rulers did were done to reach that aim.

The Ch'in rulers tried to make things the same all through the country. They set up a system of weights and measures for all Chinese to use. That was very helpful to farmers, merchants, and anyone who bought and sold goods that had to be weighed or measured. The size of the axles of wagons had to be the same for all wagons. That way, Chinese wagons would all make the same ruts in the road. Wagons from faraway places would not fit the same ruts.

Under the Ch'in dynasty, the system of writing was made simpler. It became the same for the whole country. The Ch'in dynasty also set up a strong central government. It set up 36 districts in the country. The districts were ruled by the Ch'in government, not by local lords.

The Ch'in dynasty also tried to make everybody think the same way. They burned books written by their enemies. They did not want anyone who did not agree with them to spread ideas.

The Ch'in dynasty also had to deal with the danger of invasions from people living north and west of China. The Chinese were afraid of the Huns. The Ch'in rulers built a Great Wall to keep out the Huns.

The Great Wall

There were some small walls in many parts of northern China. They were built to keep out invaders. The Ch'in emperor ordered the building of the famous Great Wall. It stretches for 1,400 miles (2,253 kilometers). People were forced to build the wall. Many thousands died building the Great Wall.

For about 500 years invaders did not cross over the wall. Later, even though the Han and Ming dynasties rebuilt the wall, invaders did manage to cross it. Besides keeping invaders out of China, the Great Wall kept people in China.

The Ch'in dynasty did not last long. The death of the first Ch'in emperor led to the end of the Ch'in dynasty.

The Han Dynasty—202 B.C. to A.D. 220

The Han dynasty had a long, fairly peaceful rule of about 400 years. During the Han dynasty, the Chinese empire grew larger. Its borders reached north to Manchuria and Korea and south to Vietnam. Most of the Chinese people today call themselves the Han people.

The Han dynasty was a time of great achievements.

- Trade to central Asia and the area along the Persian Gulf grew. Trade with Europe was carried on over the land. This land route was known as the Silk Road. It was called this because silk was one of the most important products China had to sell. The Han dynasty also kept up a great deal of trade with the Roman Empire.
- The Buddhist religion came to China from India.
- Art, literature, and architecture were important.
- The first complete history of China was written.
- Paper was invented.
- Women as well as men ruled.
- The ideas of Confucius became important in China. These ideas became the basic ideas of the government. People who wanted **civil service** jobs had to take and pass tests based on

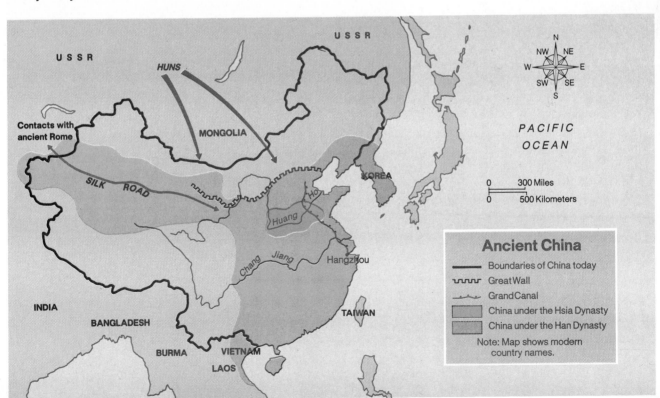

Ancient China

— Boundaries of China today

ᴜᴜᴜᴜ Great Wall

⌐ᴧᴧ Grand Canal

China under the Hsia Dynasty

China under the Han Dynasty

Note: Map shows modern country names.

the teachings of Confucius. The civil service is made up of people who work for the government in most jobs except military jobs.

Between Two Dynasties

Different Han generals began to want more and more power. Some of them became war lords. They started fighting each other for power. At first there were three kingdoms. Then other rulers came in and ruled parts of the country for a while.

During this time a canal was begun. It reached from the Chang Jiang to the Huai (HWAY) River and from the Chang Jiang to the city of Hangzhou (HAN-JOO). The canal brought grains from the south up to the north. This was the first part of what was to become the Grand Canal.

During this time, Christianity and Islam began to reach China.

The T'ang Dynasty—A.D. 618 to 906

The T'ang dynasty was a "Golden Age" for China. It was a time of great artists, poets, and scholars. It was also a time of invention. Block printing was invented. Movable type for printing was invented, too. Agriculture improved.

The T'ang dynasty also brought back the idea of tests for civil service jobs. Through the tests, the rulers hoped they would get the best people. These tests, like earlier ones in the Han dynasty, were based on the works of Confucius.

China did not have castes like India. It did not have a noble class like much of Europe. Classes in China were based on what people did. Scholars were the highest class. They were the people who passed the civil service tests. A child from a poor family could become a scholar. A scholar's child, on the other hand, might not be the same class as the parent.

Some other important things happened during the T'ang dynasty.

- China was united. Large parts to the west were gained.
- Korea was made a **protectorate** of the Chinese Empire. A protectorate is a country that depends on a stronger country that does not actually rule it but controls it to some degree.
- China's central government was made stronger.
- Trade with Japan, the Middle East, and Central Asia grew.

- Southern China became important. It was a center of Chinese culture.

Some Chinese people today think that the T'ang dynasty was China's greatest time. They call themselves "the people of T'ang." Although it had many great achievements, the T'ang dynasty fell like those before it. Constant war with neighboring people left the government weak.

The Sung Dynasty—960 to 1279

After about 50 years of war lords fighting in a divided China, the Sung dynasty began. It ruled a much smaller area of China than the T'ang had ruled. The Sung dynasty was a time of great culture and artistic growth.

There was a strong government, but a weak military system. Because of the weak military system, Sung rulers could not keep control of the whole country. The Sung dynasty began in the north but was forced to move south. Tribes from the north were invading.

A porcelain lion of the T'ang dynasty.

28

Exercises

A. Finding the Main Ideas:

Put a check next to the sentences that give the main ideas of what you have just read.

_____ **1.** The Chinese built a Great Wall.

_____ **2.** Printing was invented in China.

_____ **3.** Early Chinese dynasties had many great achievements.

_____ **4.** The teachings of Confucius developed and became important in China.

_____ **5.** Dynasties rose and fell in China.

B. What Did You Read?

Choose the answer that best completes each sentence. Write the letter of your answer in the space provided.

_____ **1.** The Ch'in dynasty gave China a uniform system of
    a. government and farming.
    b. weights and measures.
    c. weights and industry.
    d. art and sciences.

_____ **2.** The Great Wall was built to keep out
    a. Japanese invaders.
    b. Indian invaders.
    c. European invaders.
    d. Hun invaders.

_____ **3.** The idea of scholar officials and civil service tests first developed in the
    a. Ch'in dynasty.
    b. Han dynasty.
    c. T'ang dynasty.
    d. Hsia dynasty.

_____ **4.** During the T'ang dynasty
    a. Buddhism was brought to China.
    b. Confucianism became important in China.
    c. southern China became a center of Chinese culture.
    d. pottery was first made in China.

_____ **5.** The Sung dynasty had problems because
    a. it was a time of few artists.
    b. it had a greater area of China than any earlier dynasty.
    c. it had a weak central government.
    d. it did not have a strong military government.

C. Chronology Skills:

In the space provided, write the letter of the event that took place first. You may use the text and the time line on page 25 for help.

_____ **1. a.** Shang dynasty
      b. Han dynasty
      c. T'ang dynasty

_____ **2. a.** picture writing
      b. block printing
      c. invention of paper

_____ **3. a.** building of Great Wall
      b. Confucius lives
      c. fall of T'ang dynasty

_____ **4. a.** Sung dynasty
      b. building of Great Wall
      c. Buddhism is brought into China

_____ **5. a.** Buddhism is brought into China
      b. ideas of Confucius are brought back by Mencius
      c. system of civil service tests and scholar officials begins

D. Checking for Details:

Read each statement. Put a T in the space next to each statement if it is true. Put an F in that space if it is false. Put an N if you cannot tell from the reading if it is true or false.

_____ **1.** Confucius warned that it was bad to have a strong central government.

_____ **2.** The Ch'in rulers ordered the building of the Great Wall.

_____ **3.** Korea became a Chinese protectorate during the Hsia dynasty.

_____ **4.** Chinese civilization began in the Huang Ho valley.

_____ **5.** Buddhism spread from China to India.

_____ **6.** The Chou dynasty never became a part of Chinese life.

_____ **7.** Confucianism became an important part of life during the Han dynasty.

_____ **8.** China was the first country to use printing with movable type.

_____ **9.** The Chinese system of picture writing was borrowed from India.

_____ **10.** During the Han dynasty, China's borders reached to Manchuria and Vietnam.

E. Behind the Headlines:

Write two or three sentences that support or tell about each of the following headlines. Use a separate piece of paper.

CHINA ENTERS "GOLDEN AGE"

HAN DYNASTY CONTROLS CHINA

ACTION TAKEN TO MEET THREAT OF HUNS

F. Word Meanings:

Match each word in Column A with the correct meaning in Column B. Write the letter of each answer in the space provided.

Column A

_____ **1.** protectorate
_____ **2.** civil service
_____ **3.** Confucianism
_____ **4.** dynasty

Column B

a. jobs working for the government
b. a class system
c. a country that is controlled by another country but is not a colony of that country
d. a system of belief that says a person should obey and honor parents, older people, and the emperor
e. a family of rulers

G. Understanding Global History:

On page 24 you read about three factors in global history. Which of these factors applies to each statement listed below? Fill in the number of the correct statement on page 24 in the space provided. If no factor applies, fill in the word NONE.

_____ **1.** Chinese civilization began in the valley of the Huang Ho.

_____ **2.** Many people who invaded China became part of the Chinese culture. Chinese culture is a mix of many cultures.

_____ **3.** Contacts with India led to the beginning of Buddhism in China.

_____ **4.** The use of silk spread from China to Europe.

An emperor of the T'ang dynasty holding court.

Chapter 5

China—From the Mongol Dynasty to the Manchu Dynasty

Understanding Global History

   Think about the following statements as you read about the last dynasties of China.
1 Events occurring in one part of the world have influenced developments in other parts of the world.
2 The culture in which we live influences our view of other people.
3 Contact among peoples and nations can lead to cultural changes.
4 Present culture is shaped by the past.

Beijing, the capital of China. This picture shows the Temple of Heaven. Mongol, Ming, and Manchu rulers built many palaces and temples in Beijing.

Learning New Words and Terms

The following words are used in this chapter. Think about the meaning of each one.

minority: less than half the people of a country or place

majority: more than half the people of a country or place

queue: a men's hair style; one long braid is worn at the back of the neck and most of the rest of the head is shaved

barbarian: person who has no real culture and is not civilized

technology: the use of science and invention to improve people's lives in practical ways

Think As You Read

1. Who were the Mongols? How did they affect China?
2. What were some contributions of the Ming dynasty?
3. How did the Manchu dynasty affect Chinese life?

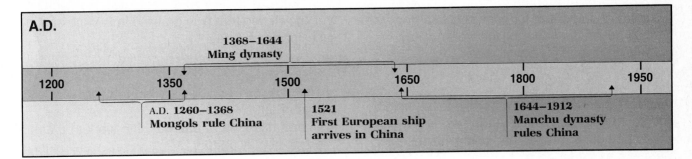

A.D.

| 1200 | 1350 | 1500 | 1650 | 1800 | 1950 |

1368–1644 Ming dynasty

A.D. 1260–1368 Mongols rule China

1521 First European ship arrives in China

1644–1912 Manchu dynasty rules China

The Mongol, or Yuan, Dynasty—1260 to 1368

The Mongol people ruled Mongolia in central Asia. Their leader was Genghis Khan. The Mongols swept out of Mongolia and gained control of much of Asia, India, Persia, and southern Russia. In the late 1200s A.D. they took over China.

Kublai Khan, a grandson of Genghis Khan, ruled Mongolia and China. He declared himself emperor in 1271. Kublai Khan founded the Yuan dynasty.

The Mongols' Way of Ruling China

The Mongol rulers did not try to change China too much. They did not force their own religion on the Chinese. They had Chinese people help run the government. They took over the Chinese form of government, the Chinese language, and even the Chinese way of dress. But they also did not change some of their own way of living. They were people who raised animals. They thought that herding animals was a better way of life than farming.

Kublai Khan

The Mongol dynasty had a central government. This was the government of the emperor. The country was divided into provinces. Each province was run by someone who ruled for the emperor and the central government.

Europeans learned about the Mongols and Kublai Khan from Marco Polo. Marco Polo spent 17 years in Beijing. This was the Mongol capital. He worked for Kublai Khan during part of that time. Marco Polo's book about his trip stirred European interest in China and in all of eastern Asia.

Achievements of the Mongol Dynasty

Two of the great achievements of the Mongol dynasty were:

- The rulers made the Grand Canal larger so that it reached Beijing, their capital city. The canal linked north and south China. As before, the canal was important for bringing grain from the south to feed people in the north. They also made the roads in China better.
- The Mongol dynasty encouraged art, architecture, literature, and plays in China.

Many Chinese people did not like to be ruled by people from outside China. After a while, the Mongol empire grew weaker, and some Chinese people decided to get rid of it.

Ming Dynasty—1368 to 1644

In 1368, a former Buddhist monk overthrew the Mongol dynasty. He started a new dynasty. He became the new emperor. The new dynasty was called "Ming," which means "glorious." The new emperor wanted to go back to what he thought were the best of the old Chinese dynasties—especially the Sung and the T'ang. He wanted to get rid of all the Mongol influences in China. The new Ming emperor brought back many old Chinese traditions and set up a code of law.

A Return to Old Ways

The Ming emperors brought back the civil service tests for government officials. Like earlier government tests, they were based a great deal on the teachings of Confucius. These tests helped bring educated people into the government. The people brought into government were not interested in science or mathematics, however. Chinese knowledge in these areas soon fell behind the knowledge that was growing in Europe and in other parts of Asia.

What the Ming Dynasty Accomplished

The Ming dynasty had some great accomplishments in other fields.

- During this time, there was fine work in crafts, especially in pottery. Ming vases were highly admired for their beauty. They are very valuable to this day.
- Great architecture developed. Some of the most famous Ming buildings are in the Forbidden City. This is in the center of Beijing.

Porcelain dish and flask. These objects were made during the Ming dynasty.

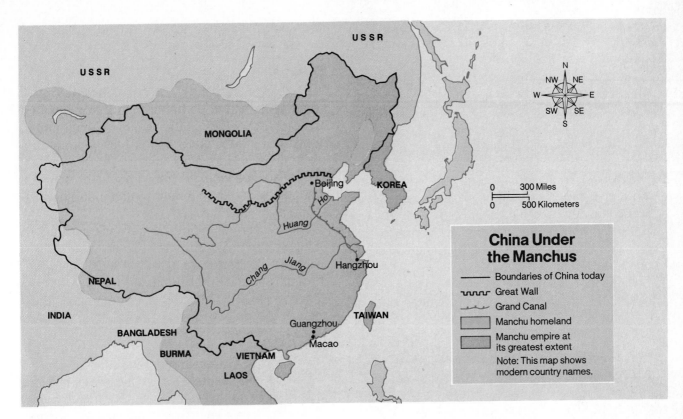

China Under the Manchus

- —— Boundaries of China today
- ᴜᴜᴜᴜ Great Wall
- ⌐⌐⌐ Grand Canal
- Manchu homeland
- Manchu empire at its greatest extent

Note: This map shows modern country names.

- Foreign trade grew. The Ming had a very good navy. A fleet of Chinese ships sailed to India. This trip took place before Vasco da Gama's first voyage from Portugal to India.

Europeans and Japanese in Ming China

The first European ship arrived in China in 1521. It was a Portuguese ship. It came to the city of Guangzhou (GWAN-JOO). Ming officials gave the Portuguese traders the same rights as the Arab and Persian traders who were already there. They did not treat them well, however, and thought the Europeans to be lower than themselves. When the Portuguese captains acted badly towards the Chinese, the officials placed limits on their trading rights. In 1557, the Portuguese settled in the city of Macao.

A fleet of Japanese ships attacked Korea and China in the late 1500s. The Chinese beat off that attack and defeated the Japanese.

In spite of its victories, the Ming dynasty was beginning to grow weak. Manchu invaders from the north kept trying to come into China. A rebellion in Beijing weakened the Ming rulers still more. The government was not able to control bandits and war lords. China was about to be taken over again.

Manchu (Ching) Dynasty—1644 to 1912

The Manchus were once part of the larger group of Mongol invaders. They had settled in the northeastern part of China. This land was called Manchuria. In 1644, they moved into northern China. A Chinese general who was trying to fight off some bandits opened a gate in the Great Wall to let the Manchus in. He wanted the Manchus' help in fighting the bandits.

The Manchus eventually took over China. They became the ruling class. Their large army put down any protests against Manchu rule. The Manchus were a **minority.** Their group made up less than half of all the people. They were able to rule the Chinese **majority.** The Chinese made up more than half of all the people.

The Manchus never became a part of Chinese life the way other rulers did. The Manchus took steps to keep the Chinese people in a lower position. They did not want to mix with the Chinese. They even made laws saying that a Manchu could not marry a Chinese person. They made Chinese men wear the Manchu hair style of the **queue** (KYOO). The queue was one long braid worn down the back of the head. Often the rest of the head was shaved.

Manchu Contributions to China

The Manchus made some important contributions to Chinese life.

- At first, their government was run better than most earlier governments.
- They improved the system of choosing scholar officials in civil service jobs.
- They accepted both Buddhism and Confucianism. Many Chinese people practice both Buddhism and Confucianism together. The teachings of both of these helped to make the Manchus' control of China stronger. For example, the Confucian teaching of obedience to the emperor made people feel that they should obey the Manchu rulers.
- They accepted Chinese art and literature. Many of China's greatest novels were written during the Manchu rule. The Manchus prepared one of the great dictionaries of the Chinese language.

The Problems the Manchus Faced

One great weakness of the Manchus was their sense of pride. They believed they were better than others. They thought that they were better than the people they ruled.

Besides the problems with the people they ruled, the Manchus had problems with the Europeans. They looked down on the Europeans and thought of them as **barbarians.** They thought Europeans were people of little or no culture or civilization. The Europeans wanted more trading rights in China. The Manchus would not let European countries gain greater trading rights. Their refusal was really a sign of Manchu weakness.

Technology and Products

For many centuries, Chinese **technology** in some fields had been better than European technology. Technology is the use of science and invention to manufacture goods and improve people's lives in practical ways. By the 1800s, European technology had improved. Chinese technology could no longer match that of the Europeans.

There were still many things—silk and tea, for example, that Europeans wanted from China. Europe's desire for trade with the Chinese burst through the shell that protected the way of early Chinese life. The Manchu rulers permitted European trade only in the cities of Guangzhou and Macao, however.

The Manchu Government Weakens

European pressure for more trade was only one thing that began to weaken the Manchu government. The government was too corrupt. The farmers were growing poorer. Landowners were charging rents that were so high people could not pay them and still have anything left for food. The peasant unrest began to be felt.

Imperialism came to China during the Manchu rule. That was one more thing that led to the end of the Manchu dynasty. The Manchu dynasty was to be China's last dynasty.

Europeans visiting the court of the Manchu emperor, 1800s.

Exercises

A. Finding the Main Ideas:

Put a check next to the sentences that give the main ideas of what you have just read.

_____ **1.** The Ming dynasty had many great accomplishments.

_____ **2.** The Manchus affected life in China.

_____ **3.** Chinese trade improved.

_____ **4.** The Mongol dynasty was noted for roads, canals, and art.

_____ **5.** Marco Polo met Kublai Khan.

_____ **6.** The Ming dynasty used tests for civil service jobs.

B. What Did You Read?

Choose the answer that best completes each sentence. Write the letter of your answer in the space provided.

_____ **1.** During the early 1500s, the Portuguese traders in China had
 a. full trading privileges.
 b. no trading rights.
 c. the same trading rights as Arab traders.
 d. to leave China.

_____ **2.** All the following were true of the Manchus except that they
 a. came to China as invaders.
 b. set up an efficient government in China.
 c. weakened Chinese art and literature.
 d. accepted Buddhism and Confucianism.

_____ **3.** The Grand Canal of China was
 a. built by the Portuguese.
 b. begun by the Ming rulers.
 c. made larger to reach Beijing by the Mongol rulers.
 d. brought farther west by the Manchu dynasty.

_____ **4.** The Manchu dynasty
 a. encouraged Manchus to marry Chinese.
 b. tried to get more trade with Europe.
 c. thought Europeans were barbarians.
 d. stopped using tests for civil service jobs.

C. Checking for Details:

Read each statement. Put an F in the space next to each statement if it is a fact. Put an O in that space if it is an opinion. Remember that facts can be proved, but opinions cannot.

_____ **1.** During the Ming dynasty, the Chinese knowledge of math and science fell behind European knowledge.

_____ **2.** Ming architecture was the best in Chinese history.

_____ **3.** The Manchu government was the most corrupt in Chinese history.

_____ **4.** Marco Polo's writings awoke Europe's interest in China.

_____ **5.** The Ming dynasty wiped out Mongol influences in China.

_____ **6.** European pressure for trade was one thing that helped weaken the Manchu government.

_____ **7.** The Portuguese were better traders than the Chinese.

_____ **8.** Kublai Khan was a greater ruler than Genghis Khan.

_____ **9.** The Ming dynasty's tests helped bring better-educated people into the civil service.

_____ **10.** The Manchus' rules helped keep the Chinese in a lower position.

D. Time Line Skills:

In which period of time did each of the following events occur? You may look at the text and the time line on page 33 of this lesson to help you.

_____ **1.** The Ming dynasty rules China

_____ **2.** The Manchus rule China

_____ **3.** First European ship arrives in China

_____ **4.** The Mongols rule China

_____ **5.** The Japanese try to invade China and Korea

E. Thinking it Over:

Answer each of the following questions in three or four sentences. Use a separate piece of paper.

1. How did the attitude of the Manchu rulers help to weaken their dynasty?

2. Does the Ming dynasty deserve to be called a "glorious" dynasty?

F. What Does It Mean?

Choose the best meaning for each of the words in capital letters.

_____ **1.** MINORITY
   a. half
   b. more than half
   c. less than half

_____ **2.** MAJORITY
   a. half
   b. more than half
   c. less than half

_____ **3.** TECHNOLOGY
   a. improvement in art and literature
   b. study of early cultures
   c. science and invention used for practical purposes

_____ **4.** BARBARIAN
   a. person of little or no culture
   b. person whose culture is better than yours
   c. person from another country

_____ **5.** QUEUE
   a. a hair style
   b. a clothing style
   c. a farming style

G. Understanding Global History:

On page 32 you read about four factors in global history. Which of these factors applies to each statement listed below? Fill in the number of the correct statement on page 32 in the space provided. If no factor applies, fill in the word NONE.

_____ **1.** The Mongol, Ming, and Manchu dynasties contributed to the art, architecture, and literature of China.

_____ **2.** Kublai Khan, ruler of Mongolia and China, began the Yuan, or Mongol dynasty.

_____ **3.** Buddhism and Confucianism remained important in China under the Manchu dynasty.

_____ **4.** Europeans learned about China and the Mongol dynasty from Marco Polo. They began to be interested in Asia.

_____ **5.** The Manchus took over China but never took on Chinese customs and ways of life.

Chapter 6

Imperialism in China

Understanding Global History

Think about the following statements as you read about imperialism in China.

1 Events occurring in one part of the world have influenced developments in other parts of the world.
2 The culture in which we live influences our view of other people.
3 People should learn to understand and appreciate cultures different from their own.
4 Present culture is shaped by the past.

Shanghai harbor today. The city of Shanghai became an important center of foreign trade in the 1800s. It is one of the world's great seaports as well as China's leading industrial city.

Learning New Words and Terms

The following words are used in this chapter. Think about the meaning of each one.

sphere of influence: an area in which one country gets the right to trade in another, weaker country and to keep out other trading countries. Usually the stronger country has some control of the government as well.

extraterritoriality: a special right the citizens of a foreign country may have. They are tried by the laws and courts of their own country.

indemnities: payments to make up for some harmful actions

Think As You Read

1. How did the Manchu rulers look upon other people and other countries?
2. How did the weakness of China affect its relations with other countries?
3. How did European imperialism affect the Chinese government?
4. What was the Boxer Rebellion?

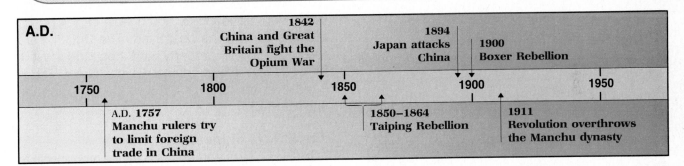

A.D.

| 1750 | 1800 | 1850 | 1900 | 1950 |

1842 China and Great Britain fight the Opium War

1894 Japan attacks China

1900 Boxer Rebellion

A.D. **1757** Manchu rulers try to limit foreign trade in China

1850–1864 Taiping Rebellion

1911 Revolution overthrows the Manchu dynasty

China—A Different Kind of Imperialism

Imperialism in China was different from imperialism in India and in most other countries. European countries never had any real colonies in China. China had a strong central government for much of the time the Europeans were there. European countries did not build schools or railroads in China. They did not set up European-run governments in China.

European Spheres of Influence

European imperialism in China took place through a **sphere of influence.** A sphere of influence is an area where a foreign country has the right to trade. Usually other countries do not have the right to trade in that country's sphere of influence. Often a country with a sphere of influence can have a say in the policy of the country it is in.

The history of European imperialism in China is a history of growing spheres of influence, not of colony building.

The Europeans in China were trying to gain as much as they could for themselves. They also helped keep the ruling dynasty in power. The Europeans were afraid that if there was no real government, they could not trade the way they wanted. They often sent in armies to help the Chinese government keep its power over its people.

The First European Traders

Europeans had been trading for Chinese goods for centuries. Usually, the Europeans did not go all the way to China for the goods. They bought Chinese goods through Arab and Persian traders. It was hard for Europeans to travel over the land to China. They were not welcome in some countries. Travel was hard and dangerous.

European traders knew they should be trading directly with China. They could make more money that way. That is why the Portuguese looked for a route to China by sea. The route over water—although it had its dangers—was safer than the land route.

The Portuguese arrived in China in the 1500s. The Ming dynasty still ruled at that time. The Spanish came later in the 1500s.

British ships bombing Guangzhou during the Opium War. China lost this war with Great Britain.

The Dutch, British, and French reached China in the 1600s. The Ming dynasty was growing weaker. The Manchus took over in 1644.

Guangzhou—the Main Trading City

In 1757, the Manchu government said that all foreign trade had to be in Guangzhou. The British wanted to trade in other ports. They sent officials to try to change the minds of the rulers. The Chinese said no.

The Chinese acted the way they had always acted all through their history. They were the great country in that part of Asia. Foreigners had to follow their rules.

Opium and the Opium War

There were many things that Europeans wanted to buy from China. Some of these things were silk, tea, and china. China also had many raw materials that the Europeans wanted.

There were not many things that the Chinese wanted to buy from the Europeans. The Chinese still thought that most of what they had was better than what other countries had. They thought of the Europeans as barbarians. By the 1800s, the Europeans had begun to think that the Chinese were barbarians.

The British found one thing that the Chinese wanted. It was opium, a drug that people become addicted to. The Chinese government passed a law, in 1729, against bringing opium into China. The rulers knew that it would ruin people's health and make them poor. Still, the British kept buying opium in India and selling more and more of it in China.

In 1839, a Chinese official was sent to Guangzhou to look into the opium problem. When he arrived, he found 20,000 chests of opium. He ordered them to be destroyed. The British were angry that their property had been destroyed. They declared war against China. Great Britain had better technology in its weapons. It won the war in 1842.

The Effects of the Opium War

In 1842 China agreed to open five more ports to trade. It also agreed to have a tariff of 5 percent on all exports and imports. That was a fairly low tariff. In addition, China agreed to give the port city of Hong Kong to Great Britain.

Another result of the war was that Europeans gained the right of **extraterritoriality.** Extraterritoriality meant that a foreigner could not be tried by a Chinese court. A foreigner could not be tried even for crimes committed in China. Foreigners did not have to obey Chinese laws. Any foreigners who broke laws were turned over to their own governments for trial. Chinese people who were hurt by a European could do nothing about it. Of course, this hurt Chinese pride. It made the Chinese helpless against foreign criminals. It also led to bitter feelings against foreigners.

More Gains for the Europeans

France, Germany, and Russia quickly began to move into China. In 1860, a force of British and French ships crushed the Chinese. They took over the capital city of Beijing and burned the emperor's palace.

Between 1858 and 1910, China lost its control over Vietnam, Burma, and other places in Southeast Asia. At the same time, more Chinese ports were opened to foreign trade. Germany took control of Shandong. Russia received a lease on Lushun and control over Manchuria.

The Taiping Rebellion—1850–1864

Meanwhile, a group of Chinese in southern China began to rebel against the Manchu rulers. They said that farmers were becoming poor because of greedy landlords and corruption in the government. They called their rebellion "Taiping," which means "Great Peace." The rebellion spread through the eastern valley of the Chang Jiang. The Taiping group even set up a capital at Nanjing.

After a while, the Taiping movement lost its spirit. The British were afraid that if the Manchu Dynasty fell apart, they would lose their trade. They helped the Manchus fight the Taiping group. Together, they put down the Taiping Rebellion.

A Change is Needed

After China lost the Opium War, its rulers realized that they would need a more modern army and navy. That was the only way the Chinese would be able to stop foreigners from gaining more and more rights that China did not want to give up. But the Manchu rulers did not see that they would also have to change their ideas and the way they ran the country. They thought they could be strong with a modern army and old-fashioned ways.

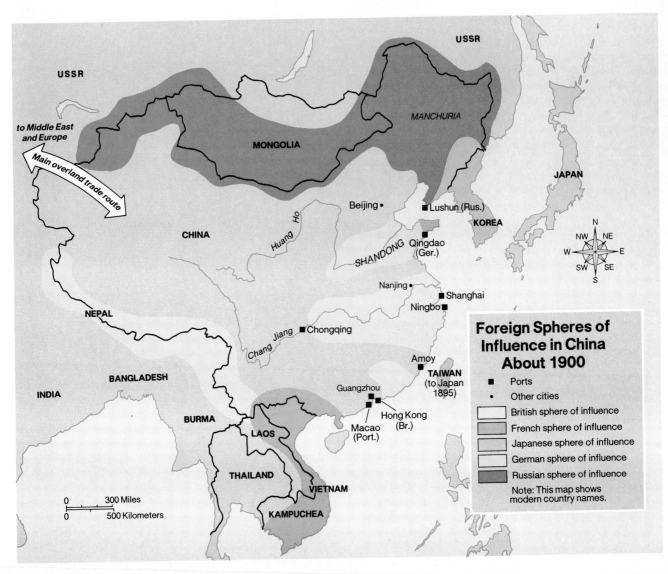

Foreign Spheres of Influence in China About 1900

■ Ports
• Other cities
British sphere of influence
French sphere of influence
Japanese sphere of influence
German sphere of influence
Russian sphere of influence
Note: This map shows modern country names.

The War with Japan

The next problem China had was with its Asian neighbor, Japan. Japan had created a modern army and navy. It had changed many of its old-fashioned ideas. It wanted to be modern. That meant that it wanted to be an imperialist country.

Japan attacked China in 1894. By 1895, the Japanese had beaten the Chinese. After the war with Japan, China had to give Taiwan to Japan. It had to give Korea its independence. In 1910, the Japanese took over Korea. The status and power of the Manchus were at an all-time low.

The Open Door Policy

Now that China had grown weaker, the countries of Europe tried to gain more and more land. It looked as if the Western countries were about to divide up China into colonies.

The United States did not have any spheres of influence in China and did not want to see China divided into colonies. The United States Secretary of State suggested the Open Door policy for China. That meant that all countries would have equal rights to trade in China. The Open Door policy gained the good will of the Chinese for the United States, but it did not really do much else. China, however, was not divided into colonies.

The Empress T'zu Hsi

In 1861, the Manchu emperor died. His empress, T'zu Hsi (TSOO-SHE), now ruled as regent for her son. When the son died, she appointed her nephew as emperor and ruled as regent for him. In 1898, she began to rule in her own name.

T'zu Hsi was against having a modern China. More than anyone else, she kept China the way it had been for many years.

Empress T'zu Hsi. She was against change in China. T'zu Hsi secretly supported the Boxers against foreigners.

A "Boxer." The Boxers wanted to drive foreigners out of China.

The Boxer Rebellion

In 1900, a group of Chinese rose to rebel against foreigners. The rebellion was led by a secret society. The name in Chinese meant something like "the society of the harmonious fists." In English, it was called the Boxers. Empress T'zu Hsi encouraged the Boxers. She hoped that the Boxers would save China by getting rid of the foreign powers.

The Boxers attacked buildings in Beijing that held representatives of foreign countries. They began a war against foreigners.

Military forces from 11 countries, including the United States, put down the Boxer Rebellion. Afterwards, the Chinese had to pay **indemnities** to the foreign governments. An indemnity is money paid to make up for some wrong act. The United States used its indemnity money to set up a fund to educate Chinese students sent to American schools. This use of the money gained good will for the United States in China.

Manchu Power Comes to An End

By the early 1900s, China had been divided into spheres of influence by the imperialist countries. China was treated as if it were a colony by the imperialists. The Manchu rulers were left with hardly any power. In parts of China, there was no real government. War lords, who were bandits or generals, ruled these parts. The Chinese government had no control here.

Imperialism had brought bitterness and shame to China. The people hated the Manchu emperor and government almost as much as they hated the foreigners.

In 1911, a Chinese doctor who had been educated outside of China led a revolution to get rid of the Manchu dynasty. Dr. Sun Yat-sen's nationalist movement ended the rule of the Manchus. In the first months of 1912, the nationalists set up a new government. This was the Republic of China. It was an end to the thousands of years of dynasties.

Sun Yat-sen

Exercises

A. Finding the Main Ideas:
Put a check next to the sentences that give the main ideas of what you have just read.

_____ **1.** China is in Southeast Asia.

_____ **2.** The Manchu rulers had to deal with European imperialists in China.

_____ **3.** War lords gained control of parts of China.

_____ **4.** The Manchu government grew weaker and weaker.

_____ **5.** China lost control of Korea.

B. What Did You Read?
Choose the answer that best completes each sentence. Write the letter of your answer in the space provided.

_____ **1.** The idea for the Open Door policy came from
    a. China.
    b. the United States.
    c. Japan.
    d. Russia.

_____ **2.** The Opium War ended up in
    a. a defeat for China.
    b. more Chinese ports being opened for foreign trade.
    c. China giving Hong Kong to the British.
    d. all of the above.

_____ **3.** Manchu rulers of China thought of themselves as
    a. religious leaders in Asia.
    b. barbarians.
    c. good as other people.
    d. better than other people.

_____ **4.** The Boxer Rebellion was aimed against
    a. the Manchus.
    b. the Open Door policy.
    c. all foreigners in China.
    d. indemnities.

C. Checking for Details:
Read each statement. Put a T in the space next to each statement if it is true. Put an F in that space if it is false. Put an N if you cannot tell from the reading if it is true or false.

_____ **1.** Most Manchu officials were corrupt.

_____ **2.** China did not have many raw materials.

_____ **3.** War lords ruled many parts of China.

_____ **4.** Extraterritoriality gave special rights to foreigners in China.

_____ **5.** The Manchu emperors became more powerful in the early 1900s.

_____ **6.** Spheres of influence were good for the imperialist countries.

_____ **7.** The British tried to end the opium trade in China.

_____ **8.** China defeated Japan in a war in 1894–1895.

D. Word Meanings:

Match each word in Column A with the correct meaning in Column B. Write the letter of each answer in the space provided.

Column A

_____ **1.** extraterritoriality

_____ **2.** indemnities

_____ **3.** sphere of influence

Column B

a. payments to make up for some harmful actions

b. an area in which a country has special rights, but does not have colonies

c. the right of foreigners to be tried in their own courts instead of in the courts of the country they are in

d. a dislike of foreigners

E. Understanding Global History:

On page 40 you read about four factors in global history. Which of these factors applies to each statement listed below? Fill in the number of the correct statement on page 40 in the space provided. If no factor applies, fill in the word NONE.

_____ **1.** When the Manchu government grew weaker in the 1800s, the imperialist powers were able to move in.

_____ **2.** The nationalist feelings of the Chinese people grew as the imperialists gained more and more power.

_____ **3.** The Manchu rulers thought they were better than other people and were not willing to accept new ideas.

_____ **4.** The European imperialists thought of China as a place to get raw materials and to sell manufactured goods.

Chapter 7

Emperors, Shoguns, and Imperialists in Japan

Understanding Global History

Think about the following statements as you read about the early rulers of Japan.
1. Contact among peoples and nations can lead to cultural changes.
2. Nations choose what they borrow and adapt from other nations.
3. People use the environment to achieve economic goals.
4. Present culture is shaped by the past.

This gate is part of a large Shinto shrine. Shinto is the oldest religion of Japan. Today, Japanese visit the many Shinto shrines that are found all over Japan.

Learning New Words and Terms

The following words are used in this chapter. Think about the meaning of each one.

daimyo: a land-owning feudal lord in Japan; a noble

samurai: a Japanese feudal knight or warrior

shogun: Japan's most important military leader; the military leader who acted as the ruler of Japan

bushido: the code of honor for the samurai

typhoon: a very powerful storm with heavy winds and rain; a heavy storm found in the Pacific Ocean

isolation: keeping apart from other countries

Think As You Read

1. How was the Japanese culture influenced by China?
2. What was a shogun? Why was he important in Japan?
3. What important events took place during the Kamakura period?
4. What important changes took place during the Tokugawa period?
5. What changes came about during Meiji times?

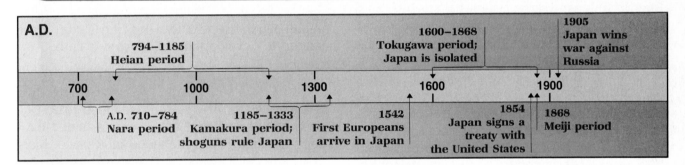

A.D.

| 794–1185 Heian period | 1600–1868 Tokugawa period; Japan is isolated | 1905 Japan wins war against Russia |

700 — 1000 — 1300 — 1600 — 1900

A.D. **710–784 Nara period** | **1185–1333 Kamakura period; shoguns rule Japan** | **1542 First Europeans arrive in Japan** | **1854 Japan signs a treaty with the United States** | **1868 Meiji period**

The Early Japanese

The first people of Japan were the Ainu (AY-noo). They most likely came from the mainland of Asia. Later, after 1000 B.C., more people came to Japan. The new people probably came from China, Korea, Manchuria, Malaysia, and Indonesia. They forced the Ainu to move north. The new people settled in the southern islands of Japan.

At first, Japan's culture had a lot that made it like the cultures of China and Korea. After 250 B.C., however, Japan had its own special culture. Buddhism reached Japan from China in A.D. 552. The Japanese practiced this new religion in their own way. This helped give Japanese culture a shape different from all other cultures.

The Emperor

The Japanese believe that the first emperor ruled about 660 B.C. The emperor's family was thought to be descendants of the sun god. Through Japanese history, only one family of emperors has ruled. This is very different from the changing dynasties of India and China. It is also very different from the countries of Europe. The Japanese believe that having just one line of emperors makes Japan different in an important way from all other countries.

The Great Reform

At first, Japanese emperors had little power. They ruled only part of Japan. Then, in A.D. 645, a new emperor began a Great Reform. This brought about great change. The emperor began to control land and taxes. A new code of laws gave greater power to the emperor.

The Nara Period—710 to 784

In A.D. 710, the Japanese emperor built a capital city at Nara. The idea for the capital city was borrowed from the capital city of China's T'ang rulers. That was only one of the ideas that Japan borrowed from China.

From the 500s through the 800s, Japan sent hundreds and thousands of people to China. There, the Japanese studied why China was so

Buddhist shrines at Nara.

great and powerful. Japanese people visited the T'ang court. When they returned to Japan, the visitors came back with new ideas and customs. People in Japan began to use the Chinese system of writing. They also used the Chinese way of dress. Many ideas of art and living that were Chinese were borrowed by the Japanese.

Nara was near some great Buddhist shrines. Buddhism was very important during the Nara period. Many older Japanese preferred Shinto, however. Shinto is the older, traditional Japanese religion. They did not like having the capital so near the most important Buddhist shrines in Japan. After less than 100 years, the capital was moved.

The Heian Period—794 to 1185

In A.D. 794, the emperor built a new capital at Heian (HAY-ahn). Heian is just about where the city of Kyoto (KYOH-toh) is today. This time in Japanese history is called the Heian period.

Some important changes came about in Japan during the Heian period.

- Buddhism and Shinto both became important in Japanese life. Many Japanese practiced both. They brought the ideas of the two religions closer.
- A feudal system of land ownership began. Peasants had small strips of land. They paid part of their crops to the noble landowners. The payments were for the right to use the land.
- The power of the **daimyos** (DI-myohs), or nobles, grew stronger. The power of the central government grew weaker.
- People started thinking of the emperor as a religious figure rather than as a government

leader. The idea that he was a descendant of a god made him a figure to worship.

Changes taking place in China began to affect Japan. The T'ang dynasty was losing its power. Japan began to end official ties with China. Japan started to develop more of its own culture.

Kana—A New Form of Writing

One example of the changes in Japan's culture is kana writing. At first, the Japanese used Chinese picture writing. Each character stood for a separate idea. Then a change took place. More and more Japanese started to use kana. Kana is a kind of phonetic writing. The writing stands for sounds, not for ideas. At first, kana writing had been used by Japanese women. In the Heian period, it began to take the place of the Chinese form of writing.

The Fujiwara Family Gains Power

During the Heian period many nobles had more real power than the emperor. From the 800s to the 1100s, one family was the real ruler of Japan. That was the Fujiwara family. Many children of the Fujiwara family married members of the emperor's family. Many Fujiwara daughters became empresses. The emperor was still said to be the ruler. The Fujiwara, however, ruled by having many nobles serve them as **samurai.** The samurai were warriors. They were somewhat like the feudal knights in medieval Europe.

By the middle 900s, the Fujiwara family began to lose its power. The central government could not keep peace in the land. Local samurai began to fight for local landowners. Then the daimyos began to fight other daimyos for power.

The Rise of the Shoguns

For many years during the 1000s and 1100s, there were feudal wars in Japan. Toward the end of the 1100s, one family won out over the others. The Minamoto family came into power in Japan. The leader of that family took the title of **shogun.** Shogun is a military title. It means military leader or chief general. For more than 600 years, Japan was ruled by military leaders called shoguns.

When the shoguns began to rule, the emperor and his court stayed at Kyoto. The shoguns set up their own capital city. This meant that Japan had two capitals. One was the emperor's city. The other was the city of the ruling shogun.

The Kamakura Period—1185 to 1333

The Minamoto family set up their capital at Kamakura. The time of their rule is known as the Kamakura period.

Yoritomo was the first shogun. He is shown here receiving the title of shogun. Notice the armor of the samurai in the picture.

The Samurai and Bushido

The Kamakura period is the first period in which the shoguns ruled. Since it was a military rule, warriors, or samurai, had a special status. Like the knights of medieval Europe, the samurai had their own code of honor. The code of honor was known as **bushido.** Samurai had to be loyal to their lord. They valued honor above all other things.

Japan in the Kamakura Period

The Minamoto shoguns set up a central government. They gave their loyal followers land in parts of the country where the Minamoto wanted friends. Trade with other countries grew. Painting, art, and poetry became important. The arts became very important at the court in Kyoto.

The status of Japanese women improved. They had more rights than European women would have in the next 500 years.

Mongol Invasions

The Mongol leader, Kublai Khan, was gaining control of China in the 1200s. He also wanted Japan. At first, Kublai sent some ambassadors to Japan. Kublai demanded that the Japanese come under his power. The Japanese refused.

Then he sent ships to attack Japan. The first ships were sent in 1274. A **typhoon,** or heavy storm, destroyed most of the Mongol ships. The Mongols tried again. In 1281, the Mongols sent about 4,000 ships to attack Japan. The Japanese began to arm themselves to fight back. This time, an even bigger typhoon destroyed the Mongol ships. The Japanese called the typhoon a *kamikaze.* This means "divine wind." The Japanese believed that their gods had sent the typhoons to protect them from invasion.

The End of the Kamakura Period

The Japanese were now safe from the Mongols. They had problems because of the attempted invasion, however. The Japanese had spent a great deal of money to arm themselves against the Mongols. Ships and towns had been strengthened. Warriors had to have weapons and armor. The government was having money troubles.

Money troubles were one reason the Kamakura period came to an end. The rule of the shogun fell apart in 1333. The central government lost control of the country. Local wars broke out.

The Ashikaga Shoguns—1338–1597

A new family of shoguns took control in 1338. They were the Ashikaga shoguns. They brought some order back to the country. They moved the capital to Kyoto. This was where the emperor had his capital.

The Ashikaga shoguns never gained as much power as the Minamoto family. They did have more power to rule than anyone else during their time, however.

The Europeans Arrive

In 1542, while the Ashikaga were shoguns, the first European ships arrived. They came from Portugal. The Portuguese brought Christian missionaries. They also brought many new ideas.

The Portuguese soon taught the Japanese about firearms. Guns and other firearms soon made the samurai, who fought with swords, seem behind the times.

An Attack on Korea and China

During this period, armed nobles gave the emperor back some of his power. The Japanese had new weapons and new feelings of power. In the 1590s, Japan decided to take over Korea and China. The Chinese, with the help of Korea, beat off the Japanese invaders. Soon after this, the Tokugawa family began its shogun dynasty in Japan.

The Tokugawa Period—1600 to 1868

Japan needed new rulers. It soon found them in the Tokugawa shoguns. The Tokugawa set up their new capital city at Edo. It is now called Tokyo.

The Tokugawa gave up the idea of invading China. Instead, they turned to setting up a strong government. They took the following steps to make this happen. The first Tokugawa shogun said that the nobles had to appear at court when court was in session. No daimyo could build a new castle or strengthen armies without permission. Each daimyo had to keep a place to live in Edo. When the daimyo left Edo, he had to leave someone behind as a hostage. (A hostage is a person held by another person or a group of people until certain demands are met.)

These rules were meant to see that no other person or group could take control of Japan.

Isolation Under the Tokugawa Shoguns

The Tokugawa shogun decided on a policy of **isolation.** Isolation means keeping apart from other countries.

All Japanese ports were closed to foreign ships. Limits were put on the rights of Chinese ships to trade in Japan. During this period Japan built larger and better ships. These ships traveled to China and the Philippines to trade. While the Japanese traded outside of Japan, hardly any other countries were allowed to trade in Japan.

Inside Japan, the Tokugawa shoguns closed Japan to foreign trade. Only one port was left open to a small amount of foreign trade. This port was at Nagasaki.

Christianity had been allowed in Japan. Many Japanese became Christians under the Ashikaga shoguns. Under the Tokugawa, however, Christianity was against the law. Foreign missionaries were ordered to leave.

Japan remained closed to foreigners until the 1850s. At that time, an American made a great change.

Commodore Perry Reaches Japan

In 1853, an American navy officer sailed into what is now Tokyo Bay. Commodore Matthew C. Perry had arrived in Japan. He came with four large U.S. ships and a letter from the President of the United States. The Japanese told him that he had to go to Nagasaki because that was the only port for foreign ships. Commodore Perry refused to leave Tokyo Bay. It was hard for the Japanese officials to argue with Perry. He had large ships and guns.

Perry made some demands of Japan. He wanted Japan to agree to treat shipwrecked American sailors well. He wanted Japan to open more ports to Americans.

Japan and the U.S. Sign a Treaty

Commodore Perry left Japan and returned in 1854 with more ships. Japan agreed to a treaty with the United States. More ports were opened for U.S. ships. American sailors would be treated well. Trade would be allowed. The treaty that Japan signed was an unequal treaty. That is, the United States gained more than Japan did. Also, Japan was no longer isolated.

Japanese officials, on the right, meet with Commodore Perry.

The Meiji Period

The feudal rule of the shoguns did not work well in the modern world. In 1868, Japan put limits on the power of the shoguns and the samurai. The emperor once again took over running the government of Japan.

This time in Japanese history was the Meiji (MAY JEE) period. The young emperor changed Japanese government. Meiji means "enlightened peace." The name did not really fit. The changes did not lead to peace. They did lead to a stronger, more modern Japan, however.

Japan and Imperialism

For a while, it looked as if Japan would be another Asian country for imperialist powers to take over. At first, Japan had to give more to the Western countries than it received.

Japan was not taken over, however. In less than 50 years of Meiji rule, Japan made some amazing changes.

- Japan put an end to feudalism and serfs. Many farmers became owners of their own small pieces of land.
- Japan wrote its own constitution. The emperor continued to rule. The constitution, however, allowed for some representatives of nobles and of elected representatives.
- Japan set up public schools. Almost everybody learned to read.
- Japan formed a strong, modern army and navy.
- Japan set up modern industries. Japan became one of the world's industrial powers.

Japan Becomes an Imperialist Nation

In the 1900s, Japan did what it had done during China's T'ang Dynasty. It studied strong nations to learn how they became successful. Then Japan set out to use what it had learned.

Japan became an industrial nation. In the spirit of nationalism, the Japanese were proud of their nation. Japan began to follow the same path as other industrial nations. Japan became an imperialist nation.

Japan did not have many of the raw materials its industries needed. If it bought those raw materials, it would have to depend too much on foreign nations. Japan saw that nearby countries in Asia had many of the raw materials it needed. It decided to take over these countries. First, Japan had to defeat any countries standing in the way of Japanese imperialism.

The War with China

From 1894 to 1895, Japan used its military might to defeat China. That victory let Japan take Taiwan from China. It also let Japan force China to give up Korea. At first, Korea was just in Japan's sphere of influence. Then Japan took over Korea in 1910.

The War with Russia

Japan's growing military power next showed itself in a war with Russia. Japan amazed the world in 1904 and 1905 by winning victories against Russia. The treaty that ended the war gave Japan possession of land in China for a certain amount of time. Japan also gained spheres of influence that used to belong to Russia.

An Imperialist Asian Country

By 1910, Japan had become one of the main imperialist countries of the world. It held Lushun in China. It had a sphere of influence in Manchuria. More and more, the Japanese began to look at China and Southeast Asia as part of Japan's special area of interest.

In about 50 years Japan had become one of the world's great imperial powers.

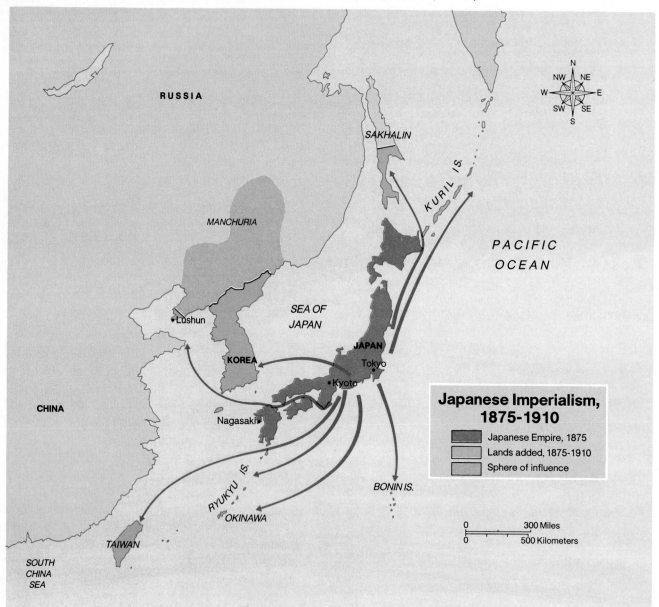

Japanese Imperialism, 1875-1910

Japanese Empire, 1875
Lands added, 1875-1910
Sphere of influence

Exercises

A. Finding the Main Ideas:

Put a check next to the sentences that give the main ideas of what you have just read.

_____ **1.** The Portuguese landed in Japan.

_____ **2.** Shinto is the traditional religion of Japan.

_____ **3.** Japan's culture borrowed a lot from China.

_____ **4.** Japan developed its own special culture.

_____ **5.** Japanese warriors were called samurai.

_____ **6.** Japan built industries and became an imperialist country.

B. What Did You Read?

Choose the answer that best completes each sentence. Write the letter of your answer in the space provided.

_____ **1.** A shogun was
   a. an emperor.
   b. a civil service employee.
   c. a military leader.
   d. an elected official.

_____ **2.** In early times people came to Japan from
   a. India and China.
   b. Korea and China.
   c. Malaysia and India.
   d. Manchuria and Africa.

_____ **3.** The Mongol attempts to invade Japan failed because of
   a. the skill of Japanese generals.
   b. typhoons.
   c. the fall of the T'ang Dynasty.
   d. all of the above.

_____ **4.** The Buddhist religion
   a. began in Japan.
   b. came to Japan directly from India.
   c. made the Japanese stop practicing Shinto.
   d. came to Japan from China and Korea.

_____ **5.** Something that is unusual about Japan's rule and is not true of any other country in Asia is
   a. it was ruled by military leaders.
   b. it had an emperor.
   c. it had women rulers.
   d. there was only one family of emperors in its history.

_____ **6.** Japan did not become a colony of a Western country because
   a. Japan became an imperialist country instead.
   b. Japan did not have anything the Western countries wanted.
   c. Westerners did not travel to Japan.
   d. Japan had enough raw materials for everything it needed.

C. Reviewing Your Reading:

Fill in the word or term that best completes each statement below.

Ainu	Japan	power	shoguns
defeated	Korea	religion	taxes
emperor	land	Shinto	trade

1. Japan's efforts to invade China in the Ashikaga period were _____ by China with the help of _____.

2. Commodore Perry opened Japan to _____ with the United States.

3. The _____ were the first people who lived in _____.

4. The Great Reform gave the _____ control over _____ and _____.

5. The older, traditional _____ of early Japan was _____.

6. _____ held _____ instead of the emperor during much of Japan's history.

D. Time Line Skills:

In which period of time did each of the following events occur? You may look at the time line on page 49 of this lesson to help you.

_____ **1.** The first Europeans arrive in Japan.

_____ **2.** Nara is the capital of Japan during this time.

_____ **3.** The Japanese defeat Russia.

_____ **4.** The United States opens Japan to greater foreign trade.

_____ **5.** The Tokugawa shoguns isolate Japan.

E. Checking for Details:

Read each statement. Put a T in the space next to each statement if it is true. Put an F in that space if it is false. Put an N if you cannot tell from the reading if it is true or false.

_____ **1.** The Chinese and Koreans were a strong influence on early Japan.

_____ **2.** The emperors of Japan were always very powerful.

_____ **3.** The rulers during the Heian period wanted to spread Buddhism and drive out Shinto.

_____ **4.** Kana writing was at first used by Japanese women.

_____ **5.** The samurai were important civil servants.

_____ **6.** The *kamikaze* were rulers of Japan.

_____ **7.** The presents that Commodore Perry brought made the Japanese realize that they were behind in technology.

_____ **8.** The Tokugawa shoguns insisted that Japan become more modern.

_____ **9.** The Meiji period brought power back to the emperor.

_____ **10.** The Portuguese brought Christianity to Japan.

F. Behind the Headlines:

Each headline has a story behind it. Write two or three sentences that support or tell about each of the following headlines. Use a separate piece of paper.

JAPAN CLOSED TO OUTSIDERS   CHIEF GENERAL APPOINTED TO RULE

NATURE WINS A BATTLE FOR JAPAN   JAPAN SIGNS TRADE TREATIES

G. Word Meanings:

Match each word in Column A with the correct meaning in Column B. Write the letter of each answer in the space provided.

Column A   Column B

_____ **1.** shogun   **a.** Japanese warrior or knight

_____ **2.** bushido   **b.** a heavy storm at sea

_____ **3.** daimyo   **c.** belief that your country is best

_____ **4.** samurai   **d.** the code of honor for Japanese warriors

_____ **5.** isolation   **e.** a Japanese feudal lord

_____ **6.** typhoon   **f.** a military ruler of Japan

                               g. keeping your country apart from other countries

H. Understanding Global History:

On page 48 you read about four factors in global history. Which of these factors applies to each statement listed below? Fill in the number of the correct statement on page 48 in the space provided. If no factor applies, fill in the word NONE.

_____ **1.** A feudal system of land ownership developed in Japan.

_____ **2.** Buddhism reached Japan from China. It then combined with Shinto in Japan.

_____ **3.** Japan kept up close contacts with China in early times. The Chinese influence was strong in Japan.

_____ **4.** During the Heian period, the special Japanese culture developed and grew.

Chapter 8

Chinese, Indian, and European Influences in Southeast Asia

Understanding Global History

Think about the following statements as you read about Southeast Asia.
1 Nations borrow and adapt ideas and institutions from other nations.
2 Contact among peoples and nations can lead to cultural changes.
3 Events occurring in one part of the world have influenced developments in other parts of the world.
4 Location, topography, and resources affect interaction among people.

Indonesia is one of the main island countries in Southeast Asia. These are rice fields on Bali, one of the 13,600 islands that make up Indonesia.

Learning New Words and Terms

The following words are used in this chapter. Think about the meaning of each one.

province: a part of a country
monsoon: a wind in the region of Southeast Asia; it blows in one direction in the summer and in another direction in the winter

Think As You Read

1. Which parts of Southeast Asia were influenced strongly by China?
2. Which parts of Southeast Asia were influenced strongly by India?
3. What Western countries had colonies in Southeast Asia? Where were the colonies found?

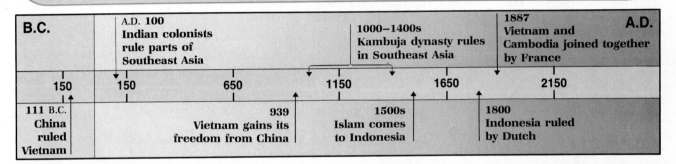

B.C.	A.D. 100 Indian colonists rule parts of Southeast Asia		1000–1400s Kambuja dynasty rules in Southeast Asia	1887 Vietnam and Cambodia joined together by France	A.D.
150	150	650	1150	1650	2150
111 B.C. China ruled Vietnam		939 Vietnam gains its freedom from China	1500s Islam comes to Indonesia	1800 Indonesia ruled by Dutch	

Where is Southeast Asia?

When you look at a map of Asia, you can see the two large countries of China and India. Tucked between China and India, there are some small countries. There are also some islands lying off the Asian continent. The countries on the mainland and the islands found off the continent are the lands of Southeast Asia.

On the mainland of Southeast Asia are the present-day countries of Burma, Laos, Thailand, Malaysia, Kampuchea (Cambodia), Singapore, and Vietnam. The main island countries of Southeast Asia are Indonesia, the Philippines, and Papua New Guinea.

A Crossroads of the World

Southeast Asia is one of the crossroads of the world. A crossroads is an area that connects two or more places. Southeast Asia is a crossroads that joins India, China, and the countries of the Pacific Ocean. A great deal of ocean traffic moves through this important crossroads.

The People of Southeast Asia

People first began to move into Southeast Asia more than 12,000 years ago. They most likely came from the north. They were related to people of central Asia. Later, other groups moved into the area.

The Malays were one group that moved into Southeast Asia. They came from northern and central Asia about 2000 B.C. The Malays settled on the coast and on the nearby islands. They brought their own system of growing rice. The Malays also brought sailing skills. In later years, Malay sailors sailed to India and the eastern coast of Africa.

Other groups of people settled in parts of Southeast Asia.

- A group known as Negritos settled in what is now Malaysia and the Philippines. Scientists believe that some of the ocean areas were once connected by land. The Negritos probably reached the Philippines traveling by land.
- The Mons people moved from China into the areas of the Mekong River delta and Burma.
- The Khmer people moved from the north into the area around Laos. Later they moved into Cambodia.
- The Vietnamese moved from southern China into Southeast Asia.

How China and India Influenced Southeast Asia

At some periods of history, India stretched farther east than it does now. At times it stretched into some of the lands of Southeast Asia. China,

Barges on the Mekong River, 1800s. The Mekong flows south from China into Laos, Kampuchea (Cambodia), and Vietnam. It is one of the great rivers of Southeast Asia.

too, reached farther south than it does today. At times it reached into parts of Southeast Asia.

At other times the lands of Southeast Asia were not actually part of India or China. They were protectorates instead. Some were under the control of India or China during certain periods.

China and India influenced Southeast Asia in other ways, too. People from China and India sometimes moved into the lands of Southeast Asia. They brought with them some of the customs and ideas from the countries they had left.

China and Vietnam

China had a great influence on the area that is now Vietnam. We know about Vietnam's early history from stories that the Vietnamese people have passed down through word of mouth.

According to these stories, the Vietnamese had their own kingdom in southern China in very early times. That kingdom ended in 333 B.C. Then the Vietnamese moved south. They lived under Chinese rule until the Ch'in dynasty fell apart in 207 B.C. For a while after that, there was another Vietnamese kingdom.

Vietnam During the Han and T'ang Dynasties

In 111 B.C., the Han rulers controlled the Vietnamese. From that time on, we have a written record of Vietnamese history. The Chinese made part of what is now northern Vietnam a **province** of China. A province is a part of a country. Later, China ruled the area even more directly.

The language of China became the basis for the early language of Vietnam. Chinese culture

60

also influenced Vietnam. The people of Vietnam showed a great respect for China. They also hated and feared Chinese rule. A love-hate relationship arose between Vietnam and China. Some of that feeling still remains today.

Vietnam Rules Itself and Others

When the T'ang dynasty fell, the people of Vietnam gained their freedom from Chinese rule. That was in A.D. 939. For the next 900 years, the northern part of Vietnam was ruled by its own dynasties. This northern area of Vietnam began to gain control over kingdoms to the south. It also gained control over the southern part of Cambodia.

The Vietnamese gave their land the name of Dai-Viet, this means "Greater Viet." They kept the name until the 1800s. After that time, the name was changed to Vietnam.

The people in the southern part of what is now Vietnam were different from the Vietnamese people. Many belonged to a people called the Champa. The Vietnamese began to take over the Champa in the 900s A.D. The Champa hated and feared the Vietnamese. The feelings of hate and fear began in the days of the Dai-Viet. Some of these feelings continue to this day.

India and Southeast Asia

Most of China's contact with Southeast Asia was by land. A great deal of India's contacts were made by water. Sailors and traders who lived on the southern and eastern coasts of India sailed to Southeast Asia.

India's People and Ideas Travel

India and much of Southeast Asia has **monsoon** winds. Monsoons are winds that blow in one direction in the summer and in another direction in the winter. The sailors and traders used the monsoon winds that blow across the Indian Ocean to reach Southeast Asia. They also used the monsoon winds to return home.

Indian travelers began to influence the western areas of the Southeast Asian mainland. Indian colonies also began to appear in Southeast Asia.

By A.D. 100, Indian colonists ruled several kingdoms in Southeast Asia. One of these was the Champa kingdom in the southern part of Vietnam. As you know, the Vietnamese began to take over the Champa kingdom in the 900s A.D.

The Kambuja Dynasty of the Khmer People

The Kambuja dynasty ruled most of the rest of the mainland of Southeast Asia from A.D. 1000 to the 1400s. The people of this kingdom are the Khmer (kuh-MER).

The Khmer were strongly influenced by Indian religions and culture. The Kambuja dynasty built the capital city of Angkor Thom in what is now Kampuchea. The famous temple buildings of Angkor Wat are in the city of Angkor Thom. These buildings show a lot of Indian influence.

The Malay Peninsula and the Nearby Islands

Other Indian influences were found in the Malay peninsula. They were also found in some of the islands of what is now Indonesia. Indian traders and Buddhist and Hindu monks brought Indian culture with them. There were kingdoms in these areas that were connected with India, even though they were not a part of India.

The island of Java had a great Hindu kingdom in the late 1200s. At one time this kingdom controlled a great deal of the Indonesian islands and the Malay peninsula.

Religions of Southeast Asia

The cultures that traveled across Southeast Asia included a number of religions. Buddhism began in India. It then moved to China. By A.D. 500, it had moved to Southeast Asia. Another Indian religion, Hinduism, was also brought to many parts of Southeast Asia.

By the 1500s, Arab traders brought their religion of Islam to much of Indonesia. Since that time, most of the people of Indonesia have been Muslims. An exception is the island of Bali. The people of Bali remained Hindus.

Christianity did not reach Southeast Asia until European explorers and traders arrived. At first, the Portuguese, then the Spanish, brought Roman Catholicism. The English and Dutch brought the Protestant faith to Southeast Asia. The Philippines is the only country in Southeast Asia that is mostly Christian. Elsewhere, Christianity is the religion of only a small minority of the people of Asia.

Europeans in Southeast Asia

Europeans began trading in Southeast Asia in the 1500s. The first European traders were Portuguese and Dutch. The Portuguese were the first to set up trading posts to trade for spices. Then the Dutch came in the late 1500s. The Dutch were followed by the British in the early 1600s.

Indonesia—After a while, the Dutch forced the Portuguese to leave most of Indonesia. The Dutch East India Company gained control of the trade. By 1800, the Dutch government had taken over Indonesia.

The Philippines—The Spanish were the first to reach the Philippines. The ships that Magellan was taking around the world (1519–1522) landed at the Philippines. By 1564, Spain had taken over most of the Philippines.

Malaysia—The Portuguese took over Malacca on the Malay peninsula in 1511. Then Dutch traders took it over. Finally, the British in the early 1800s took control of the land then called Malaya.

This area was very important. The Strait of Malacca is one of the world's most important waterways (see map below). The country that controlled the strait and other nearby waterways could control a lot of the trade in Southeast Asia.

Imperialism in the 1800s

The race for colonies reached its height in the 1800s. The Manchu government in China had ruled much of the mainland of Southeast Asia. As the Manchu government grew weaker, the European countries gained more control of the mainland.

Southeast Asia had many of the raw materials the industrial countries needed. The large population of Southeast Asia could also be a market for manufactured goods. This was just what the imperialist countries wanted—a place to get raw materials and a place to sell manufactured goods.

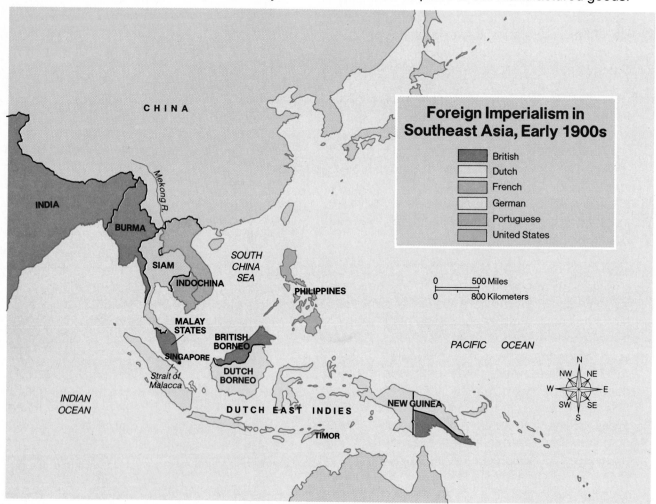

Foreign Imperialism in Southeast Asia, Early 1900s

- British
- Dutch
- French
- German
- Portuguese
- United States

The British in Burma—By the 1800s, Great Britain and France had become the imperialist leaders in Southeast Asia. The British took over northern Burma between 1824 and 1826. By 1885, the British gained control of the southern part. The British made Burma part of British India.

The French in Indochina—The French took the land that was known as Indochina. That land included what are now Vietnam, Laos, and Kampuchea (Cambodia). The southern part of Vietnam became a French colony. The rest became protectorates. They were ruled by native rulers who were controlled by the French. In 1887, France joined Vietnam and Cambodia. Laos came under French control in 1893. This area was called French Indochina.

The Philippines—The Spanish ruled the Philippines from the middle 1500s until the late 1800s. In 1896, the Philippine people started to fight the Spanish to gain their freedom. The United States sent some help to the fighters for freedom.

In 1898, Spain and the United States fought the Spanish-American War. Spain lost. The United States got the Philippines at the end of that war.

In the early 1900s, the United States began to prepare the Philippines for its freedom. All of the people in the United States did not agree that the Philippines should be free. Some U.S. citizens wanted many colonies. Others felt that the Philippines should be free.

Although the Philippines had been promised its freedom, it did not come very quickly.

Papua New Guinea—The British also took the area now called Papua New Guinea. It became a protectorate. In 1905, that land was ruled by Australia, which was part of the British family of nations. Australia was also near Papua New Guinea.

The Germans ruled the northern part of Papua New Guinea in the late 1800s and early 1900s. Most of Papua New Guinea was ruled by Australia, however.

Thailand

Only one country in Southeast Asia remained free. That country was Thailand. Thailand was then called Siam.

The people of Siam had come from their own kingdom. That kingdom had been in part of southern China. The Mongols destroyed their kingdom in 1253. Then the people moved south into an area that used to belong to the Khmer. The people of Siam learned the Khmer alphabet. They were in contact with India, too.

The first Europeans to reach Siam were the Portuguese. They came in 1511. The Burmese ruled part of Siam in the late 1500s. By the 1600s, Siam had become an important kingdom.

Siam was closed to foreigners in the late 1600s and in the 1700s. In the 1800s, it ended its isolation. Siam began to deal with Western countries. Siam also became more modern.

King Choulalonkorn of Siam. He ruled from 1869 to 1910. Notice his Western-style uniform. Siam had contact with Western countries in the 1800s.

Siam was located between British colonies and French colonies. It took advantage of this. Siam played the French against the British. That is probably why Siam was able to remain independent while the other countries in Southeast Asia were ruled by the imperialists.

63

Exercises

A. Finding the Main Idea:
Put a check next to the sentence that gives the main idea of what you have just read.

_____ **1.** The people of Southeast Asia belong to many different groups.

_____ **2.** Southeast Asia has monsoon winds.

_____ **3.** There were many Chinese influences on Vietnam.

_____ **4.** Parts of Southeast Asia were Hindu.

_____ **5.** India influenced the western parts of Southeast Asia.

_____ **6.** There are several crossroads in the world.

B. What Did You Read?
Choose the answer that best completes each sentence. Write the letter of your answer in the space provided.

_____ **1.** The religions that had the strongest influence on Southeast Asia were
    a. Buddhism, Islam, and Christianity.
    b. Hinduism, Islam, and Christianity.
    c. Hinduism, Buddhism, and Islam.
    d. Islam, Hinduism, and Judaism.

_____ **2.** The most important foreign influence on the Khmer of Cambodia came from
    a. Thailand.
    b. China.
    c. Vietnam.
    d. India.

_____ **3.** Monsoon winds were helpful in spreading
    a. the system of rule in Vietnam.
    b. Chinese ideas in Southeast Asia.
    c. Indian influences in Southeast Asia.
    d. all of the above.

_____ **4.** The fall of the T'ang dynasty ended Chinese rule of
    a. Cambodia.
    b. Indonesia.
    c. Malaya.
    d. Vietnam.

_____ **5.** The Dutch had most of their colonies in
  a. Thailand.
  b. Indonesia.
  c. Vietnam.
  d. Cambodia.

_____ **6.** All of the following were part of French Indochina *except*
  a. Laos.
  b. Vietnam.
  c. Burma.
  d. Cambodia.

C. Checking for Details:

Read each statement. Put a T in the space next to each statement if it is true. Put an F in that space if it is false. Put an N if you cannot tell from the reading if it is true or false.

_____ **1.** China's influence on Southeast Asia was stronger than India's.

_____ **2.** Under the Han dynasty, China controlled Vietnam.

_____ **3.** Southeast Asia is a crossroads that links Asia, Europe, and Africa.

_____ **4.** India was the country that the Vietnamese respected and feared.

_____ **5.** Dai-Viet was ruled by China.

_____ **6.** The Malays were the best sailors in Asia.

_____ **7.** Thailand was part of French Indochina.

_____ **8.** At one time, Angkor Thom was the largest city of Southeast Asia.

_____ **9.** The Champa kingdom was located in part of Vietnam.

D. Understanding Global History:

On page 58 you read about four factors in global history. Which of these factors applies to each statement listed below? Fill in the number of the correct statement on page 58 in the space provided. If no factor applies, fill in the word NONE.

_____ **1.** Chinese contact with Southeast Asia was by land. Indian contacts were by sea.

_____ **2.** While the Vietnamese were under Chinese rule, the language of China became the basis for the early language of Vietnam.

_____ **3.** Malay settlers in Southeast Asia brought a system of rice farming to the region.

_____ **4.** Angkor Wat was built during the Kambuja dynasty in Cambodia.

_____ **5.** Chinese rule over Vietnam ended with the fall of the T'ang dynasty.

Chapter 9

Early Kingdoms of Black Africa

Understanding Global History

Think about the following statements as you read about the early kingdoms of black Africa.
1. Nations are linked by a network of economic interdependence.
2. The physical environment can encourage or limit contact among people.
3. Contact among peoples and nations can lead to cultural changes.
4. Events occurring in one part of the world have influenced developments in other parts of the world.
5. Nations borrow and adapt ideas and institutions from other nations.

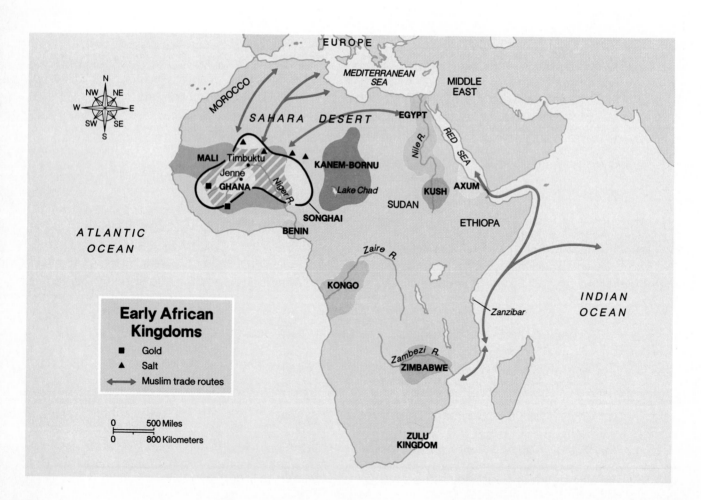

Early African Kingdoms

- ■ Gold
- ▲ Salt
- ←→ Muslim trade routes

0   500 Miles
0   800 Kilometers

Learning New Words and Terms

The following words are used in this chapter. Think about the meaning of each one.

Sudan: a grassland area that lies south of the Sahara and Libyan deserts; the Sudan area stretches from the Atlantic Ocean to the mountains of Libya

pagan: a person who believes in many gods

hadj: a pilgrimage to Mecca required of all Muslims

refugees: people forced to leave their homeland and find a new place to live

Think As You Read

1. What kind of trade was carried on between the people of the Sudan and traders from northern Africa?
2. How did the Muslim religion affect the African kingdoms of Ghana, Mali, and Songhai?
3. What were the great kingdoms of eastern Africa?
4. How did the actions of the Zulus affect southern Africa?

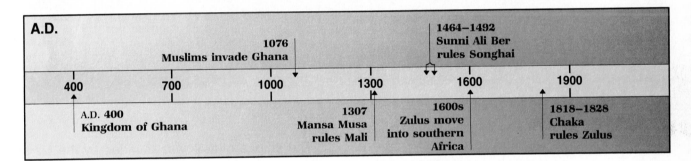

Early Kingdoms

Black Africans live mainly in the parts of Africa that are south of the Sahara desert. There have been kingdoms in black Africa for hundreds of years. We know about many of these early kingdoms through the writings of people from Europe, Asia, and the northern part of Africa.

The kingdom of Kush was found in eastern Africa. Axum was also in the east. The kingdoms of Ghana, Mali, and Songhai were in western Africa. The Zulus were in the south.

The Sudan

The area called the **Sudan** stretches from the Atlantic Ocean to the mountains of Ethiopia. The Sudan area lies between the Sahara and Libyan deserts to the north and the rain forests to the south. The Sudan is mainly an area of grasslands and some dry lands.

For many centuries, trade was carried on between the Sudan and northern Africa. Traders from northern Africa led caravans across the Sahara Desert. Caravans are groups of travelers moving together over the land with their goods. The caravans from northern Africa wanted to get to the markets in the Sudan.

Goods and Ideas Are Traded

Northern Africans had salt, tools, clothing and fine swords. They wanted to trade these for the Sudan's gold, ivory, and slaves. There was not much salt in the Sudan. Salt was very important, however. It was needed to keep food from spoiling. It was also needed to keep people healthy.

The traders from northern Africa brought more than salt and other goods. They also brought the religion of Islam to the Sudan. Islam played an important part in the early Sudan kingdoms. Most of these kingdoms were ruled by Muslims. Most of these kingdoms had Muslims in their courts as scholars and judges.

Ghana

The earliest known kingdom of the Sudan was Ghana. Nobody is sure when it began. Many people think it was about the 400s A.D. It was found in

The city of Timbuktu as it is today. The houses are made of dried mud.

a crossroads area. Ghana joined northern Africa, the western part of the Sudan, and eastern Africa (see map, p. 66). Ghana controlled the gold mines in the western Sudan. Control of the gold helped Ghana keep control of the trade with northern Africa.

Religion helped lead to Ghana's downfall. Ghana's rulers were Muslim. Most of the people of Ghana were not Muslim. Many of those who were Muslim did not practice their religion very strictly. They kept many of their **pagan** beliefs along with Islam.

Invasions from Northern Africa

In 1076, Muslims from northern Africa invaded Ghana. They wanted to force people to practice Islam more strictly. The Muslims killed many pagans. They also took control of Ghana's gold trade.

Within ten years, Ghana got its freedom back. The northern invaders were defeated. Ghana was left weaker, however. The different states that had been ruled by the emperor started to fight among themselves. Ghana never got back its strength as an empire. In the early 1200s, it fell to the kingdom of Mali.

Mali

The empire of Mali was founded by the Mandingo people. They saw that the empire of Ghana was growing weaker. A group that was north of Mali tried to destroy the Mandingo kings. Their plot failed. Instead of losing the battle, the Mandingo king got his army together. He destroyed the northern group's army in about 1240. Then, feeling strong from his victory, the king turned to take over the area that had been Ghana.

Mali took over the gold fields that Ghana had ruled. The new empire also widened the trade between the Muslim traders and the people of the Sudan. Mali's cities became centers of trade, religion, and culture. Timbuktu was one of the most famous Mali cities.

A Great Mali Emperor

In 1307, a Mali emperor called Mansa Musa came to the throne. Mansa means "king," so his name really means "King Musa." Mansa Musa became famous in Africa, Asia, and Europe for a **hadj** he made in 1324. A *hadj* is a pilgrimage to Mecca. Mecca is a city in Arabia. It is holy to Muslims.

People along the way who saw Mansa Musa could not believe his wealth. He had about 500 slaves and 100 camels. As he traveled, he gave out gold and gifts. He and the people with him bought many things. For years afterward, people spoke of Mansa Musa's wealth and generosity. His fame grew. Mali was shown on many European maps of the time.

When Mansa Musa returned to Mali, he had new mosques built in Mali's cities. A mosque is a Muslim place of worship.

The Weakening of Mali

After Mansa Musa's death, Mali weakened. His son could not keep a strong rule over the empire. Local village chiefs began to rise up against the Mali rulers. The rulers were Muslim. So were many of the people. But there were also many in Mali who held on to their pagan beliefs. The religious differences helped weaken the empire.

One of the local groups who rose against Mali was from Songhai (SAWNG-hi). In the 1400s, Songhai overthrew Mali's rule. Now it was Songhai's chance to have the great empire of the Sudan.

Songhai

Songhai was a little to the east of where Ghana and Mali had their empires. For a long time, Songhai had been a trade center. It gained strength during the 1300s under its Sunni dynasty.

In 1464, a new Sunni ruler came to power. He was Sunni Ali Ber, or Sunni Ali the Great. Sunni Ali was in many ways a cruel ruler and a tyrant. He had many scholars and religious people killed.

Sunni Ali Ber took the cities of Jenne and Timbuktu from Mali. He made the Songhai government stronger. He also spread the reach of its power. A fleet of boats helped Songhai control trade along the Niger River. Sunni Ali Ber died in 1492.

The Askia Dynasty

After Sunni Ali Ber's death, one of his fellow soldiers took the throne from the Sunni son. The new leader took the title Askia. His dynasty was known as the Askia dynasty. The Askia dynasty enlarged Songhai's borders. It also increased trade with other parts of Africa. At its height, Songhai's rule reached from the Sahara in the north to the rain forest in the south. It also reached from

Artists of Benin made this ivory mask. Benin was a kingdom in western Africa.

the Atlantic Ocean almost to Lake Chad (see map, p. 66).

Under the Askia ruler, Islam was encouraged. In the cities, Muslim beliefs were strong. Songhai's leaders were Muslim. However, most village people kept their pagan customs. Therefore, most of the people in the empire were pagans. Muslim scholars and religious leaders were favored by the rulers of Songhai.

Attack from Northern Africa

In the late 1500s, the northern African kingdom of Morocco attacked Songhai. The Moroccan king Ahmed al-Mansur wanted to control the Sudan's trade in salt and gold.

The Moroccans had to try more than once. On the first try, almost all of the army of thousands died crossing the Sahara. Their biggest trouble had been finding enough water.

Then al-Mansur, "The Victorious," sent more soldiers to take the salt mines. They took the mines, but the miners escaped. There was nobody left to mine the salt.

Finally, the Moroccan king sent another army in about 1590. Only about 1,000 out of the 4,000 soldiers lived through the desert march to attack Songhai. Their guns were too much for the spears and arrows of the Songhai warriors, however. Songhai was defeated. Its once-great empire became just a group of small village-states.

Kingdoms of Eastern Africa

To the east of the Sudan region, there were other great kingdoms. The kingdom of Kush rose from small settlements on the upper part of the Nile. It was influenced by Egypt, Greece, and Rome. During the 300s A.D., the nearby kingdom of Axum crushed Kush.

Axum's rulers made Christianity the religion of the kingdom. Trade with Rome, India, and the central parts of Africa helped Axum become stronger. When Rome fell, Axum was ruined. It had lost an important trading partner. Then, in the 500s, Axum's trade with India ended. Muslim conquests in the 600s cut off Axum's trade with Egypt and northern Africa. Axum's power weakened rapidly.

Ethiopia

After A.D. 700, many people in Axum moved south. They took over lands that were held by pagan peoples. They converted the pagans to Christianity. The new kingdom of Ethiopia began. Axum's Christians were its nobles.

After the early 1100s, the nobles lost control of Axum. A new form of Christianity began to develop in Ethiopia. When the nobles got back their power after 150 years, an Ethiopian form of Christianity had been formed.

Christian Ethiopia faced many attacks from its Muslim neighbors over the years. In the 1500s, Ethiopia asked Portugal for help. With the use of guns from Portugal, Ethiopia defeated the invaders. Even so, Ethiopia had been weakened by Muslim attacks and by disputes inside Ethiopia.

The Zulu Kingdom of the South

The Zulus were a Bantu-speaking people in southern Africa. Bantu is a group of African languages. The people of Africa south of the Sahara speak Bantu languages. The Zulus had moved into southern Africa in the 1600s. In the late 1700s, they were ruled by a chief named Dingiswayo. Dingiswayo died in battle in 1818. Chaka, one of his military leaders, took over.

Chaka's Military Rule

Chaka set up a military system. He had young men of about the same age form a group of warriors. They had good weapons, a strong plan for battle, and strict discipline. These factors made them excellent warriors.

Chaka had a military plan. He wanted to bring all Bantu-speaking people under his power. He called this military plan the *mfekane*. This means "crushing." To do what he wanted, Chaka had to crush the other Bantu-speaking people.

The *mfekane* succeeded. Many Bantu people fled in fear in all directions. They became **refugees**. They had to leave their homeland and find a new home. Many refugees decided to fight back. They became fierce warriors. Huge movements of people, many wars, and some new kingdoms came about as a result of Chaka's *mfekane*.

Chaka was killed by his half brother in 1828. The brother, Dingane, was not able to continue Chaka's military successes.

Europeans were beginning to move into southern Africa. Soon the Zulus were fighting the Europeans.

Zulu warriors.

Exercises

A. Finding the Main Ideas:

Put a check next to the sentences that give the main ideas of what you have just read.

_____ **1.** Ghana was a black, Islamic kingdom.

_____ **2.** Ethiopia developed its own religion and its own monarchy.

_____ **3.** Many black kingdoms existed in Africa before 1800.

_____ **4.** The Sunni dynasty ruled Songhai.

_____ **5.** Islam played an important part in the kingdoms of the Sudan.

_____ **6.** The Zulus had a great effect on events in southern Africa.

B. What Did You Read?

Choose the answer that best completes each sentence. Write the letter of your answer in the space provided.

_____ **1.** Merchants from northern Africa traded their goods in the Sudan for
a. slaves.
b. gold.
c. ivory.
d. all of the above.

_____ **2.** Islam was the religion of all the following *except*
a. Ghana.
b. Ethiopia.
c. Mali.
d. Songhai.

_____ **3.** The people of Axum were later the leaders of
a. Mali.
b. Songhai.
c. Ethiopia.
d. Ghana.

_____ **4.** The Zulu kingdom was located in
a. northern Africa.
b. southern Africa.
c. the Sudan.
d. western Africa.

_____ **5.** Mansa Musa was the emperor of
a. Morocco.
b. Ghana.
c. Songhai.
d. Mali.

_____ **6.** The Askia dynasty ruled the kingdom of
a. Songhai.
b. Mali.
c. Ethiopia.
d. Ghana.

C. Checking for Details:

Read each statement. Put a T in the space next to each statement if it is true. Put an F in that space if it is false. Put an N if you cannot tell from the reading if it is true or false.

_____ **1.** All the people of Ghana accepted Islam.

_____ **2.** The Sudan region is mostly grassland.

_____ **3.** Timbuktu was a religious center in the Mali kingdom.

_____ **4.** Salt was scarce in the Sudan.

_____ **5.** Ghana was a kingdom in eastern Africa.

_____ **6.** Black Africans live mainly in the part of Africa that is south of the Sahara.

_____ **7.** Ghana was the last of the black kingdoms of Africa.

_____ **8.** Zulu warriors followed strict discipline.

_____ **9.** Chaka's *mfekane* was a religious war.

_____ **10.** Ethiopia got along well with its Muslim neighbors.

D. Who Were They?

Name the person or groups of people described in each sentence. Write the answer in the space provided.

_____ **1.** We overthrew the Mali rule.

_____ **2.** We were defeated by attacks from Morocco.

_____ **3.** We defeated the kingdom of Kush.

_____ **4.** We were a military power in southern Africa.

_____ **5.** We were the first black kingdom to control the gold mines of the western Sudan.

_____ **6.** We are the people who founded the Mali kingdom.

_____ **7.** I began the *mfekane*.

_____ **8.** I began the Sunni dynasty in Songhai.

_____ **9.** We were ruined by the fall of Rome.

_____ **10.** We developed a new form of Christianity.

E. Chronology Skills:

In the space provided, write the letter of the event that took place first. You may use the text and the time line on page 67 for help.

_____ **1. a.** kingdom of Kush
 b. kingdom of Ethiopia
 c. kingdom of Axum

_____ **2. a.** kingdom of Mali
 b. kingdom of Ghana
 c. kingdom of Songhai

_____ **3. a.** kingdom of Ghana
 b. Zulu kingdom
 c. kingdom of Axum

_____ **4. a.** Mansa Musa's *hadj*
 b. Askia dynasty
 c. Chaka's *mfekane*

_____ **5. a.** rule of Dingiswayo
 b. Europeans settle in southern Africa
 c. Chaka's *mfekane*

_____ **6. a.** Portuguese help Ethiopia
 b. rise of Axum
 c. Christianity develops in Ethiopia

F. Thinking it Over:

Answer each of the following questions in three or four sentences. Use a separate piece of paper.

1. Several African nations today have taken the names of earlier black kingdoms. They include Mali, Benin, Ghana, and Zimbabwe. Why do you think they chose these names? What does it tell about how Africans feel about their history?

2. Mansa Musa's *hadj* was one of the most famous of any Muslim in history. What good could such fame have done for his empire? How has it helped people today learn about his empire?

G. Understanding Global History:

On page 66 you read about five factors in global history. Which of these factors applies to each statement listed below? Fill in the number of the correct statement on page 66 in the space provided. If no factor applies, fill in the word NONE.

_____ 1. The northern African regions were separated from the Sudan by the Sahara Desert.

_____ 2. The rulers of Ghana were Muslims.

_____ 3. The fall of Rome ruined the kingdom of Axum.

_____ 4. Northern Africans traded salt, tools, and fine swords for gold, ivory, and slaves from the Sudan.

_____ 5. Islam became the religion of many rulers of the Sudan.

_____ 6. A new form of Christianity arose in Ethiopia.

Chapter 10

Imperialism in Africa

Think about the following statements as you read about imperialism in Africa.

1 The physical environment can encourage or limit contact among people.

2 Events occurring in one part of the world have influenced developments in other parts of the world.

3 People should learn to understand and appreciate cultures different from their own.

4 Contact among peoples and nations can lead to cultural changes.

Victoria Falls of the Zambezi River. The falls were discovered in 1855 by Dr. David Livingstone, an explorer and missionary. He named them after Queen Victoria of England.

Learning New Words and Terms

The following words are used in this chapter. Think about the meaning of each one.

Boer: a farmer from the Netherlands who settled in the area that is now South Africa

assegais: thin spears with iron tips; used by Zulu warriors in southern Africa

trek: a long and hard journey on foot

Think As You Read

1. Why were the Europeans able to take over so much of Africa?
2. How did events in Europe affect the taking of colonies in Africa?
3. What European countries held colonies in Africa? Where were the colonies? Which African countries remained free?
4. What were the good and bad effects of imperialism on Africa?

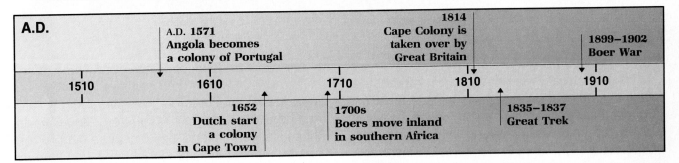

A.D.

A.D. **1571**
Angola becomes a colony of Portugal

1814
Cape Colony is taken over by Great Britain

1899–1902
Boer War

| 1510 | 1610 | 1710 | 1810 | 1910 |

1652
Dutch start a colony in Cape Town

1700s
Boers move inland in southern Africa

1835–1837
Great Trek

Knowledge of Africa Before 1400

Europeans knew little about Africa until the 1400s. Sailors from Europe were afraid to sail too far into the southern Atlantic. They had no maps. They did not know if there were places to stop and get fresh food and supplies. These problems limited travel by sea to western Africa.

Travel by land from Europe was blocked by the Sahara Desert. Only the traders of northern Africa dared to cross the Sahara.

Even Africans did not know all of Africa. Many rivers in Africa have waterfalls that make them poor waterways for boats. Travel over land was the only way to get somewhere. This often meant traveling through different climates. It also meant finding people who might not be friendly. Most Africans knew only their own places and the places they traded with.

Some people in Asia had sailed to the eastern coast of Africa from time to time. Malay sailors and others had reached the eastern coast.

The First Europeans in Black Africa

Life in Europe changed during the 1400s. This was the time of the Renaissance. Europeans improved their sailing ships. They made better in-struments for sailing. Better ships and better equipment made sailors from Europe feel ready to try new waters. The Renaissance was a time of growing interest in trade. In the 1400s sailors and shipowners were more willing to take the risk of exploring the African coast.

The Portuguese Sail Along Africa's Coast

Sailors from Portugal were the first Europeans to make direct contact with Africa south of the Sahara. Prince Henry of Portugal encouraged exploration. Ship captains were trained in Prince Henry's navigation school. They used their skill to explore the western coast of Africa in the middle 1400s.

Sailors from Portugal learned about the gold trade of the Sudan. The southern part of the Sudan coast became known as the "gold coast." Portugal soon had hopes of finding gold in Africa. Their main goal, however, was to find a new sea route to India.

In November 1497, Vasco da Gama found the new sea route around Africa. He reached India in May 1498. Before long, Portugal set up trading posts along eastern Africa and in India. The Portuguese were also active in the slave trade.

The city of Loango in western Africa, 1700s. This city was in the Kingdom of Congo. European visitors to the city made this drawing.

Portuguese Aims in Africa

At first, Portugal was interested in Africa as a place to stop over on the way to India. A few Portuguese did settle on the African coast. They did not set up colonies for a long time, however. It was not until 1571 that Portugal took Angola as a colony (see map, p. 79).

How Problems in Africa Helped the Europeans

When sailors from Portugal first explored the coast of Africa, there were some strong African kingdoms. Songhai was still powerful. There was also a kingdom at the mouth of the Zaire River (then called the Congo River).

The Portuguese usually made agreements with the rulers of the places where they stopped. The Portuguese agreed to exchange goods for food, water, and supplies. At the time, the Portuguese did not seem to be a threat to the Africans.

Songhai grew weak. The kingdom at the mouth of the Zaire disappeared. There were no strong empires left in Africa. Songhai had already learned that spears, swords, and bows and arrows could not win against guns. When European countries were ready to take colonies, there was no longer a strong African kingdom to stop them.

The Slave Trade

There were stories in Europe about the profits to be made in the slave trade. These stories brought more Europeans to Africa. England and France joined the slave trade in the middle 1600s.

The slave trade made things even worse. Africa had traded in slaves for centuries. As more and more Europeans entered the slave trade, greater numbers of slaves were taken from Africa. To get these slaves, Africans had to capture people from nearby tribes. Because of that, tribes fought each other. This kept different groups of Africans from working together to keep out the Europeans.

A slave market in Africa, 1800s.

The Dutch in Africa

The Dutch are the people of the Netherlands. In the late 1500s, the Dutch gained their freedom from Spain. They became a seagoing power.

Dutch ships moved into the slave trade in the early 1600s. The Dutch took trade centers on Africa's gold coast. They also moved farther south. In 1652 they set up a trading station in southern Africa. Their trading station was near where the city of Cape Town is today. A Dutch colony, known as the Cape Colony, grew at that site.

The Boers Move Inland

More Dutch settlers continued to arrive at the Cape Colony. They were called **Boers** (BORS). This is a Dutch word meaning farmer or peasant. The Boers were very independent. They did not like the rules that the Dutch officials set up.

Many Boers moved inland. They started large cattle farms. By the late 1700s, they found themselves fighting with the Bantu-speaking peoples of southern Africa. They came into conflict with the well-trained Zulu warriors. The Boers had better weapons, however. The arrows and **assegais,** or spears, of the Africans were no match for the Boers' guns. By the early 1800s, the Boers ruled large parts of the inland part of southern Africa.

For a while it looked as if the Boers would control southern Africa. Then, around 1800, the British began to settle there.

Great Britain Adds to Its Colonies

England took the name Great Britain in the early 1700s. At that time, England joined with Scotland. Great Britain added to its colonies in North America and other parts of the world. The British lost some of their North American colonies in 1783. This is when the thirteen British colonies became the independent United States of America. Canada, however, remained a North American colony. In Asia, the British still held India.

During the 1800s, Great Britain became a major imperialist power in Africa.

The Congress of Vienna Helps Great Britain

Events in Europe in the early 1800s helped the British gain control of southern Africa. The first defeat of Napoleon in Europe, in 1814, led to the Congress of Vienna. This congress was called mainly to settle the boundaries of Europe after Napoleon's wars had destroyed them. It also was supposed to settle who was the ruler of each European country.

Besides doing these things, the Congress of Vienna decided which European countries would hold some colonies in other parts of the world.

Great Britain, Austria, Prussia, and Russia controlled the Congress of Vienna. They changed boundaries and colonies. One result of their work was that the Netherlands lost the Cape Colony in Africa. The Cape Colony became a British possession in 1814.

Fighting in South Africa

The Boers were now British subjects. They did not like that. The black Africans, especially the Zulus, thought all Europeans were enemies. It did not matter whether they were Boers or British.

The stage was now set for many kinds of fighting. The Boers and British fought each other. The Boers and Zulus fought each other. The British and Zulus fought each other.

The Great Trek

During the 1830s, the Boers moved away from the Cape area. Their movement north is known as the Great **Trek.** A trek is a long and hard walk. The Great Trek lasted from 1835 to 1837.

The Boers found themselves fighting the Zulus. The Zulus were led by Chaka's brother Dingane (see p. 70). They fought, and the Boers won. This left the way open for the Boers to settle in the northern part of southern Africa.

The Boers Against the British

The Boers set up the Orange Free State and the Transvaal as independent areas. Then diamonds and gold were discovered in the area. Many British settlers rushed into the region. They hoped to get rich. When the Boers tried to stop the British, fighting broke out.

Some British settlers helped bring about a war. Many imperialists in Great Britain wanted this war. The Boer War was fought from 1899 to 1902. It ended with the Boers losing. The British set up a colony called the Union of South Africa.

Europeans Explore the African Continent

Until about 1850, most European settlements were just along the coast of Africa. Even after more than 300 years, little was known about the inside of the continent.

Dr. David Livingstone was a Scottish doctor. He went to Africa as a medical missionary in the mid-1800s. He also explored Africa. When nobody heard from Dr. Livingstone for a long time, a U.S. newspaper sent a reporter to find him. This was Henry Stanley. This picture shows the meeting of Stanley, on the left, and Livingstone in 1871.

Many explorers began to travel through Africa. Some wanted to make maps of the continent. Many of them were there for adventure. A few were really trying to help the Africans.

King Leopold and the Congo

European countries wanted to learn more about the center of Africa. King Leopold II of Belgium formed a private company. The company was formed to explore the area then called the Congo. This was in the central part of Africa. The equator passes through the Congo. This company was also supposed to help improve the area. This meant building railroads and bringing in other modern things.

King Leopold hired Henry Stanley (see above) to explore the area around the equator.

The Conference of Berlin

Other European countries were moving into Africa. Many countries were worried about free trade. In 1884, Germany called a conference of all European nations to decide what to do about Africa. The United States and Turkey also attended the Conference of Berlin. The conference was called to set up some system of free trade in Africa. It was also supposed to set up rules for forming colonies in Africa.

The Conference of Berlin did not really do either of these things. It set up a system that helped Europeans gain rule over almost all of Africa. It also gave King Leopold II of Belgium the right to the Congo.

Shortly after the conference, King Leopold began to rule the Congo as his own private property. After a while, stories came out of the Congo about very cruel treatment of the African people. Leopold was forced to turn the Congo over to his country, Belgium.

The Europeans Race for Colonies

The race was on! Great Britain took over colonies on both the west and east coasts of Africa. Great Britain also controlled the Suez Canal. The canal had been built between 1859 and 1869. It was Britain's fastest route to India.

France took over some colonies, too. Some of France's colonies were in northern Africa, on the Mediterranean Sea. Other colonies were in the part of Africa south of the Sahara. The map on page 79 shows which European countries had colonies in Africa. Can you find any free countries?

How Imperialism in Africa Worked

The European countries wanted the same things in Africa that they wanted in other places. They wanted places to get raw materials. They wanted places to sell manufactured goods.

Most of the time, the European countries did not have to fight the Africans to get colonies. They often were able to make agreements with local rulers. These agreements gave the rulers good chances for trade. They also promised that modern goods would flow into Africa. Often the rulers gained something from dealing with the Europeans. Most of the rest of the African people did not.

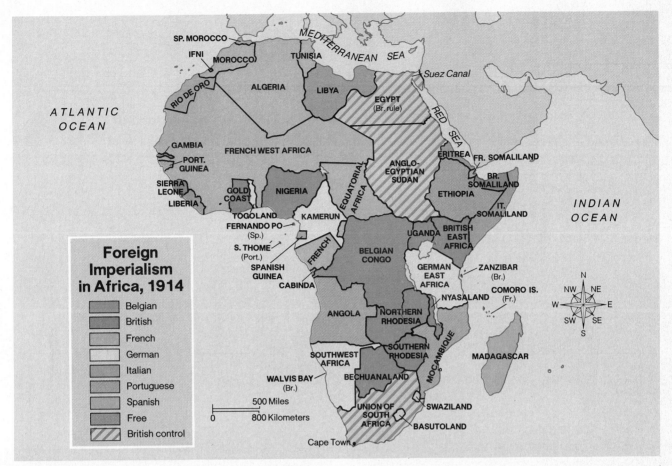

Foreign Imperialism in Africa, 1914

- Belgian
- British
- French
- German
- Italian
- Portuguese
- Spanish
- Free
- British control

500 Miles
0   800 Kilometers

Most of the imperialist countries also sent missionaries to Africa. The missionaries went to convert Africans to Christianity. They were not always welcome, however. Often, the African people saw the missionaries as just another way of pushing the interests of the imperialist countries.

The Borders of the Colonies

The Europeans set up borders between African colonies. These borders made sense from the European point of view. They did not make sense from the African point of view. Often, tribes that did not get along were brought together in one colony. Sometimes one tribe was split up into two or more colonies. This was not always done on purpose. Often, the European countries did not know about the tribal groups.

The Good and the Bad of Imperialism

It is fairly easy to figure out some of the bad points of imperialism in Africa. The African cultures were not thought of as important. Europeans tried to make Africans feel that they were inferior to Europeans. African languages were not even used.

Many Europeans treated Africans badly. For many years Africans who worked on plantations or in mines were expected to do a certain amount of work a day no matter what. If they could not do it, they were punished. Many Africans were treated like slaves.

Families and tribes were often separated because of the imperial powers. The main interest of the imperialist countries was getting the raw materials. They didn't care how the African people might suffer.

Some Africans did gain something from imperialism. Many received an education. A few were even sent to schools in Europe for more education. Cities and factories were built. Transportation was improved. Much of this was done for the Europeans. It helped the Africans, too.

One important result was that the people of Africa began to make contacts with people in other continents and on their own continent. Ideas were exchanged. Cultural contact was having an effect.

Exercises

A. Finding the Main Ideas:
Put a check next to the sentences that give the main ideas of what you have just read.

_____ **1.** The Boer War took place in southern Africa.

_____ **2.** The Zulus used spears called *assegais*.

_____ **3.** European imperialism in Africa began in the 1500s and grew strongest in the 1800s.

_____ **4.** The Renaissance in Europe affected Africa.

_____ **5.** By the 1900s, most of Africa had been taken over by imperialists.

B. What Did You Read?
Choose the answer that best completes each sentence. Write the letter of your answer in the space provided.

_____ **1.** The gold coast of Africa was in
  a. northern Africa.
  b. the southern part of
    the western Sudan.
  c. the eastern coast of Africa.
  d. the southern tip of Africa.

_____ **2.** The first Europeans in the
  Cape Colony were the
  a. Dutch.
  b. Portuguese.
  c. British.
  d. Spanish.

_____ **3.** The Great Trek was made by the
  a. Zulus.
  b. British.
  c. Boers.
  d. Portuguese.

_____ **4.** European efforts to explore Africa
  were helped by
  a. a growing interest in trade.
  b. better ships.
  c. better sailing instruments.
  d. all of the above.

_____ **5.** The Congress of Vienna gave
  the Cape Colony to
  a. the Dutch.
  b. the French.
  c. Napoleon.
  d. the British.

_____ **6.** The Conference of Berlin
  was called to
  a. settle European borders.
  b. try to get free trade in Africa.
  c. settle a problem between
    the Boers and the British.
  d. explore the center of Africa

C. Who Were They?

Name the country, groups of people, or person described in each sentence. Write the answer in the space provided.

_____ **1.** Our country's sea captains were trained in Prince Henry's school.

_____ **2.** Our country gained its freedom from Spain. It became a seagoing power.

_____ **3.** We moved inland and settled in southern Africa.

_____ **4.** Our country received the Cape Colony as a result of the Congress of Vienna.

_____ **5.** We fought agains the Boers and the British in southern Africa.

_____ **6.** I owned the Belgian Congo after the Conference of Berlin.

_____ **7.** Our country controlled the Suez Canal.

_____ **8.** Vasco da Gama established a sea route around Africa for our country.

D. Matching:

Match each imperialist power in Column A with the areas it controlled in Column B. Use the map on page 79 for help.

Column A

_____ **1.** Great Britain
_____ **2.** France
_____ **3.** Germany
_____ **4.** Portugal
_____ **5.** Italy

Column B

a. Tunisia
b. Angola
c. Cameroon
d. Nigeria
e. Libya

E. Understanding Global History:

On page 74 you read about four factors in global history. Which of these factors applies to each statement listed below? Fill in the number of the correct statement on page 74 in the space provided. If no factor applies, fill in the word NONE.

_____ **1.** The Congress of Vienna helped the British gain control of southern Africa.

_____ **2.** Most Europeans did not try to understand the cultures of the different African peoples.

_____ **3.** England and France moved into the slave trade in the middle 1600s.

_____ **4.** Europeans could not reach the Sudan by land because it was hard to cross the Sahara Desert.

_____ **5.** Some Africans were sent to schools in Europe. There, they made contacts with other peoples.

Chapter 11

Imperialism and the Americas

Understanding Global History

Think about the following statements as you read about imperialism in the Americas.
1 Nations are linked by a network of economic interdependence.
2 Events occurring in one part of the world have influenced developments in other parts of the world.
3 The culture in which we live influences our view of other people.

The United States fought Spain in 1898. Fighting took place in Cuba, shown here, and in the Philippines. Cuba won its freedom from Spain as a result of the war. The United States gained Puerto Rico and the Philippines as well as Guam.

Think As You Read

1. What was the United States' main interest in the Americas after 1865?
2. How did the Spanish-American War in 1898 affect the United States' move toward imperialism?
3. How did the United States extend the meaning of the Monroe Doctrine?
4. What did Latin Americans think of the "big stick" policies of the United States?

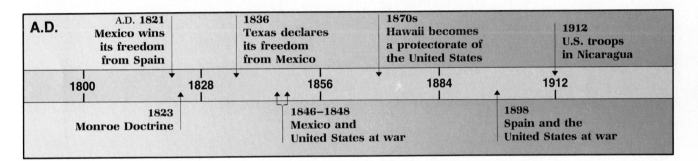

A.D.

| A.D. 1821 Mexico wins its freedom from Spain | 1836 Texas declares its freedom from Mexico | 1870s Hawaii becomes a protectorate of the United States | 1912 U.S. troops in Nicaragua |

1800 — 1828 — 1856 — 1884 — 1912

1823 Monroe Doctrine | 1846–1848 Mexico and United States at war | 1898 Spain and the United States at war

Early Imperialism in the Americas

Europeans had brought an early form of imperialism to North and South America. From the 1500s to the 1800s, people from European countries came to settle in the colonies in the Americas. After a while, the imperial countries started treating the settlers differently from the way the people who stayed in Europe were treated. Sometimes they were treated like other colonial people.

The European countries lost most of their American colonies by the middle 1800s. The British still held Canada. Russia owned Alaska. Most of the Caribbean islands were still colonies of European countries. British, Dutch, and French Guiana in South America were colonies. Most of the rest of the Americas had become independent (see map, p. 84).

Independence in the Americas

The thirteen British colonies that became the United States were the first to gain their freedom. England had tried to use these colonies as a place to get raw materials and to sell finished products. The colonists rebelled.

The United States gained its freedom in 1783. Other countries in the Americas fought for their freedom, too. Haiti declared its independence in 1804. Mexico became free of Spain in 1821. Central America gained independence from Spain between 1821 and 1823. Simón Bolívar helped free what are now the countries of Venezuela, Colombia, Panama, Ecuador, Peru, and Bolivia. By the 1820s, they were free of Spain. José de San Martín and Bernardo O'Higgins helped free Argentina and Chile.

The United States had hoped that these freed countries would become democracies. Most of them were ruled instead by **dictators.** These were rulers who have all the power in a country. They do not allow others to make decisions. They forbid the people to vote in open elections.

The Monroe Doctrine

In 1823, President James Monroe of the United States made an important speech. He said that no more colonies could be set up on the continents of North and South America. He also said that the United States would stay out of European affairs.

83

Latin America Becomes Free

PARENT COUNTRY

- Spain
- Portugal
- Great Britain
- Netherlands
- France

Note: Nicaragua, Honduras, and Costa Rica became free in 1821. In 1838, they became separate republics. Venezuela became free in 1821 also. It separated from Colombia in 1830.

In turn, European countries should stay out of the Americas.

This statement is called the Monroe Doctrine. There was an important reason why it was made. The United States was afraid that European countries would try to take over the countries in South America that were just gaining their freedom.

The United States Grows

The United States began to grow from thirteen colonies to many states. People moved west. As they did so, they took over the land from the Native Americans who lived there. The new country bought the Louisiana Territory from France in 1803. People pushed on westward.

By the middle of the 1800s, the United States began to disagree with its neighbors. These were Mexico to the south and Canada to the north. The disagreement was about the borders of the United States. The United States managed to settle most of its difficulties with England about the border with Canada without going to war. (At the time, Canada was still a colony of England.)

Texas

The United States fought with Mexico over Texas. At one time Texas was part of Mexico. Mexico had welcomed settlers from the United States. After a while, there were more U.S. settlers in Texas than Mexicans. In 1836, the U.S. settlers in Texas declared their freedom from Mexico.

Mexican forces storming the Alamo during the Texas war for independence, 1836. Less than 200 Americans held the Alamo for 12 days against 4,000 Mexican soldiers.

In 1845, Texas became a state of the United States. This led to war with Mexico. The war lasted from 1846 to 1848. At the end of the war, Mexico had lost most of the land between Texas and California to the United States. That was about half of all Mexico's land.

Mexico was angry. Many other countries of Latin America began to worry about imperialist interests of the United States.

The United States After the Civil War

After the Civil War (1861–1865) the United States underwent a big change. Its industry was growing very fast. The United States was becoming an industrial power. It began to show an interest in nearby Central and South America and the Caribbean islands. By the end of the 1800s the United States was also showing an interest in Asia.

Alaska

In 1867, the United States bought Alaska from Russia. The United States paid a little more than seven million dollars. One of the main reasons for buying Alaska was to keep Russia out of North America. At the time, many people thought it was foolish to spend so much money on Alaska. They thought it was little more than an icebox. Later, buying Alaska turned out to be a smart move.

The United States Goes to War With Spain

The United States wanted to get the Spanish out of the Caribbean area. Spain still held Cuba and Puerto Rico. Its hold was growing weaker on these places, however. People in those islands had been fighting for freedom. The Philippines in the Pacific also wanted its freedom.

Many people in the United States wanted to see independence in Cuba and in the Philippines. Relations between the United States and Spain were growing worse. Then, in 1898, the battleship the U.S.S. *Maine* was blown up and sank in the harbor of Havana, Cuba. Nobody knew exactly what happened. The United States blamed Spain. That led to the Spanish-American War.

The war was fought in the Caribbean and in the Pacific. The United States destroyed the Spanish naval forces at Manila Bay in the Philippines. It wiped out the Spanish forces outside Santiago harbor in Cuba. At the same time, American soldiers captured the city of Santiago in Cuba.

The United States Gains Territory

After the war, Spain gave Cuba its freedom. The United States gained from Spain the colonies of Puerto Rico and the Philippines. It also gained Guam, an island in the Pacific.

Puerto Rico and Cuba

Puerto Rico became a possession of the United States. Its people became limited American citizens in 1917. Puerto Ricans could elect representatives to the government of the United States. The governor of Puerto Rico and its important officials were appointed by the U.S. government.

Cuba gained its freedom. However, it remained under the influence of the United States. Cuba had to allow the United States to use a naval base. This was Guantanamo Bay, at the eastern tip of Cuba. The United States also got the right to step into Cuban affairs.

Queen Liliuokalani of Hawaii. She was the last ruler of Hawaii.

Hawaii

American traders had begun to trade with Hawaii in about 1810. American missionaries began to work in Hawaii in about 1820. U.S. business interests there grew. By the 1870s, Hawaii was almost a protectorate of the United States.

The United States made a treaty to have a naval base at Pearl Harbor. This was in Hawaii. Americans helped to overthrow the Hawaiian queen in 1893. Then the United States began to rule Hawaii. By 1900, Hawaii had been made a territory of the United States.

Extending the Monroe Doctrine

The United States played a big role in the Americas. This was true during the 1890s and early 1900s. The United States used the Monroe Doctrine to gain even greater control of what went on in the Americas. For example, Great Britain and Venezuela had been disagreeing about the border between Venezuela and Guyana (then British Guiana). The two countries had been arguing about the border for years. Venezuela asked the United States for help.

The United States said that the countries should settle it by **arbitration**. This is a decision made by someone who has listened to both sides. That someone does not favor either side. The United States was the arbitrator. The United States warned the British that if they refused they would be acting against the Monroe Doctrine.

The British refused at first. For a time there was a danger of war. Finally, the United States did settle the border dispute by arbitration. The danger of war was gone. Europeans and Latin Americans felt some relief. They still worried about the growing American power, however.

Venezuela's Debts to Europe

In 1902, Venezuela was again in trouble. The government of Venezuela owed money to Great Britain, Germany, Italy, and some other European countries. Venezuela was not able to pay the money it owed. The European countries sent warships to force payment. Many Latin American countries were angry. They wanted the United States to protect Venezuela from the European warships. If the Monroe Doctrine meant anything, they thought, the United States should act to help Venezuela.

American pressure did get the Europeans to go to arbitration. The United States refused to act as the arbitrator, however.

The Dominican Republic

In 1904, the Dominican Republic could not pay its debts to European countries. The United States warned the European countries that it would not permit them to do anything to force the Dominican Republic to pay. In 1905, U.S. armed forces took control of the Dominican Republic. The United States arranged for the payment of the debt.

The "Big Stick" Policy

President Theodore Roosevelt called the action in the Dominican Republic an extension of the Monroe Doctrine. He spoke of it as a "big stick" policy. This was part of a saying of his. Roosevelt said that the United States should "speak softly and carry a big stick."

Many Latin American countries were angry about the "big stick" policy. They took the idea to mean that the United States had imperialist control over Latin America. Bad feelings in Latin America grew deeper and deeper.

A Canal in Central America

The United States wanted to build a canal across Central America. Without a canal, the only way ships could travel from the east coast to the west coast was to go around the tip of South America. This was a long trip. The waters at the southern tip of South America made it a dangerous trip, too. Some travelers would go by boat to the isthmus of Panama. (An isthmus is a narrow strip of land. It connects two larger bodies of land.) Travelers would cross the isthmus and then go by boat for the rest of the trip. That was also a long, hard trip.

Panama Rebels

Panama was part of the country of Colombia. In 1903, people from the United States encouraged a rebellion in Panama. It succeeded. Panama declared its independence from Colombia. The United States thus gained the right to build a canal. The United States owned the canal. It also had control of land on each side of the canal.

After it was built, the canal was used by the seagoing countries of the world. Even though many countries liked having the canal, they did not like the way the United States got the right to build it.

Nicaragua

The United States also took part in actions in Nicaragua. For some years Great Britain and the United States had been thinking of building another canal through Nicaragua.

In 1912, the U.S. Marines moved into Nicaragua to support one side in a civil war. (A civil war is a war within a nation.) That led to a treaty giving the United States the right to build a canal. The U.S. Marines stayed in Nicaragua. They left for a short while in 1925. The Marines returned, however. This time they stayed until 1933. The United States used the marines to keep the government it wanted in Nicaragua. It never built the canal.

The Strongest Country in the Americas

In the early 1900s, the United States was the strongest country in the Americas. The gains the United States made from the Spanish-American War and other activities made U.S. nationalism stronger. At the same time, its control over other areas helped increase feelings of imperialism in the United States.

Imperialist countries usually thought that it was their right or their duty to step into the affairs of other countries. The United States had protectorates and spheres of influence. It moved in when it did not like the way some other American country was acting. The countries in Latin America remembered the fact that the United States did not treat them as equals.

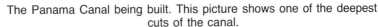

The Panama Canal being built. This picture shows one of the deepest cuts of the canal.

Exercises

A. Finding the Main Ideas:

Put a check next to the sentences that give the main ideas of what you have just read.

_____ **1.** Alaska was important to the United States.

_____ **2.** The United States developed a policy of imperialism in the Americas.

_____ **3.** Europeans had interests in the Americas.

_____ **4.** The Panama Canal was important.

_____ **5.** The United States extended the Monroe Doctrine in several ways.

B. What Did You Read?

Choose the answer that best completes each sentence. Write the letter of your answer in the space provided.

_____ **1.** The main interests of European imperialist countries were in
  a. Asia.
  b. the Middle East.
  c. Africa.
  d. all of the above.

_____ **2.** The United States bought Alaska from
  a. Russia.
  b. France.
  c. Spain.
  d. Great Britain.

_____ **3.** Panama gained its freedom from
  a. the United States.
  b. Mexico.
  c. Colombia.
  d. Spain.

_____ **4.** The "big stick" policy was used by
  a. Great Britain.
  b. the United States.
  c. Spain.
  d. all of the above.

_____ **5.** The U.S. Marines remained for about twenty years in
  a. Venezuela.
  b. Santo Domingo.
  c. Mexico.
  d. Nicaragua.

_____ **6.** Between 1898 and 1900, the United States got control of all the following countries *except*
  a. the Philippines.
  b. Hawaii.
  c. Colombia.
  d. Puerto Rico.

C. Map Study Skills:

Look at the map of Latin America. Identify the countries shown by the letters on the map. Place the correct letter in the space provided. You may use the map on page 84 for help.

_____ **1.** Panama

_____ **2.** Cuba

_____ **3.** Puerto Rico

_____ **4.** Venezuela

_____ **5.** Dominican Republic

_____ **6.** Colombia

_____ **7.** Nicaragua

_____ **8.** Brazil

_____ **9.** Bolivia

_____ **10.** Argentina

_____ **11.** El Salvador

_____ **12.** Mexico

D. Checking for Details:

Read each statement. Put a T in the space next to each statement if it is true. Put an F in that space if it is false. Put an N if you cannot tell from the reading if it is true or false.

_____ **1.** Most of the countries in the Americas were still colonies in the middle 1800s.

_____ **2.** After 1865, the United States turned most of its attention to Asia.

_____ **3.** Spain ruled Cuba harshly.

_____ **4.** Building the Panama Canal was a hard job.

_____ **5.** In the 1890s and early 1900s, the United States did not change the ideas of the Monroe Doctrine.

_____ **6.** The United States bought Alaska from Russia.

_____ **7.** Spain faced a war for independence in Cuba but not in the Philippines.

_____ **8.** Puerto Rico had less chance to rule itself under the United States than it had under Spain.

_____ **9.** The United States had spheres of influence.

_____ **10.** The "big stick" policy was the idea of President Monroe of the United States.

_____ **11.** The United States wanted to build a canal through Nicaragua.

_____ **12.** The United States went into Santo Domingo to help European countries get back the money owed to them.

E. Behind the Headlines:

Each headline has a story behind it. Write two or three sentences that support or tell about each of the following headlines.

UNITED STATES AND GREAT BRITAIN NEAR WAR OVER BORDER IN SOUTH AMERICA

_____

_____

_____

PANAMA GRANTS CANAL RIGHTS TO UNITED STATES

_____

_____

_____

UNITED STATES USES "BIG STICK" IN THE DOMINICAN REPUBLIC

_____

_____

_____

MARINES LEAVE FOR NICARAGUA

_____

_____

_____

F. What Does It Mean?

Choose the best meaning for each of the words in capital letters.

_____ **1.** ARBITRATION
   a. settling an argument by using force
   b. making people talk to each other
   c. having a third party decide how to settle an argument

_____ **2.** DICTATOR

   a. a democratic ruler
   b. a member of a ruling group
   c. a ruler who has complete power

G. Understanding Global History:

On page 82 you read about three factors in global history. Which of these factors applies to each statement listed below? Fill in the number of the correct statement on page 82 in the space provided. If no factor applies, fill in the word NONE.

_____ **1.** The United States did not treat Latin American nations as equals and showed little interest in their culture.

_____ **2.** Imperialist countries in the 1800s were mostly interested in the raw materials and the markets they needed.

_____ **3.** Great Britain held Canada, and Russia owned Alaska in the middle 1800s.

_____ **4.** Spain's weakness made the United States feel that the time was good for taking over Spanish colonies in the Caribbean and the Pacific.

Chapter 12

Imperialism and Nationalism

Understanding Global History

Think about the following statements as you read about imperialism and nationalism.
1. Nations are linked by a network of economic interdependence.
2. The culture in which we live influences our view of other people.
3. Contact among peoples and nations can lead to cultural changes.
4. Present culture is shaped by the past.

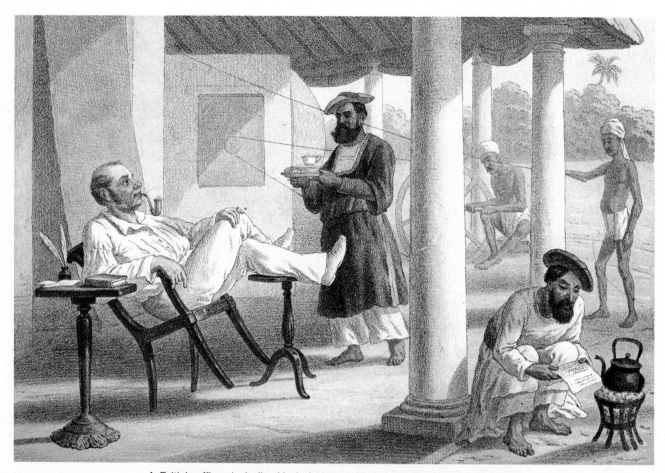

A British officer in India. He is being waited on by his Indian servants. Many foreigners lived well in their colonies. Colonial peoples were poor, however. For this and other reasons, they began to dislike foreign rule.

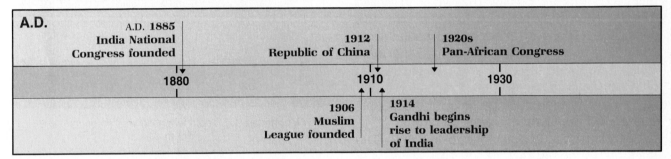

A.D.

A.D. 1885 India National Congress founded — 1880

1912 Republic of China — 1910

1920s Pan-African Congress — 1930

1906 Muslim League founded

1914 Gandhi begins rise to leadership of India

Imperialism and the Industrial Revolution

The kind of imperialism that came about in the 1800s was an answer to the needs of the Industrial Revolution. The imperialist countries were industrial countries. They made goods. They needed colonies to supply raw materials for their goods. They also needed colonies for places to sell finished goods. Raw materials for factories and a market for factory-made goods—those were the main ideas behind imperialism in the 1800s.

Nationalism in the Imperialist Countries

It was more than economic needs that helped imperialism grow. Nationalism also played a part. Nationalism in the imperialist countries gave them reasons for taking colonies.

The imperialist countries saw their own culture and their own economic needs. What they saw made them believe that imperialism was right. They did not think about the cultures of their colonies. People from imperialist countries usually looked down on the cultures of colonial peoples. They also ignored the economic needs of their colonies.

Who Gained by Imperialism?

Some people gained a great deal from imperialism. Owners of factories could get cheap raw materials. They also had markets for their goods. There were jobs in the colonies, too. Many people from the imperialist countries took these jobs. Some of these people might have had trouble finding good jobs at home. Shipowners gained from imperialism. So did people who built railroads and factories.

There were many people in the imperialist countries who did not gain anything in the way of money, however. Factory workers did not make lots of money because of imperialism. There were more factory jobs. But there was not a lot more pay for the workers. People who paid taxes had to support the armies and navies of the imperialist countries. Soldiers from the imperialist countries risked their lives fighting to get the colonies.

Even so, people who had little to gain in money had a sense of pride in their country. People in an imperialist country felt that their country was better than others. This kind of national pride made them feel important.

Nationalism in Colonies

The people in imperialist countries felt a national pride. People in the colonies also began to feel a growing nationalism. This growing national spirit led people in most colonies to want freedom. The colonies wanted to get rid of imperialist rule.

The English colonies in North America felt the desire for freedom early. They became the independent United States before the 1800s. Latin American countries soon followed. Nationalism led many Latin American countries to gain their freedom from Spain in the early 1800s.

Nationalism Grows in India

Many of the early Indian nationalists got their education from the British. They went to British schools. Then they returned to India with new ideas. They spoke of freedom and nationalism.

In 1885, a group of Indians formed the India National Congress. The Congress was formed to try to get the British to give the Indians more of a say in running their country. Most of the people who formed the Congress were Hindus.

A Muslim League was formed in 1906. The League was formed to work for a Muslim part in running the country.

There were bad feelings between Hindus and Muslims even before the British took over India. The British helped these feelings continue with their divide-and-rule policy. Keeping the two groups suspicious of each other helped Great Britain rule India.

Gandhi

In 1914, Mohandas K. Gandhi began his rise to Indian leadership. Gandhi was born in India. He studied law in Great Britain. Then he moved to South Africa. This was a British colony at the time. Gandhi practiced law in South Africa. He worked for the rights of Indians who lived in South Africa. Gandhi left South Africa after he had made the government agree to give Indians more rights.

Gandhi returned to India in 1915 at the age of 46. He brought with him a new idea for the Indian nationalists. The idea was **civil disobedience.** This is a kind of non-violent action. Civil disobedience meant disobeying laws that people thought were wrong or unfair. It meant disobeying the law without physical fighting and without violence.

Mohandas K. Gandhi when he was a young lawyer in South Africa.

Gandhi called his kind of civil disobedience by an Indian name that meant "keeping to the truth."

The Salt Tax

The British placed a tax on salt in India. Indians felt that it was unfair to tax salt. People needed salt for their food. The British had also made it against the law to make salt in India.

Gandhi marched 200 miles (320 kilometers) to the ocean. His plan was to make salt from the sea. The British arrested Gandhi for this non-violent protest against the salt tax. Peaceful acts like this made people in India and around the world admire Gandhi.

Many Indians called Gandhi *Mahatma.* This means "great soul." They respected his ideas. Sometimes people found it hard not to fight back. It was hard being non-violent when the British used violence. Some of the Indians did use violence at times. Civil disobedience and non-violence were beginning to work, however.

Muhammad Ali Jinnah

Muhammad Ali Jinnah (JIN-na) was a Muslim Indian lawyer. He was also trained in England. Then he returned to India to practice law.

At first, Jinnah joined the National Congress. He hoped that Muslims and Hindus could work together for India's freedom.

The Muslim League

The Muslim League was formed in 1906. Its aim was to see that Muslims were represented in a free India. Jinnah joined the Muslim League. He began his rise to leadership of the Muslim League at about the same time that Gandhi began to lead the growing National Congress.

Muslims wanted freedom. They were afraid, however, that they would be a minority in a free India. They feared that laws would not be fair to them.

Hindus were afraid that Muslims would try to make Muslim religious laws the law for all Indians. Indians were afraid this might happen in some places where there were more Muslims than Hindus. Hindus remembered the Mogul rule. During the time of the Moguls, the Hindu majority had been treated badly.

For the next 30 years, Gandhi and Jinnah led Hindus and Muslims in the struggle for freedom. At first, they worked together. Later they each worked for different goals. Gandhi and the National Congress wanted a united, free India. The Muslim League began to work for a separate, independent Muslim country in part of what was British India.

Nationalism in China

A spirit of nationalism arose in China in the late 1800s and early 1900s. The first leaders were young Chinese people who had gone to study in other countries. These people felt that China had been shamed by its Manchu rulers. They believed that the Manchu rulers had not been able to keep the imperialists from taking control of China.

Sun Yat-sen's Program

The Chinese nationalists organized a secret organization. It was called the Young China Party. Dr. Sun Yat-sen was its leader. He gave up the practice of medicine to work for Chinese freedom. He had been made to leave China in 1895.

Sun Yat-sen lived in Hawaii, Japan, the United States, and Great Britain for the next few years. While he lived outside of China, he drew up a program for China.

His program had three principles. They were

- nationalism—a strong national government for China
- democracy—a democratic form of government for China
- livelihood—an improvement of the standard of living in China

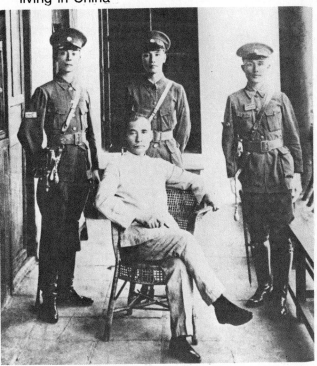

Sun Yat-sen, seated in the middle. Chiang Kai-shek stands directly behind him.

The End of Manchu Rule

In 1911, the nationalists overthrew the Manchus. In 1912, the nationalists set up a republic. Civil war, however, kept China from being joined together. China was split into different parts. These were ruled by generals and war lords. In 1917, Sun Yat-sen was able to take control of the republic. The republic held only a small part of southern China, however.

Sun Yat-sen and his followers organized the **Kuomintang** (KWO-MIN-DAHNG). This was a nationalist party. They wanted the Kuomintang to unite China.

The Chinese Communist Party

The Chinese Communist party was formed in 1921. At first, it worked with the Kuomintang. They tried to unite China. Their goal was to free the country of the war lords and generals who were keeping it divided.

Chiang Kai-shek

Sun Yat-sen died in 1925. His place as head of the Kuomintang was taken by General Chiang Kai-shek (CHANG KHY-SHEK). Chiang did not want to work with the Chinese Communist party.

In 1927, civil war broke out once again. Chiang Kai-shek and his army brought most of China under the rule of the national government. He also fought the Chinese Communists.

Mao Zedong

Mao Zedong (MOW DZOO-DOONG) became leader among the Chinese Communists. The Communists and Nationalists fought each other for nearly 20 years. This civil war kept China from growing strong.

Nationalism in Southeast Asia

Nationalism grew stronger in India and China. It also began to grow in Southeast Asia. In this part of the world, as in China and India, many of the early nationalist leaders were young people. These young people had gone to local schools. Many had also studied in the Netherlands, France, and Great Britain. They returned home with many new ideas. Among their ideas was a spirit of nationalism.

Malaysia—Malaysia was a colony of Great Britain. It was called Malaya then. The people of Malaysia wanted to get rid of the British imperialists. They also wanted to get rid of the Chinese living in their land.

The British had brought the Chinese to Malaysia to work. Before long, the Chinese had much of the trade and business. Malaysian nationalists did not like that at all. Some nationalists took out their angry feelings on the Chinese in their country.

Burma—Burma had been part of British India since 1885. In the 1920s, Great Britain began to let some Burmese have a say in the government. The main decisions still belonged to the British, however. Burma was not separated from British India until 1935.

Indonesia—The Dutch had ruled Indonesia for hundreds of years. In the 1800s, the Indonesians tried several times to get rid of the Dutch rulers. All the attempts failed. In 1927, an Indonesian nationalist party was formed. Its leader was Achmed Sukarno. The Indonesians worked for about 20 years to gain freedom.

Indochina—Feelings against the French were growing in Indochina. Anti-French feelings were very strong in Vietnam, a part of Indochina. It would be many years, however, before Indochina would become strong enough to get the French out.

Nationalism in Africa

Small groups of Africans who were educated by the colonial powers became leaders of the nationalist movement in Africa.

In the early 1900s, African nationalists formed some links with blacks in the United States. Dr. W. E. B. Du Bois (doo-BOYS) was a black scholar and teacher from the United States. He was attracted to the African heritage. During the late 1890s and early 1900s, he studied this heritage. He later helped organize a **pan-African** Congress in the 1920s. Pan-African means "all African."

African nationalism developed slowly in the years before 1945. It was hard to develop a national spirit in colonies that did not have a common language and history.

Nationalism in the Middle East

In 1900, most of the Middle East and North Africa was ruled by what was left of the Ottoman Empire. It had once been very strong. By the early 1900s, the Ottoman Empire had grown weak. The Ottoman Empire suffered some very bad losses in wars. It was on the losing side in World War I.

A Turkish nationalist movement had been growing in the Ottoman Empire during the early 1900s. The nationalists were called "Young Turks." They wanted to set up a Turkish republic. They wanted to be proud of their country. One of the leaders was a young general named Mustafa Kemal (moos-tah-FAH keh-MAL). He later became the president of Turkey. He ruled under the name Atatürk.

Arab Nationalism

Arab nationalists made up a second group in the Ottoman Empire. Both the Ottoman rulers and the Arabs were Muslim. Religion had once joined much of the empire. During World War I the Arabs fought to get rid of Ottoman control of their lands.

Most of the Arab lands did get rid of Ottoman control. They did not gain freedom right away, however. Instead, they came under control of the Western imperialist nations. After World War I, the

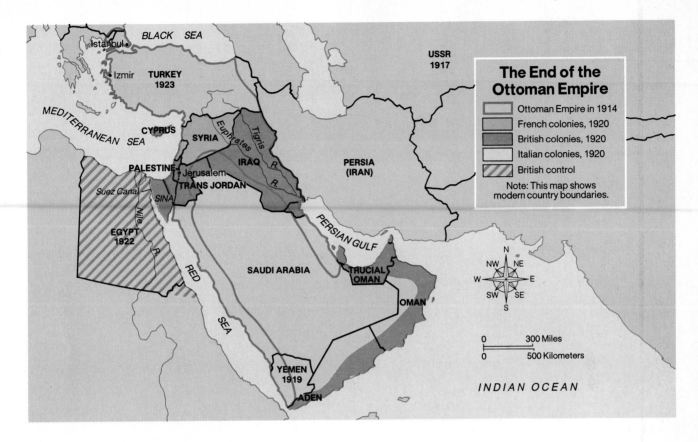

The End of the Ottoman Empire

- Ottoman Empire in 1914
- French colonies, 1920
- British colonies, 1920
- Italian colonies, 1920
- British control

Note: This map shows modern country boundaries.

Arab lands that had been part of the Ottoman Empire became colonies of Great Britain, France, and Italy.

Arab nationalists continued to fight for freedom from the imperialist powers.

Jewish Nationalism

A third group in the Ottoman Empire was moved by the spirit of Jewish nationalism. This spirit of nationalism was called **Zionism.** Many Jews had been forced to leave the Palestine area during Roman times. This scattering of Jews was called the **Diaspora** (dy-AS-pur-uh). The Jews had been forced to move into other countries in Europe, the Middle East, and North Africa.

The Diaspora was remembered in Jewish life and religion in all parts of the world. Some Jews still thought of Jerusalem and Palestine as their real home.

Theodor Herzl (HEHR–tsuhl) was a Jew who was born in Hungary. Herzl wrote a book that suggested that Jews should begin to settle once again in Palestine. This idea became known as Zionism. Those who supported Zionism were called Zionists. Attacks against Jews in France and Russia in the late 1800s made Zionism stronger.

Zionists wanted Jews to have a safe homeland in Palestine. Many began to move there. The Ottoman rulers were against the development of a Jewish state in their territory.

The Effects of Rising Nationalism

The rise of nationalism in colonies helped join people in a feeling that they should get rid of imperialist rule. The nationalism that was growing in Asia, Africa, the Middle East, and South America also had a dangerous side.

In some cases, the new nationalists were against neighboring groups as well as against imperialist rulers. Sometimes nationalists were against other groups of people living in the same country. Each of these problems would continue to cause wars and bad feelings in the years to come.

Exercises

A. Finding the Main Ideas:

Put a check next to the sentences that give the main ideas of what you have just read.

_____ **1.** Nationalism helped promote imperialism in industrial countries.

_____ **2.** Latin Americans did not like the "big stick" policy of the United States.

_____ **3.** Nationalism helped promote independence movements in the colonies.

_____ **4.** Dr. Sun Yat-sen had an important influence on the Chinese nationalist movement.

_____ **5.** There were at least three nationalist groups that were against Ottoman rule in the Middle East.

_____ **6.** The Ottoman Empire lost several wars.

_____ **7.** Mohandas K. Gandhi had a major influence on the Indian nationalist movement.

B. What Did You Read?

Choose the answer that best completes each sentence. Write the letter of your answer in the space provided.

_____ **1.** The imperialist countries depended on their colonies mainly for
   a. cultural needs.
   b. economic needs.
   c. a spirit of nationalism.
   d. all of the above.

_____ **2.** The Indian National Congress was
   a. against Hindus.
   b. against nationalism.
   c. against the British.
   d. none of the above.

_____ **3.** Dr. Sun Yat-sen's principles included all of the following *except*
   a. a strong national government.
   b. a better standard of living.
   c. a stronger Manchu emperor.
   d. a democratic form of national government.

_____ **4.** The national groups that were against rule by the Ottomans included
   a. Indians, Turks, and Arabs.
   b. Turks, Jews, and Indians.
   c. Chinese, Arabs, and Turks.
   d. Arabs, Turks, and Jews.

C. Checking for Details:

Read each statement. Put an F in the space next to each statement if it is a fact. Put an O in that space if it is an opinion. Remember that facts can be proved, but opinions cannot.

_____ **1.** There was too much nationalism in the 1900s.

_____ **2.** Gandhi brought the idea of civil disobedience to the Indian nationalist movement.

_____ **3.** Chinese nationalists were not as well organized as Indian nationalists.

_____ **4.** Dr. Sun Yat-sen was not able to unite China.

_____ **5.** Zionism had its roots in Jewish history and religion.

_____ **6.** Some blacks in the United States took part in the pan-African movement.

D. Word Meanings:

Match each word in Column A with the correct meaning in Column B. Write the letter of each answer in the space provided.

Column A

_____ **1.** pan-African
_____ **2.** Zionism
_____ **3.** Diaspora
_____ **4.** civil disobedience
_____ **5.** Kuomintang

Column B

a. Jewish nationalism
b. Indonesian nationalism
c. all African
d. disobeying laws without violence
e. the scattering of Jews from Palestine to other countries
f. Chinese national party

E. Understanding Global History:

On page 92 you read about four factors in global history. Which of these factors applies to each statement listed below? Fill in the number of the correct statement on page 92 in the space provided. If no factor applies, fill in the word NONE.

_____ **1.** Imperialist countries were industrial countries.

_____ **2.** Many colonial nationalist leaders picked up their ideas while studying in universities in Europe.

_____ **3.** Imperialist countries depended on their colonies for raw materials and markets for finished goods.

_____ **4.** The Diaspora was a feature that is remembered in Jewish life and religion.

_____ **5.** Imperialist countries thought highly of their own culture and looked down on the cultures of colonial countries.

Unit 2
Wars, Revolutions, and Efforts for Peace in the Twentieth Century

The early years of the twentieth century saw the outbreak of World War I. For four years (1914-1918), the countries of Europe fought one another in a bloody conflict (see photo opposite). The peace was finally won in 1918. But bitterness and hatred remained. In a little over 20 years time, war would break out again. The early years of the twentieth century also saw a revolution in Russia. The absolute rule of the czars came to an end. A communist-led government came to power in the Soviet Union.

The years after World War I found most of Europe suffering from economic depression. Fear of communism led to the rise of fascist dictatorships in Europe. Fascism was on the rise elsewhere. Military leaders took over the government of Japan.

Some efforts were made to prevent future wars, however. An international organization called the League of Nations was set up in 1919. But the league was weak. It could not stop the dictators of Germany, Italy, and Japan from seizing land. Various acts of aggression during the 1930s set the stage for a bigger conflict. The invasion of Poland by Germany in 1939 started World War II. The war ended in 1945 with the complete defeat of Germany and Japan.

Two important events took place in 1945. One was the use of the first atomic bombs. The second was the forming of a new international organization. This was the United Nations. Its members work to build peaceful relations among the nations of the world.

Despite the efforts of the United Nations to keep peace, wars broke out in the 1950s, 60s, and 70s. Conflicts took place in East Asia, Southeast Asia, and the Middle East. Today, the nations of the world are still trying to find ways to peace.

In Unit 2, you will read the following chapters:

Chapter 1

World War I

Understanding Global History

Think about the following statements as you read about World War I.
1. Events occurring in one part of the world have influenced developments in other parts of the world.
2. Nations are linked by a network of economic interdependence.
3. The culture in which we live influences our view of other people.
4. Present culture is shaped by the past.

United States Marines fighting German troops during World War I. Several million soldiers died in the trenches dug along the battle fronts.

Learning New Words and Terms

The following words are used in this chapter. Think about the meaning of each one.

nationalism: a feeling of pride in and devotion to one's country

chauvinism: extreme patriotism

alliances: agreements between two or more nations to help each other

balance of power: a situation in which no one nation has more power than its neighbors or other nations

mediation: settlement of a dispute by use of another party; his or her proposals are not binding

neutral: not taking sides in a dispute

czar: the title of the ruler of Russia

armistice: an agreement to stop fighting

communism: a system of government in which the state owns all businesses, factories, and farms

Think As You Read

1. What were the two groups of alliances in Europe in 1914?
2. What were the major threats to peace in Europe in 1914?
3. What was the direct cause of World War I?

A.D.

1917 United States enters the war; Revolution in Russia — 1917

1919 Treaty of Versailles is signed — 1919

1914 · 1917 · 1918 · 1919

A.D. 1914 Archduke Francis Ferdinand is assassinated; World War I begins

1918 World War I ends; Germany is defeated

Changes in the World in the 1800s

Many important changes took place in the world during the 1800s. The two Industrial Revolutions changed the way goods were made. They also caused more goods to be made. The Agricultural Revolution changed the ways of farming. More crops were produced. Transportation and communication improved because of inventions.

Many of the changes during the 1800s helped the world. For example, living standards improved in many parts of the world. Feelings of **nationalism** helped join together Italy and Germany. Many countries of Latin America gained their freedom. Some of the changes of the 1800s brought harmful results, however. By the early 1900s, nationalism was changing to **chauvinism** and imperialism. These two things hurt relations between countries.

Europe Moves Towards War

Between 1910 and 1914, Europe moved closer to war. By 1914, Europe was divided into two groups of **alliances.** On one side were Britain, France, and Russia. They were known as the Allied Powers. On the other side were Germany, Austria-Hungary, and Italy. They were called the Central Powers. At first, these alliances were formed to try to prevent war. They were meant to keep a **balance of power** in Europe. Leaders believed that if no one nation had more power than the others, war could be avoided. The threat of war grew in spite of these alliances, however.

Threats to Peace

There were four major reasons for the rising danger of war in Europe in the early 1900s. These reasons were imperialism, nationalism, militarism, and the lack of international organizations.

Czar Nicholas II of Russia on the left and Kaiser William II of Germany on the right. Both rulers wanted to build military strength in their countries. This created tensions that helped lead to war.

Imperialism

During the late 1800s and the early 1900s the major nations of Europe were searching for colonies throughout the world. The Industrial Revolutions had increased the amount of goods that were made. To continue making more goods, industrial countries needed more raw materials that were less costly. They also needed new markets in which to sell their goods. The desire of more than one country for the same colonies sometimes led to dangerous rivalries. These rivalries sometimes threatened to end in war.

Imperialist Tensions in the Balkans

There were also imperialist tensions between Austria-Hungary and Russia in the Balkan region. Both Austria-Hungary and Russia looked toward eastern Europe for new lands. Each was a threat to the other's interests in the area. Russia also thought of itself as the protector and leader of the Slavic people in the Balkans. Russia's interest in eastern Europe strained its relations with the Ottoman Empire (Turkey). The Russians made no secret of wanting to gain an entrance from the Black Sea to the Mediterranean Sea. This entrance was through the Bosporus Straits. This is a narrow seaway connecting the Black Sea (by way of the Sea of Marmara) and the Mediterranean Sea. Turkey ruled the Bosporus and had no intention of losing that rule.

Nationalism

Feelings of national pride were very strong in 1914. They divided many of the nations of Europe. This was especially true of France and Germany. These two nations fought the Franco-Prussian war in 1870–1871. France lost that war. It was forced to give some of its territory to Germany. The French wanted to get back Alsace and Lorraine, areas that were once theirs. Feelings of national pride made France and Germany bitter enemies. Though the two countries had a common border, their cultures had little in common. Each thought its own culture to be better than the other.

Nationalism Creates Tensions in the Balkans

Nationalism also created many tensions in the Balkans. That part had once been ruled by the Ottoman Empire. By 1914, a large part of the Balkans was ruled by Austria-Hungary. The kingdom of Austria-Hungary was made up of many national groups. They wanted freedom from either Turkish or Austrian rule. Other national groups wanted to be joined together. One of these groups was the Serbs. They were a Slavic people. The Serbs did not like Austria-Hungary. They wanted to be part of Serbia, a neighboring country.

Also, many Slavic peoples looked to Russia as the leader of the Pan-Slavic movement. This movement called for the freedom and unification of the Slavic peoples. Russia, therefore, also found itself in conflict with Austria-Hungary.

Militarism

Industrialism brought new machines and goods to the world. It also brought many new weapons of war. The industrial countries made and sold many new weapons. These included steel warships, long-range cannons, machine guns, powerful explosives, and poison gases. Every major country in Europe had a large army and navy. Countries spent large amounts of money on building strong armies and navies. They also spent money on making new weapons. As countries built their military power, their neighbors became alarmed. They began to build their own military power.

Lack of International Organizations

Fights between nations in the early 1900s always carried the danger of war. There was no international organization that could settle these fights. **Mediation** and arbitration were sometimes used to settle fights. These efforts failed to keep peace for long, however.

The Direct Cause of World War I

In 1914, new tensions arose between Austria-Hungary and Serbia. On June 28, a young Serbian nationalist named Gavrilo Princip assassinated Archduke Francis Ferdinand and his wife. The archduke was the heir to the throne of Austria-Hungary. Francis Ferdinand and his wife were on a visit to Sarajevo (sahr-uh-YEH-voh), a city in Bosnia. Bosnia was then part of Austria-Hungary. However, Bosnia was home to Serbs as well as other Slavic peoples. The Serbs believed Bosnia should be part of Serbia. The assassination of Francis Ferdinand started a chain reaction that began World War I.

The assassination of Archduke Francis Ferdinand of Austria-Hungary. This was the spark that set off World War I.

The angry government of Austria-Hungary threatened to hold Serbia responsible for the deaths. Austria-Hungary also saw the chance to crush Serbian nationalism. Serbia then asked Russia to support it in the crisis that followed. When Austria-Hungary declared war on Serbia, the Russians began preparing for war. Germany was an ally of Austria-Hungary. It demanded that Russia stop their war plans. They also demanded that France, Russia's ally, remain **neutral.** When Russia and France refused, Germany declared war on them. The Germans then moved across the neutral country of Belgium to invade France. Britain spoke out against this action. It demanded that Germany respect Belgium's neutrality. When the Germans would not, Britain entered the war on the side of France and Russia.

World War I

Thus, within a few days, in 1914, Europe slid into a war that no one really wanted. Britain, France, and Russia (the Allied Powers) were soon fighting against Germany, Austria-Hungary, and later, Turkey (the Central Powers). Italy did not enter the war until 1915. It deserted its alliance with Germany and joined the Allied Powers. In 1917, the United States declared war on Germany. It became an ally of Britain, France, Russia, and Italy.

World War I was not really a "world" war. Most of the fighting took place in Europe. However, all the major countries of the time were in the war. Also, the war's effects were felt all over the world.

World War I lasted from 1914 to 1918. It brought death and destruction to most of Europe. Nearly 10 million soldiers died of wounds and sickness.

At least another 20 million soldiers were wounded in battle. Also, millions of men, women, and children who were not fighting died of sickness and hunger.

The Situation in 1917

By 1917 the Central Powers seemed to be doing well. They held a strong position on both battle fronts. They also ruled most of the Balkans. Then, in April 1917, the United States joined the Allies. The United States decided to declare war on Germany because of submarine warfare. The submarine was one of the new war weapons. The Germans had decided that their submarines would attack ships of neutral countries as well as enemy countries. This helped convince the United States to enter the war on the side of the Allied nations.

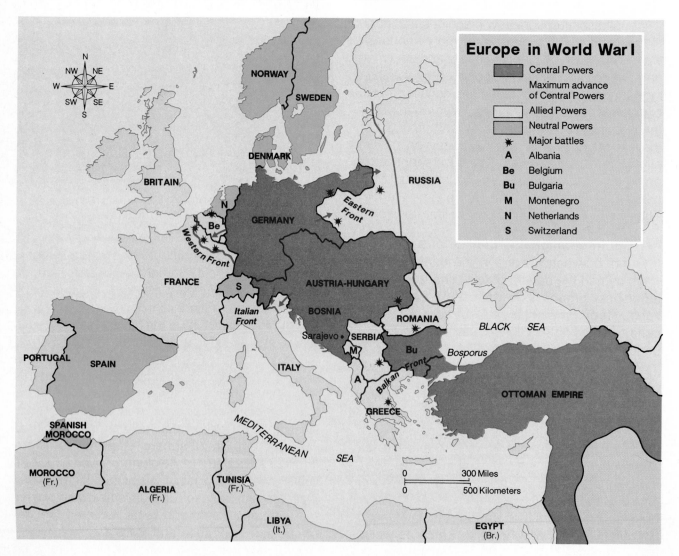

The entrance of the United States brought fresh supplies, more weapons, and two million soldiers to the Allied cause. This help came at an important time. In March of 1917, the czar (ZAHR) of Russia, Nicholas II, gave up the throne. The new government that replaced the czar continued to fight the war. In November 1917, that government was taken over by the Bolsheviks. The Bolsheviks took Russia out of the war. They signed a peace treaty with Germany.

For a time, the Russian collapse helped Germany. By November 1918, however, Germany was exhausted. Fresh American troops and supplies had helped the Allies. The Germans arranged an end to the fighting. On November 11, 1918 an **armistice** was signed. The war was over.

The Terms of Peace

The Treaty of Versailles (vair SIGH) was the peace treaty between the Allied nations and Germany. It was signed in 1919. The Treaty of Versailles was very hard on Germany. Because of the peace treaty, the following came about:

- Germany lost all its colonies and much of its European territory.
- Germany had to admit that it had caused the war. Germany also had to pay damages to the Allies.
- Germany was to be disarmed. It was to have no air force, almost no navy, and an army of only 100,000 soldiers.

Other Important Changes

There were other important changes that came about after the war. Several nations that had not existed before the war or had not been free were set up. These nations were formed from land that had belonged to Russia, Austria-Hungary, and Germany. The new nations included Poland, Latvia, Lithuania, Estonia, Finland, Yugoslavia, Hungary, and Czechoslovakia (see map, p. 110).

The League of Nations

Finally, an international organization was formed. This was the League of Nations. It was formed to find solutions for international disputes other than war. The League of Nations was the idea of Woodrow Wilson, the president of the United States. The United States, however, never joined the League of Nations.

Revolution in Russia

World War I was a disaster for Russia. Millions of Russian soldiers and people not even fighting died of wounds, sickness, or hunger. Russian factories and farms could not make enough for both those who fought and those who didn't. Hunger became a real problem. People were not happy. They blamed the government for this.

Russia's problems were made worse by its government. The czar of Russia was an absolute ruler. He had almost total power. He had the power to make laws. He also ruled the police and the armies.

Russia suffered military defeats in the war. Many people could not stand the situation any longer. A revolt in March 1917 led to the overthrow of the czar. A new, democratic government took power. The new government said it would bring greater democracy to Russia. It also wanted to continue the war against Germany, however. This was a mistake. The war was very unpopular with the Russian people. Unrest grew.

Lenin Takes Power in Russia

In 1917, Vladimir Ilyich Lenin returned to Russia from exile in Switzerland. Lenin believed in **communism.** He had read the works of Karl Marx. Lenin believed that private property should be done away with. He wanted a classless society. Lenin believed that only a revolution could bring this about. Lenin became the leader of a small group of revolutionaries. They planned to take over the government. This group called themselves Bolsheviks. This means "member of the majority." Their numbers, however, were small.

The Bolsheviks promised "Peace, Bread, and Land." This won them much support. In November 1917, the Bolsheviks overthrew the government. They set up a new, communist government. The Bolsheviks said that workers' and soldiers' councils should govern Russia. These councils were called "soviets." The soviets would be led by the Bolsheviks. The new name given to the nation was the Union of Soviet Socialist Republics (U.S.S.R.). Another name for the U.S.S.R. is the Soviet Union.

Exercises

A. Finding the Main Ideas:

Put a check next to the sentences that give the main ideas of what you have just read.

_____ **1.** Imperialism was a reason for the increasing danger of war in Europe.

_____ **2.** The Central Powers included Germany and Austria-Hungary.

_____ **3.** The Industrial Revolution changed the way people lived.

_____ **4.** Nationalism was a reason for the increasing danger of war in Europe.

_____ **5.** Militarism was a reason for the increasing danger of war in Europe.

_____ **6.** Mediation and arbitration are ways of settling disputes.

_____ **7.** Lack of an international organization was a reason for the increasing danger of war in Europe.

_____ **8.** The assassination of Archduke Francis Ferdinand was a direct cause of World War I.

B. What Did You Read?

Choose the answer that best completes each sentence. Write the letter of your answer in the space provided.

_____ **1.** During the 1800s, the world had a revolution in
    a. agriculture.
    b. industry.
    c. transportation.
    d. all of the above.

_____ **2.** The nation that wanted a warm water outlet to the Mediterranean Sea was
    a. Turkey.
    b. Serbia.
    c. Russia.
    d. Germany.

_____ **3.** Which of these nations did Serbia look to for protection?
    a. Turkey
    b. Russia
    c. Germany
    d. Austria-Hungary

_____ **4.** Which of the following were allies during World War I?
    a. Turkey, Spain, and Germany.
    b. Turkey, Britain, and France.
    c. France, Italy, and Britain.
    d. Germany, the United States, and Austria-Hungary.

_____ **5.** One of the results of World War I was
    a. the formation of the League of Nations.
    b. the unification of Germany.
    c. the defeat of France.
    d. a democratic government in Russia.

C. Checking for Details:

Read each statement. Put a T in the space next to each statement if it is true. Put an F in that space if it is false. Put an N if you cannot tell from the reading if it is true or false.

_____ **1.** By the 1900s, nationalism was changing to chauvinism.

_____ **2.** The Allied Powers were stronger than the Central Powers.

_____ **3.** Britain held the most desired colonies.

_____ **4.** The United States joined the war on the Allied side.

_____ **5.** The Treaty of Versailles, after World War I, was very easy on Germany.

_____ **6.** Turkey ruled the Bosporus.

_____ **7.** The czar of Russia was a weak ruler.

_____ **8.** Poison gas killed many soldiers.

D. Word Meanings:

Match each word in Column A with the correct meaning in Column B. Write the letter of your answer in the space provided.

Column A

_____ **1.** czar
_____ **2.** mediation
_____ **3.** armistice
_____ **4.** balance of power
_____ **5.** chauvinism
_____ **6.** nationalism
_____ **7.** communism

Column B

a. an agreement to stop fighting
b. a situation in which no one nation has more power than its neighbors or other nations
c. a feeling of pride in and devotion to one's country
d. the title of the ruler of Russia
e. settlement of a dispute by use of another party; his or her proposals are not binding
f. extreme patriotism
g. a system of government in which the state owns all businesses, factories, and farms

E. Understanding Global History:

On page 102 you read about four factors in global history. Which of these factors applies to each statement listed below? Fill in the numbers of the correct statement on page 102 in the space provided. If no factor applies, fill in the word NONE:

_____ **1.** France and Germany had a common border. However, their cultures had little in common.

_____ **2.** By the early 1900s, nationalism in Europe was turning to chauvinism and imperialism. This situation created tensions in many places.

_____ **3.** The Serbs had once been under the rule of the Ottoman Turks. In 1914 they were ruled by Austria-Hungary. The Serbs wanted to be part of a separate Serbian nation.

_____ **4.** The industrial nations of Europe needed raw materials and markets. So, they searched for colonies.

Chapter 2

After World War I

Understanding Global History

Think about the following statements as you read about the years after World War I.

1 Events occurring in one part of the world have influenced developments in other parts of the world.

2 The culture in which we live influences our view of other people.

3 Nations are linked by a network of economic interdependence.

Europe After World War I

New and enlarged countries shown in red.

Prewar Germany
Prewar Austria-Hungary
Prewar Russia

Major transfers:

1 Alsace-Lorraine
2 Eupen-Malmédy
3 Saar (to League of Nations)
4 Polish Corridor
5 South Tyrol
6 Istria
7 Transylvania
8 Galicia
9 Upper Silesia
10 Bessarabia
11 Montenegro
12 Serbia

Learning New Words and Terms

The following words are used in this chapter. Think about the meaning of each one.

capitalism: an economic system in which private individuals own businesses; they hope to gain a profit after all the expenses of running the business have been met

dictatorship: a situation in which one person or one party rules the government

fascism: a political idea that glorifies one nation; in a fascist state, the power is held by a dictator

socialism: a system in which society as a whole owns all property and runs all businesses

totalitarian: a system of government that has total power over the lives of the people

inflation: an increase in prices and a decline in the value of money

economic depression: a time when many people are out of work and business is poor

collective security: a plan of defense in which members agree to act together if any one is attacked

isolationism: a policy of avoiding relations with other nations

Think As You Read

1. What were the main problems in Europe after World War I?
2. What caused the weakness of the German republic in the 1920s and 1930s?
3. What effect did the economic depression have on Europe?
4. Why did the League of Nations fail?

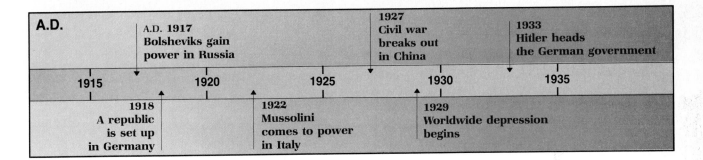

A.D.

| 1915 | A.D. 1917 Bolsheviks gain power in Russia | 1920 | 1925 | 1927 Civil war breaks out in China | 1930 | 1933 Hitler heads the German government | 1935 |

1918 A republic is set up in Germany — 1922 Mussolini comes to power in Italy — 1929 Worldwide depression begins

Europe in 1918

Europe was almost crushed by economic and political problems after World War I. It was a time of great worry and tensions. In many countries different political groups fought for power. Economic life came to a stop. Billions of dollars in damage had been done to homes, farms, and factories. Roads, bridges, and railways had been destroyed or were in poor shape. Millions of people had no food or shelter. The war had left a torn and broken society. In several countries, new political groups came into power because of these problems.

A New Government in Russia

In November 1917 a revolution in Russia had brought the Bolsheviks to power. The Bolsheviks brought communism to Russia. Many Europeans were in favor of the Communists' ideas. Commu-

nist parties were formed in most European countries and in other parts of the world, too. Strikes and demonstrations by supporters of communism led to fear among many Europeans. These were the industrialists and politicians. Many middle-class people also feared communism. They saw it as a threat to **capitalism.** They saw it as a threat to democracy.

The government set up by the Bolsheviks in the Soviet Union was a **dictatorship.** The Communists called the government a dictatorship of the proletariat. This is another name for workers. The first Soviet Communist leader was Lenin. Lenin wanted to change the Soviet Union into a communist state. This meant that the government would take over all businesses and farms. No private person could own the means of making goods. No private person could make profits. There would be no rich or poor classes of people. Lenin believed that the state would eventually disappear. Everyone would share in the wealth. This was the ideal communist state. That is not quite the way it turned out in the Soviet Union, however.

Fascism

Dictatorships existed in many other parts of the world after 1918. There were fascist dictatorships in Italy and Germany. **Fascism** is a political idea that glorifies one nation. Fascism also places power in the hands of one person and one party. This person is a dictator.

Fascism in Italy

Several revolutionary groups formed in Italy after World War I. One group was the Fascists. They were led by Benito Mussolini. Mussolini had once believed in **socialism.** He turned to other ideas, however. In 1919, Mussolini formed the Fascist party. Mussolini knew how to take advantage of the problems and unrest in Italy. He promised everything to everybody. He promised to end unemployment. He promised to make Italy strong and to get more land. He also promised to fight communism. Mussolini organized his own group of followers. They were called Black Shirts.

Mussolini and his followers came to power in Italy in 1922. He put an end to free elections, freedom of the press, and freedom of speech. Those who were not in favor of the Fascists were jailed or forced to leave Italy. The armed forces were made stronger. Mussolini often spoke of using force to win greatness for Italy. Under Mussolini's rule, Italy was militaristic, imperialistic, and antidemocratic. Italy became a **totalitarian** state.

Germany After the War

After the war, Germany was a troubled country. The economy was weak. The political situation was unstable. The German monarch, the kaiser, had been overthrown in 1918. A German republic had been set up. From the start the German republic lacked the trust of the German people. Most Germans felt that France and the Allied powers had treated Germany unfairly. German national pride was hurt by the terms of the Treaty of Versailles. That peace treaty took away Germany's colonies. It also made Germany pay damages to the Allies. Worst of all, it made Germany accept full guilt for the war.

Anger and shame led many Germans to dream of revenge. German nationalism, which was strong, became stronger. By 1923, Germany was in crisis. The economy was ruined. German pride was at a low point. Germans were ready for someone to solve their problems.

Germany, 1923. This was the worst year of inflation in Germany. This woman is burning money in her stove. It was cheaper to start fires with the almost worthless German money than to buy wood with it.

The Rise of Nazism

A new political party began in Germany in the 1920s. This was the National Socialist Workers' Party. They were also called the Nazis.

The Nazis were led by Adolf Hitler. He was an Austrian ex-soldier whose life was marked by one failure after another. Hitler thought of himself as German and had many ideas for Germany. He wanted to make Germany a powerful military state. He wanted to expand its territory. Hitler said that Germans were a superior race. He also felt that Germany should ignore the Treaty of Versailles.

Many Germans were in favor of Hitler's ideas. They felt that Hitler would give Germans back their self-respect. Hitler spoke of a super-nationalism. He also hated Jews. Hitler blamed the Jews for most of Germany's problems.

The Nazi party grew slowly. But by 1932, the Nazis had gained many followers. In 1933 Hitler was appointed chancellor, or prime minister, of Germany. This made him the head of the government. The Nazis began to take over Germany. They began to set up a dictatorship. All political parties except the Nazis were outlawed. People who were against Hitler were jailed or killed. Freedom of speech and the press was gone. Hitler's word was law.

Economies Decline

Europe's political situation was changing after World War I. Europe also faced serious economic problems. There was not enough food after 1918. Many people went hungry. Not enough food resulted in sharp rises in the price of food. **Inflation** was a big problem. Prices of goods rose as the value of money fell. Paper money had little value because most governments had no gold to back their paper. By 1923, the paper money in Germany was almost worthless. In that year a German newspaper cost 100 billion marks. People had to carry money around in wheelbarrows or carts to buy eggs or bread.

In the 1920s, Europe's economic life got somewhat better. The years from 1926–1929 were, on the whole, good ones. Inflation had slowed down. Goods were made in greater numbers. Trade started up again. Much of the world's economic well-being depended on the United States.

World Depression

Disaster struck in October 1929. The American stock market crashed. What followed was a great **economic depression.** Factories closed down. Millions of people had no jobs. Farmers could not pay their debts. They lost their farms. The economic depression in the United States was felt all over the world. Trade between nations grew less. Each nation raised taxes on imports. They did this to protect their own industries. The world economic system broke down. World trade came to a near stop.

The world economic depression in the 1930s caused much suffering. Even worse, it shook the confidence of many people in their governments. It was a turning point in Europe. Many people turned toward strong governments. They wanted greater economic security. They thought stronger governments could give them this security. The economic depression and the rise of dictatorships were closely tied together. Growing nationalism also made new tensions between countries. The world stage was being set for another conflict.

Adolf Hitler, left, and Benito Mussolini, right.

Problems of International Peace

The League of Nations had been set up after World War I. It was part of the Treaty of Versailles. The purpose of the League was to settle international disputes peacefully. The League's goal was to prevent future wars. The League of Nations lasted 20 years. It was not successful in preventing wars between nations. It was also not successful in preventing another world war.

The idea behind the League was **collective security.** All the member nations agreed to act together if any attack was made on any of them. The League of Nations never had a fair chance of success. The U.S. Senate would not agree to the Treaty of Versailles or join the League of Nations. Many people in the United States wanted the country to stay out of world affairs. They favored a policy of **isolationism.**

The failure of the United States to join the League left the organization weak. For a system of collective security to work, nations must be members of the system. Besides the United States, the League lost other important members. In 1931, Japan invaded Manchuria. When the League spoke out against the invasion, Japan withdrew from the organization. Italy invaded Ethiopia in 1935. The League tried to put pressure on Italy. Italy then withdrew. Germany withdrew in 1933. Russia was forced out in 1940 for attacking Finland. The League of Nations was a failure. This failure made the possibility of a future war a real danger.

Other Nations in the Postwar World

The years after the war saw changes throughout the world. One nation that underwent great change was China. A revolution in China in 1911 had overthrown the emperor. A republic was set up. There was, however, very little unity among the new leaders of China. The country had no order. Sun Yat-sen saw the need for a strong central government. He formed a nationalist party. It was called the Kuomintang. One of the goals of the Kuomintang or Nationalists was to bring China together. Dr. Sun first asked the United States to aid his country. When it refused, Sun Yat-sen turned to the Soviet Union. The Soviet Union sent money, equipment, and advisors. In return Sun Yat-sen let members of a small Chinese Communist party take part in his government.

Sun Yat-sen died in 1925 before China could be united. After his death, General Chiang Kai-shek became leader of the Kuomintang. He tried to place all of China under Nationalist rule. The Communists became alarmed at Chiang's growing power. Before long the Communists and Nationalists did not trust each other. Chiang Kai-shek decided to destroy communism in China. In April 1927, he began a long and bloody civil war between the two groups.

Ten years of civil war followed. The Communists were weakened. But they were not defeated. In 1937 the Nationalist-Communist struggle was temporarily stopped when Japan invaded China. The two Chinese groups stopped fighting each other. They joined to fight the Japanese. The civil war had been postponed, but not ended.

Mao Zedong, center, led the Communist forces during China's civil war. In 1934, Mao led his forces north and west in a "Long March." They finally reached Yanan. There, they set up a base of operations.

Exercises

A. Finding the Main Ideas:
Put a check next to the sentences that give the main ideas of what you have just read.

_____ **1.** The problems after World War I were felt in all parts of the world.

_____ **2.** Communism was a major problem in Europe after World War I.

_____ **3.** Germany did not like the terms of the Treaty of Versailles.

_____ **4.** The League of Nations failed in its efforts to stop international conflict.

_____ **5.** Inflation and the depression were great problems in Europe after World War I.

_____ **6.** Isolationism was a reason why the United States did not join the League of Nations.

_____ **7.** After World War I, several nations in Europe looked to dictatorships to solve their problems.

B. What Did You Read?
Choose the answer that best completes each sentence. Write the letter of your answer in the space provided.

_____ **1.** The rise in inflation in Europe after World War I resulted in
  a. great prosperity.
  b. a drop in prices.
  c. rising prices and a decline in the value of money.
  d. rising prices and a rise in the value of money.

_____ **2.** The terms of the Treaty of Versailles
  a. hurt German national pride.
  b. brought democracy to Germany.
  c. had little effect on Germany.
  d. brought Germany and France closer together.

_____ **3.** The new German republic
  a. was welcomed by most Germans.
  b. was led by the emperor.
  c. lacked the confidence of many Germans.
  d. brought the German people democracy.

_____ **4.** A serious weakness of the League of Nations was that
  a. it tried to end wars.
  b. the Soviet Union ran it.
  c. the United States did not become a member.
  d. it did not favor democracy.

C. Checking for Details:

Read each statement. Put a T in the space next to each statement if it is true. Put an F in that space if it is false. Put an N if you cannot tell from the reading if it is true or false.

_____ **1.** Inflation could have been avoided in Europe in the 1920s.

_____ **2.** Europe had been badly damaged during World War I.

_____ **3.** Revolution had brought the Bolsheviks to power in Russia.

_____ **4.** The United States had many reasons for not joining the League of Nations.

_____ **5.** The economic depression of 1929 affected the whole world.

_____ **6.** Economic life in Europe improved during the 1920s.

_____ **7.** All classes of people in Europe favored communism.

_____ **8.** German nationalism declined after 1918.

_____ **9.** France suffered the most losses of any nation in World War I.

_____ **10.** The Treaty of Versailles was turned down by the United States.

D. Understanding What You Have Read:

Tell whether each of the following involves (P) political or (E) economic issues. Place the correct answer in the space provided.

_____ **1.** A republic was set up in Germany.

_____ **2.** As trade grew less, nations raised tariffs to protect their industries.

_____ **3.** Communist parties were formed in most European nations.

_____ **4.** Paper money had little value in Europe after World War I.

_____ **5.** The kaiser of Germany was overthrown in 1918.

_____ **6.** Farms and factories were in poor shape in Europe after World War I.

_____ **7.** Inflation caused prices to rise and the value of money to fall.

_____ **8.** Mussolini formed the Fascist party in Italy.

_____ **9.** Hitler became chancellor of Germany in 1933.

_____ **10.** People lost their jobs in the depression.

E. Word Meanings:

Match each word in Column A with the correct meaning in Column B. Write the letter of each answer in the space provided.

Column A

_____ 1. isolationism
_____ 2. economic depression
_____ 3. fascism
_____ 4. totalitarian
_____ 5. collective security
_____ 6. socialism
_____ 7. inflation
_____ 8. dictatorship

Column B

a. a political idea that glorifies one nation
b. a system in which society as a whole owns all property and runs all businesses
c. a policy of avoiding relations with other nations
d. a sharp increase in prices and a decline in the value of money
e. a time when many people are out of work and business is poor
f. a mutual plan of defense
g. a system of government that tries to control the total lives of people
h. a situation in which one person or one party rules the government

F. On Your Own:

Read the following sentence. Give your opinion on this statement in ten sentences or less.

It has been said that the Allies won World War I on the battlefield, but lost it in the peace settlement.

_____

_____

_____

_____

_____

G. Understanding Global History:

On page 110 you read about three factors in global history. Which of these factors applies to each statement listed below? Fill in the number of the correct statement on page 110 in the space provided. If no factor applies, fill in the word NONE.

_____ 1. High taxes on imported goods lessened world trade. High taxes on imported goods led to a breakdown of economic interdependence among nations.

_____ 2. The Russian Revolution led to the forming of communist parties in many parts of the world.

_____ 3. After World War I, Germany felt badly towards France and its Allies. German national pride was hurt by the peace terms set down by the Allies.

117

Chapter 3

World War II

Understanding Global History

Think about the following statements as you read about World War II.
1 The culture in which we live influences our view of other people.
2 Present culture is shaped by the past.
3 Nations are sometimes dependent upon other nations for economic and political survival.
4 Location, topography, and resources affect interaction among people.

Normandy beach, 1944. The Allies (Americans, British, Canadians, Free French, and others) crossed the English Channel and landed in Normandy, France. Their invasion of Europe marked the beginning of the end of Hitler's rule over Europe.

Learning New Words and Terms

The following words are used in this chapter. Think about the meaning of each one.

demilitarized: the removal of all military forces and equipment from an area

blitzkrieg: lightning war; a method of warfare used by the Germans involving a quick, all-out attack

anti-Semitism: a feeling of hatred toward Jews

Holocaust: a word used to describe the murder of Jews during World War II; the term also means "devastation by fire"

blockade: stopping the passage of ships or troops into an area

Think As You Read

1. What did Germany accomplish in the first year of World War II?
2. What was the Battle of Britain?
3. What happened to Hitler's plan to take over the Soviet Union?
4. How did U.S. policy toward the war change between 1939 and 1941?
5. How did the United States influence the outcome of World War II?

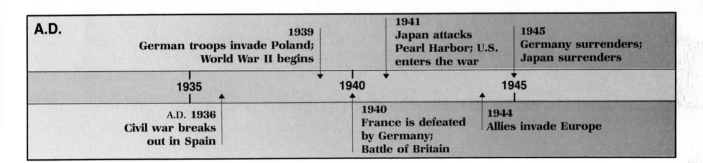

A.D.		1939 German troops invade Poland; World War II begins	1941 Japan attacks Pearl Harbor; U.S. enters the war	1945 Germany surrenders; Japan surrenders
1935		1940		1945
	A.D. 1936 Civil war breaks out in Spain	1940 France is defeated by Germany; Battle of Britain	1944 Allies invade Europe	

The years between 1918 and 1938 brought tensions and fears to the world. Economic depressions, especially after 1929, ruined many nations. Dictatorships arose in the Soviet Union, Italy, Spain, and Germany. Military rulers held power in many Latin American countries. Rioting broke out in India. Nationalists in India wanted freedom from British rule. Civil wars raged in China and Spain.

In Asia, Japan was getting ready to take over a large empire. Germany began getting ready for a war of conquest. It wanted revenge for its defeat in 1918. Worst of all, nations seemed powerless and unwilling to take actions that might stop a war.

Events Leading to War

Probably the most important steps leading to war were acts of aggression by countries that were not stopped. An act of aggression is an uncalled for attack by one country on the land of another. These acts of aggression included the following:

1931—Japan invaded Manchuria. The League of Nations said Japan was wrong for this act. Japan's answer was to leave the League. Japan then took over all of Manchuria.

1935—Nazi Germany added to its armed forces. This was forbidden by the Treaty of Versailles. Nothing was done to stop Germany.

1935—Italy invaded Ethiopia. This was a free African country. The League of Nations said Italy was wrong. The League could not keep Italy from taking over Ethiopia, however.

1936—A civil war broke out in Spain. Forces led by General Francisco Franco received aid from Fascist Italy and Nazi Germany. The elected government of Spain was overthrown by General Franco's forces.

1936—Germany sent troops into the Rhineland (see map, p. 120). This area had been **demilitarized** by the Treaty of Versailles.

1937—Japan invaded China. Japan took over much of China's coast.

1938—Nazi Germany occupied Austria. Austria became part of Germany. Great Britain and France spoke out against this, but nothing was done.

1938—Germany's leaders demanded that Czechoslovakia give up a border region called the Sudetenland (soo-DAYT-un-land). Many German-speaking people lived in that area. Great Britain and France quickly became involved. However, they agreed to Hitler's demands at a conference held in Munich, Germany. The Sudetenland was given to Germany.

1939—Italy invaded and took over Albania. This was a small nation in the Balkans (see map this page).

1939—Hitler demanded land in Poland. This land had once belonged to Germany. Britain and France promised to help Poland. At the same time, the Germans signed a treaty with the Soviet Union. With this treaty, Hitler no longer had to fear the Soviet Union if Germany moved against Poland. The treaty shocked the world because the two nations were thought to be enemies.

The War Begins

On September 1, 1939, German troops invaded Poland. This time France and Britain did not back down. They kept their promise to help Poland. France and Britain declared war on Germany on September 3. World War II had begun.

Poland was no match for Germany. The modern German army quickly crushed the out-of-date Polish army. The Germans used a new warfare called **blitzkrieg** (BLITS-kreeg). This term means lightning war. It combined quick attacks by air, tanks and armored cars, and troops. The blitzkrieg was very successful. Poland was taken over in less than a month.

Germany Looks West

Having taken over Poland, Germany now turned to the west. In April 1940, Germany launched its blitzkrieg on Norway and Denmark. Denmark was overrun in a day. Norway fell within a month. Germany next turned toward France. German troops swept through the Netherlands, Belgium, and Luxembourg. These countries were defeated within two weeks. French and British armies rushed to meet the Germans. They were trapped in Belgium, however. Instead of moving in quickly against the French and British, the German army made a mistake. It waited. This gave British and French troops time to escape across the English Channel. The survivors formed the basis for a new army.

World War II in Europe

- Axis powers
- Farthest Axis advance
- Under Axis control in 1942
- Unconquered
- Neutral

* Major battles
1. Rhineland
2. Sudetenland

A. Albania
B. Belgium
D. Denmark
L. Luxembourg
N. Netherlands
S. Switzerland

London during World War II. Nazi bombing attacks left many English cities in ruins.

The Fall of France

Germany now planned a full attack against France. At the same time, Italy entered the war as an ally of Germany. Germany and Italy called themselves the Axis powers. Italy declared war on both France and Britain. France was defeated and surrendered on June 22, 1940. Now only Britain stood in the way of Germany's conquest of western Europe. Germany began to plan its invasion of Britain.

The Battle of Britain

After the fall of France, only Britain was left to fight the Axis powers. A German invasion of Britain with ships seemed hard. This was because the British navy ruled the seas. So Hitler decided to attack Britain by air. The Battle of Britain began in August 1940. More than a thousand German planes attacked Britain. They tried to bomb the British into defeat. The German air force bombed British cities and airfields for several months. The British air force, however, fought back bravely. With the help of a new secret weapon, radar, they were able to avoid defeat.

Moving Eastward

Germany could not take over Britain. Germany and its ally, Italy, then turned toward eastern Europe. Romania, Hungary, Bulgaria, Yugoslavia, and Greece were either taken over or forced to join the Axis powers.

Next, Germany moved against the Soviet Union. It ignored the treaty of 1939 and invaded the Soviet Union in June 1941. The Soviet army was caught off guard. By October the Germans were at the gates of Moscow and Leningrad. Fortunately for the Soviets, the bitter cold of winter slowed down the Germans. Moscow and Leningrad were later saved.

Hitler's Europe

By 1941, Germany and its ally, Italy, controlled most of Europe. They began to force their rule and their ideas on the defeated peoples. Nazism was based on violence and hate. From the moment Adolf Hitler and the Nazis rose to power in Germany they used violence against anyone who disagreed with them. As they took over other nations, the Nazis planned a "new order" for Europe. People like themselves would be treated quite well. But "inferior" people would be treated harshly. Special prisons called concentration camps were built to keep these people separate. Many prisoners were used as slave labor. Some were used in medical experiments. Many starved to death.

A special program of terror was carried out against Jews. Soon after the Nazis took power in Germany, Jews were persecuted. Strong feelings of **anti-Semitism** among many people permitted this. Jews were forced out of their jobs, their businesses, their homes, and their schools. Many Jews, including famous writers and scientists, were forced to flee Germany to save their lives.

The Holocaust

Nazi actions against Jews grew worse during World War II. As the German armies took over parts of Europe, they began their persecutions of Jews in those parts. At first, the rights and property of Jews were taken away. Then, they were made to live in special areas. In 1941, the Nazis made plans for what they called a "final solution" to the Jewish "problem" in Europe. That solution was nothing less than the killing of all Jews in Eu-

Jews in Warsaw, Poland, 1943. The women and children shown here are being rounded up by the Nazis. They were sent to concentration camps.

rope. Millions of Jews throughout Europe were forced into concentration camps. These became death camps. In the camps Jews were starved, shot, and killed with poison gas. Giant furnaces were built to burn the bodies.

By 1945, more than six million European Jews had died in the Nazi death camps. This attempt to wipe out all the Jews is known as the **Holocaust.** In addition to the Jews, another six million people were murdered by the Nazis. Many of these were Gypsies and Slavic peoples. The Nazis also considered them inferior.

The United States Becomes Involved

The United States stayed out of the war from 1939 to 1941. It was a neutral nation during this time. The United States began, however, to feel that its security was threatened by the successes of Germany and Japan. So the United States began to help Germany's enemies. The Neutrality

Act of 1935 kept the Americans from selling military goods to any country at war. A new neutrality act was passed in November 1939. This new act made it possible for the United States to sell arms and raw materials to any nation on a "cash and carry" basis. This act helped the British and French. They could "carry" the materials across the Atlantic in their own ships. The Germans were stopped from crossing the Atlantic by a British naval **blockade.** Germany was, therefore, not able to buy and carry U.S. products on its own ships.

Then, in March 1941, the U.S. Congress passed the Lend-Lease Act. This made it possible for the United States to give goods and services to Britain and the Soviet Union. The Act stated that the United States could either sell, transfer, exchange, or lend any defense goods to those countries that it felt needed them. Between 1941 and 1945 Britain and the Soviet Union received over $43 billion in aid under the Lend-Lease program.

The United States at War: 1941–1945

In Asia, Japan had been taking advantage of the war in Europe to spread its own empire. Japan signed treaties with Germany, Italy, and the Soviet Union. Japan felt safe in increasing its control in Asia and the Pacific Ocean. On December 7, 1941, Japanese planes attacked the U.S. fleet at Pearl Harbor in Hawaii. The surprise attack destroyed about half the U.S. navy and much of the air force.

Within a few hours of the attack on Pearl Harbor, Japan also attacked American bases in the Philippines and on other Pacific islands. The shock of this attack caused the United States to act. On December 8 the United States declared war on Japan. Japan's allies, Germany and Italy, then declared war on the United States on December 11. Now all the major powers of the world were at war.

The location of the United States kept it free from bomb attacks. This meant that the huge resources of the United States could be used for the war effort. Americans produced food, weapons, and ammunition during the war. This effort helped turn the tide of war.

The Allies Win Victories in North Africa

Fighting had been going on in North Africa since 1940. In 1942 British forces under Field Marshal Bernard L. Montgomery defeated the Germans at El Alamein and drove them west to Tunisia. Meanwhile, British and American forces under General Dwight D. Eisenhower landed in Morocco and Algeria. They soon joined up with the British forces to the east. In May 1943 the German and Italian forces in North Africa surrendered. The stage was now set for the Allies to invade Europe.

The Allies Invade Italy

Shortly after the United States entered the war, the Soviet Union asked for help. The Soviet Union wanted the British and the Americans to open a new zone of fighting in Europe. This would relieve some of the pressure on the Soviet Union. The Russians had been fighting off the Nazis since 1941. So, in 1943, Allied forces invaded Sicily and pushed on into southern Italy. The Italian government removed Mussolini from office. They also started peace talks with the Allies. German armies moved in to take over the rest of Italy. Bitter fighting took place between Allied and German forces. The Allies freed Rome on June 4, 1944.

The Eastern Front

In the spring of 1942 the Germans began a new push into the Soviet Union. They drove all the way to the city of Stalingrad. After a long fight, the Russians defeated the German forces in the winter of 1943. By the fall of 1944 the Russians had pushed their attack into Poland, Yugoslavia, Bulgaria, and Hungary. The Germans were now pulling back in the east.

The Normandy Invasion

The Allies had begun making air attacks on Germany in 1942. By 1944 they were ready to invade France. The Allies used Britain as a base for their attack. Soldiers and equipment were brought together in England. Then, on June 6, 1944, the D-Day invasion began. Over 130,000 Allied soldiers landed on the beaches of Normandy in France. For a while, the Germans were able to hold back Allied forces. Then the Allies were able to break through German lines. By August, the Allies had freed Paris. By October they had freed France, Belgium, and Luxembourg.

The Fall of Germany

The Germans made a final effort to stop the Allied invasion in December 1944. The German advance, however, was stopped at the Battle of the Bulge. Early in 1945 both Allied forces in the west and Soviet forces in the east were moving toward Germany. The German capital of Berlin fell on May 2. A couple of days before this, on April 30, Hitler reportedly had killed himself. On May 8, 1945, Germany surrendered. The war in Europe was over.

The War in the Pacific

The Allied victories in North Africa had not been matched by victories in Asia. The Japanese won battle after battle. After the Pearl Harbor attack the Japanese took over the Philippines. During the next several months they moved on to take over much of Southeast Asia. Hong Kong, Singapore, Malaya, the Dutch East Indies, and Burma fell to Japan. The Japanese took over a number of small islands throughout the Pacific. Japan then began to threaten India and Australia.

The Japanese got their first setbacks in May of 1942. A Japanese fleet preparing for an invasion of Australia was caught in the Coral Sea by part of the U.S. Navy. The battle raged on for two days. This was the first naval battle in history fought entirely by airplanes. This battle stopped the Japanese invasion of Australia. In June, the Japanese attacked Midway, an island held by the United States. The Battle of Midway lasted four days. The Japanese suffered a big defeat. This battle was the last time Japan would attack another territory.

The United States Against Japan

In the Pacific, the United States began driving back the Japanese in 1942. Led by General Douglas MacArthur, U.S. forces began a campaign of "island hopping." Their aim was to take a number of important islands held by Japan. It was a slow and costly campaign. It worked, however. In October 1944, U.S. forces invaded the Philippines. Manila fell in February 1945.

From the islands they had captured, American bombers began attacking dozens of Japanese cities. Japan seemed to be close to defeat. However, Japan's military leaders would not give up. President Harry S. Truman of the United States decided to use a new weapon against Japan. On August 6, 1945, the United States dropped the world's first atomic bomb on the Japanese city of Hiroshima (hir-uh-SHEE-muh). Three days later another atomic bomb was dropped on the city of Nagasaki (nag-uh-SAHK-ee). These bombs destroyed more than half of each city. More than 130,000 people were killed. An equal number were injured. On August 10 the Japanese government asked for peace. The Allies agreed on August 14, and a peace treaty was signed by Japan on September 2, 1945. World War II was over.

Planning for Peace

During the war many plans were made for winning the war and for keeping peace after the war. Meetings were held and these plans were talked about. The three major Allied leaders were Winston Churchill of Britain, Franklin D. Roosevelt of the United States, and Joseph Stalin of the Soviet

Hiroshima, Japan, after the atomic bomb blast, 1945. Nearly every building within a half mile of the blast had been flattened.

Union. They took part in wartime conferences to plan for peace after the war.

At one of these conferences the Allies decided to set up an international organization. Its job would be to keep world peace. This organization would take the place of the old League of Nations. It would be called the United Nations.

The United Nations

After the war ended, representatives of 50 nations met in San Francisco. They agreed upon a charter for this new international organization. In October 1945 the United Nations (UN) was set up. The United States was the first nation to sign the UN charter and become a member.

The charter made it possible for member nations to bring international disputes to the UN for discussion and peaceful settlement. The members of the UN also agreed to work together to solve world problems. These problems include disease, hunger, and lack of education.

There are six bodies in the UN. The most important bodies are The General Assembly and the Security Council. Delegates from every member nation have a seat in the General Assembly. The Security Council has 15 members. Five members are permanent—Great Britain, the United States, the Soviet Union, China, and France. The United Nations thus became a new international organization devoted to keeping world peace.

Exercises

A. Finding the Main Ideas:

Put a check next to the sentences that give the main ideas of what you have just read.

_____ **1.** General Eisenhower led Allied forces in Europe in World War II.

_____ **2.** German armies won victories in Poland and France in the early years of World War II.

_____ **3.** There were many acts of aggression before the outbreak of World War II.

_____ **4.** The Soviet Union suffered many defeats. It was able to help defeat the Germans, however.

_____ **5.** The Japanese attack on Pearl Harbor brought the United States into World War II.

_____ **6.** The United States gave aid to Britain and the Soviet Union before Americans joined the fighting in World War II.

_____ **7.** The American use of atom bombs led to the surrender of Japan.

_____ **8.** The Neutrality Act of 1935 kept the United States from selling war goods to nations at war.

B. What Did You Read?

Choose the answer that best completes each sentence. Write the letter of your answer in the space provided.

_____ **1.** In World War II, the blitzkrieg was used by
  a. Britain.
  b. Germany.
  c. France.
  d. the Soviet Union.

_____ **2.** In the Battle of Britain, the Germans
  a. tried to invade Britain by sea.
  b. defeated Britain's air force.
  c. failed to defeat Britain by air bombings.
  d. used heavy guns to bomb Britain.

_____ **3.** The Battle of Stalingrad (1942–43) was a great defeat for
  a. Poland.
  b. Germany.
  c. the Soviet Union.
  d. none of the above.

_____ **4.** The attack on Pearl Harbor was made by
   a. Germany against the United States.
   b. Japan against Britain and the United States.
   c. Japan against the United States.
   d. Japan against the United States and the Soviet Union.

_____ **5.** The Allies planned to keep peace after World War II by setting up the
   a. League of Nations.
   b. Lend-Lease Act.
   c. Neutrality Act.
   d. United Nations.

C. Checking for Details

Read each statement. Put a T in the space next to each statement if it is true. Put an F in that space if it is false. Put an N if you cannot tell from the reading if it is true or false.

_____ **1.** British and American troops defeated the Germans in North Africa.

_____ **2.** The civil war in Spain was a very bitter and bloody war.

_____ **3.** Japan was close to defeat when the atom bomb was dropped on its cities.

_____ **4.** The policy of "cash and carry" was of little help to the British.

_____ **5.** Many Soviet soldiers were killed during World War II.

_____ **6.** Germany ignored its 1939 treaty with the Soviet Union and invaded that country.

_____ **7.** Italy and Germany called themselves the Axis powers.

_____ **8.** The United States helped the Soviet Union during World War II.

_____ **9.** Germany's treatment of the Jews improved as the war went on.

_____ **10.** The Battle of the Bulge was one of the final battles in Europe during World War II.

D. Word Meanings:

Match each word in Column A with the correct meaning in Column B. Write the letter of each answer in the space provided.

Column A

_____ **1.** demilitarized
_____ **2.** blockade
_____ **3.** anti-Semitism
_____ **4.** blitzkrieg
_____ **5.** Holocaust

Column B

a. feeling of hatred toward Jews
b. a word used to describe the murder of Jews during World War II
c. preventing the passage of ships or troops into an area
d. removal of military forces and equipment from an area
e. soldiers trained and equipped to fight on foot
f. lighting war; a method of warfare used by the Germans involving a quick, all-out attack

E. On Your Own:

In 1940, the students of an American college were asked, "Do you favor giving arms and ammunition to Britain if that is the only way to save it from defeat?"

Most students were against giving such aid even though lack of aid might lead to a victory for Nazi Germany.

Write at least 100 words telling what the above suggests about the feelings of many Americans in 1940. Use a separate sheet of paper for your answer.

F. Understanding Global History:

On page 118 you read about four factors in global history. Which of these factors applies to each statement listed below? Fill in the number of the correct statement on page 118 in the space provided.

_____ **1.** Britain was dependent upon the United States for aid in World War II.

_____ **2.** Many young people today want to learn more about why millions of Jews were killed by the Nazis in World War II.

_____ **3.** The location of the United States kept it free of the damage suffered by European nations.

_____ **4.** The Germans, led by the Nazis, looked on the Slavic peoples as an inferior group.

Chapter 4

Changes After World War II

Understanding Global History

Think about the following statements as you read about the years after World War II.

1 Nations are sometimes dependent upon other nations for economic and political survival.
2 The culture in which we live influences our view of other people.
3 Nations are linked by a network of economic interdependence.
4 Environmental problems can affect people who live miles apart.

The United Nations buildings in New York City. The United Nations (UN) was set up in 1945. Member nations try to settle differences peacefully. They also agree to work together to solve world problems.

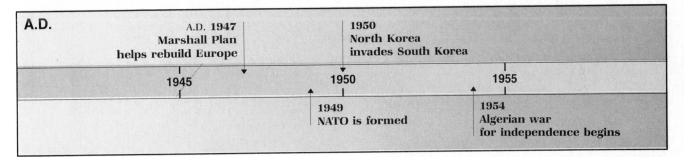

Learning New Words and Terms

The following words are used in this chapter. Think about the meaning of each one.

satellites: countries that are politically or economically controlled by another country
bloc: a group of countries joined together to help one another or to take some action
mandates: former colonies whose governments are watched over by other nations
cold war: a feeling of tension and bad feelings without real fighting; the state of relations between the Soviet Union and the United States after World War II

Think As You Read

1. How was Europe affected by World War II?
2. What were some causes of the cold war in Europe?
3. How has the growth of nuclear weapons affected relations among nations?

A.D.					
	A.D. 1947 Marshall Plan helps rebuild Europe		**1950** North Korea invades South Korea		
	1945		1950		1955
		1949 NATO is formed		**1954** Algerian war for independence begins	

Europe After the War

Almost every nation in Europe suffered during the war. The number of soldiers killed and wounded was huge. The Allies, including the United States, Britain, France, the Soviet Union, and China lost over 10 million soldiers. Germany, Italy, and Japan lost over 4 million.

People who did not take part in the fighting were also killed and wounded. Six million Jews died in Nazi concentration camps. Hundreds of thousands of men, women, and children suffered in bombing raids carried out by both sides. Factories and farms were ruined. Those people who survived faced hunger and disease.

Europe was in a state of chaos. Railroads didn't run. Seaports couldn't receive ships. Meat and vegetables could not get to the markets. Many people had no place to live. These refugees had lost everything. Whole countries needed rebuilding. How were their citizens to be fed, clothed, and housed?

American Aid

The United States helped Europe in this time of great need. The United States gave food, clothing, and medicine. These were needed right

European refugees on the road with their belongings. Thousands of people were left homeless as a result of World War II.

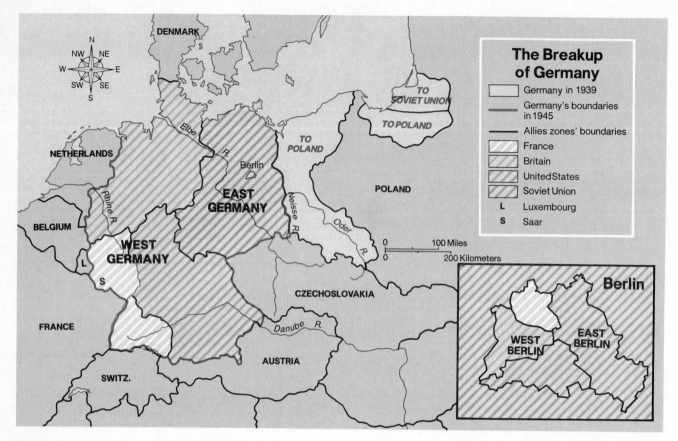

The Breakup of Germany

	Germany in 1939
	Germany's boundaries in 1945
	Allies zones' boundaries
	France
	Britain
	United States
	Soviet Union
L	Luxembourg
S	Saar

away. Then, in 1947, the United States began a big relief program. It was known as the Marshall Plan. It was named for the United States Secretary of State, General George C. Marshall. From 1947 to 1951, the United States gave over $20 million in aid to Europe. That aid included food, machinery, and raw materials. The Marshall Plan was welcomed by all nations of Europe except the Soviet Union and its communist allies.

New Governments in Europe

New governments had to be set up in many parts of Europe after the war. Britain, France, and the United States wanted to bring back democratic governments to all the freed countries. A republic was set up in France. Charles De Gaulle (duh-GAWL) became its president. The monarchy returned to Norway and to the Netherlands. Eastern European nations, however, had been freed by Soviet troops. The Soviets set up communist governments in those countries. The countries of Eastern Europe became **satellites** of the Soviet Union. They were in the Soviet sphere of influence. They were dominated by the Soviet Union.

Italy fell to the Allies in 1943. The Italian people did not want to return to the monarchy that had existed before Mussolini. They elected a parliament. Italy set up a democracy with free elections.

Germany is Divided

Germany's future was decided by the Allies at several secret meetings. The Soviets, British, French, and Americans divided Germany into four zones. Each of these countries ruled a zone. The German capital of Berlin was inside the Soviet zone. Berlin was also divided into four zones. It was called an international city because of the Allies' control (see map above).

The United States, Britain, and France wanted to bring together Germany's four zones. They wanted to create a single German republic. The Soviet Union didn't agree to this. They set up a separate communist government in their zone. Germany was therefore divided. East Germany belonged to the Soviet **bloc** of nations. West Germany allied itself with the United States, Britain, and France. Cooperation among the Allies had broken down. Because of political differences, the Soviet Union decided to follow its own course.

Other Nations Gain Freedom

The years following World War II saw the rise of freedom movements in many colonies throughout the world. Europe's colonial empires were breaking up.

- The defeated Axis powers had few colonies to deal with. Germany had lost all of its colonies in World War I.
- Japan had only Korea. Korea was divided between the Soviet Union and the United States.
- Italy had colonies in Libya, Eritrea (er-IT-tree-uh) and Somalia in Africa. These were given to the British and the French as **mandates.** This meant that their governments would be watched over by the British and French. Libya achieved its full freedom in 1951. Eritrea was joined to Ethiopia in 1952. Somalia won its freedom in 1960.
- The Philippines won its freedom from the United States in 1946.
- The British colony of India became the free countries of India and Pakistan in 1947.
- Burma became free of British control in 1948.
- Indonesia became free in 1949. The Netherlands agreed to give up its control at that time.

Freedom Movements Grow Stronger

By the late 1950s freedom movements were getting stronger. They were also getting violent. Former parent countries were under pressure to give their colonies freedom. Most parent countries were worried about the safety of Europeans left behind in a new country where they were in the minority. Britain eased many of its colonial problems by forming the British Commonwealth. This was a loose federation of countries with economic or cultural ties to Britain.

Some Nations Fight to Be Free

Freedom came easily to most countries. There were some, however, that had a hard time. Algeria began a long war with France in 1954. Mozambique won its freedom from Portugal only after a long bitter struggle. In 1965, Rhodesia, a country in southern Africa, declared itself independent. The only other nation to ever do this was the United States. That was in 1776. Rhodesia set itself up as a white-ruled African state. However, other nations in Africa and elsewhere did not like this. They thought black Africans in Rhodesia should also take part in government. In 1979, blacks came into power in Rhodesia. They renamed the nation Zimbabwe.

The United States and the Soviet Union Disagree

After World War II, the United States and the Soviet Union become the two strongest nations in the world. Each nation has its own group of allies. The United States and the Soviet Union are separated by many cultural, political, and economic differences. This has made it hard for them to understand each other. The Soviet Union has been accused of trying to spread communism by revolution. Soviet leaders deny this. They say the United States and its allies want to destroy the Soviet Union.

West Berlin was totally rebuilt after World War II. A bombed-out church was left standing as a reminder of the war.

The Cold War

By the end of World War II, there were communist governments in Eastern Europe. Yugoslavia, Poland, Czechoslovakia, Romania, Hungary, Bulgaria, Albania, and East Germany all had communist governments. These countries were satellites of the Soviet Union. Many people felt that the Soviet Union had dropped an "iron curtain" on Eastern Europe. The democratic nations of Europe feared the further spread of communism.

Tension and bad feelings rose up between these two groups of nations. The division of Germany was one cause of the tension. This time of tension and bad feelings came to be known as the **cold war.** Most disputes in the cold war were fought with words. Sometimes countries used economic and political pressures to get their way. The cold war usually involved the United States and the democratic nations of Europe and the Soviet Union and its communist allies.

Fighting in Korea

The cold war became a shooting war in Korea in 1950. Korea had been held by Japan until the end of World War II. It was then divided into two

parts. The 38th parallel of latitude was the dividing line. The Soviet Union occupied the northern part. The United States occupied the southern part.

In June 1950, North Korean troops suddenly crossed over into South Korea. The United States came to the aid of the South Koreans. At the same time, the United Nations ordered the North Koreans to pull back to their own side. The North Koreans did not obey the order. Ten member nations of the United Nations sent military forces to help South Korea. Most of these troops were American, however. When it seemed as if these troops and the South Korean allies might win, the Chinese communists acted. Hundreds of thousands of Chinese troops moved to aid North Korea.

There was heavy fighting between United Nations forces and North Korean and Chinese troops. The fighting went on until 1953. Both sides finally decided to end the fighting. A truce was signed. Both sides returned to the point where the fighting began, the 38th parallel. In spite of the bitter fighting, the United States Congress never officially declared war on North Korea. The fighting was known only as a "police action."

Effects of the Cold War

The cold war led to the formation of new military ties between countries. In 1949, the United States helped organize the North Atlantic Treaty Organization (NATO). This organization joined the United States, Britain, France, and other Western nations in a military alliance. Each country promised to help its allies if the need arose. In 1966, France withdrew from most NATO military affairs. The alliance has kept its other members, however. In 1955 the Soviet Union set up the Warsaw Pact. This was a military alliance between the Soviet Union and its communist allies in Eastern Europe. It was created to balance the growing power of NATO in Europe.

Economic Ties

The cold war also led to the forming of economic ties among nations. The Soviet Union set up a network of economic ties with its satellite nations. Economic agreements gave the communist nations the markets they needed for their goods. Factories in the Soviet Union, for example, traded

The Korean War

DMZ Demilitarized zone created by 1953 truce

SOVIET UNION

CHINA

Tumen R.

Yalu R.

Farthest United Nations advance, 1950

NORTH KOREA

•Pyongyang

DMZ

38°N

•Panmunjom
Inchon• •Seoul

38th Parallel

Farthest North Korean-Chinese advance, 1951

YELLOW SEA

SOUTH KOREA

SEA OF JAPAN

•Pusan

0   100 Miles
0   200 Kilometers

JAPAN

Soldiers in the Korean War.

their manufactured goods for raw materials from Poland or East Germany.

At the same time, a Common Market was set up by Western European countries. The idea behind the Market was to lower tariffs and improve trade in Western Europe. Today, Common Market nations include the United Kingdom (Great Britain, Northern Ireland, Scotland, and Wales), Belgium, Denmark, France, West Germany, Greece, Ireland, Luxembourg, Italy, and the Netherlands.

The Nuclear Weapons Problem

When the atomic bombs were dropped on Hiroshima and Nagasaki, a terrible new weapon of war was introduced. In 1945, the United States was the only country with atomic bombs. This made the United States very powerful. Other countries wanted to gain power also. They soon learned how to make atomic bombs. The following timetable shows the spread of nuclear weapons since World War II.

- **1945**—the United States uses atomic bombs on Hiroshima and Nagasaki.
- **1949**—the Soviet Union explodes its first atomic bomb.
- **1952**—Britain develops an atomic bomb.
- **1960s**—More powerful hydrogen bombs are developed.
- **1964**—The People's Republic of China explodes its first atomic bomb.
- **1974**—India tests an atomic bomb.

The more nations that have nuclear weapons, the greater danger there is to the entire world. Nuclear war has become a greater possibility. One of the greatest challenges today is to deal with this problem.

Exercises

A. Finding the Main Ideas:

Put a check next to the sentences that give the main ideas of what you have just read.

_____ **1.** Life in Europe had to be reorganized after World War II.

_____ **2.** The Soviet Union suffered severe damage in World War II.

_____ **3.** Britain is a member of the Common Market.

_____ **4.** The cold war divided the Soviet Union and the Western powers.

_____ **5.** New nations have helped change global politics.

B. Remembering What You Have Read:

Use the following words to complete each sentence below. Each word is used only once.

parliament   mandates   aid
military   international city satellite

1. The North Atlantic Treaty Organization (NATO) was a _____ alliance.

2. Berlin has been an _____ since Allied troops took control of it in 1945.

3. The _____ nations of Eastern Europe followed the lead of the Soviet Union.

4. Libya, Eritrea, and Somalia became _____ of Britain and France after World War II.

5. A new Italian government was set up with a _____ and free elections.

6. The Marshall Plan gave over $20 million in _____ to Europe.

C. Checking for Details:

Read each statement. Put an F in the space next to each statement if it is a fact. Put an O in that space if it is an opinion. Remember that facts can proved, but opinions cannot.

_____ **1.** The Axis nations lost World War II.

_____ **2.** The United States did not send enough aid to Europe after World War II.

_____ **3.** All nations were equally to blame for world tensions after World War II.

134

_____ **4.** The Common Market has been a success.

_____ **5.** Nuclear weapons are a threat to world peace.

_____ **6.** The Soviet Union ruled the satellite nations of Eastern Europe.

_____ **7.** The Warsaw Pact was created to balance NATO.

_____ **8.** Britain, France, and the Netherlands waited too long to give freedom to their colonies.

_____ **9.** The Korean War involved China and the United States as well as Korea.

_____ **10.** NATO has not been as strong as it might have been.

D. What Does it Mean?

Choose the best meaning for each of the words in capital letters. Write in the letter of the answer in the space provided.

_____ **1.** SATELLITE
    a. an agreement among nations
    b. a country that is ruled or dominated by another
    c. used for a special purpose

_____ **2.** BLOC
    a. a communist country
    b. soldiers trained for military action
    c. countries that act as one

E. Understanding Global History:

On page 128 you read about four factors in global history. Which of these factors applies to each sentence below? Fill in the number of the correct statement on page 128 in the space provided.

_____ **1.** Nuclear tests give off radioactive materials. These materials fall upon parts of the world that are far away from the testing area.

_____ **2.** The Soviet Union has economic ties with its satellite nations in Eastern Europe. The countries of Western Europe are joined economically in the Common Market.

_____ **3.** Europe was in a state of chaos at the end of World War II. The United States helped rebuild Europe by giving economic aid.

_____ **4.** Cultural differences made it hard for the Soviet Union and the Western democracies to understand each other.

Chapter 5

The Soviet Union Since World War II

Understanding Global History

Think about the following statements as you read about the Soviet Union after World War II.

1 The culture in which we live influences our view of other people.

2 Basic human needs—food, clothing, and shelter—are influenced by our environment and our culture.

3 Providing for individual and group needs is a common goal of all peoples and cultures.

4 Nations borrow and adapt ideas and institutions from other nations.

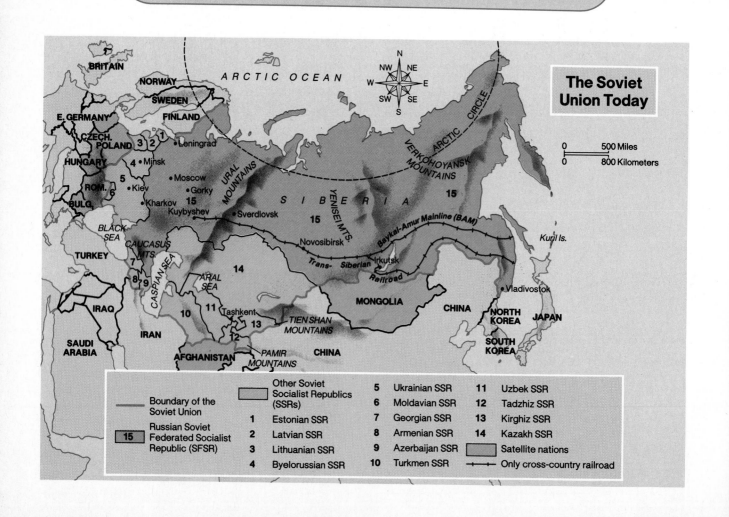

The Soviet Union Today

0 — 500 Miles
0 — 800 Kilometers

—	Boundary of the Soviet Union		Other Soviet Socialist Republics (SSRs)	**5** Ukrainian SSR	**11** Uzbek SSR
			1 Estonian SSR	**6** Moldavian SSR	**12** Tadzhiz SSR
15	Russian Soviet Federated Socialist Republic (SFSR)		**2** Latvian SSR	**7** Georgian SSR	**13** Kirghiz SSR
			3 Lithuanian SSR	**8** Armenian SSR	**14** Kazakh SSR
			4 Byelorussian SSR	**9** Azerbaijan SSR	Satellite nations
				10 Turkmen SSR	Only cross-country railroad

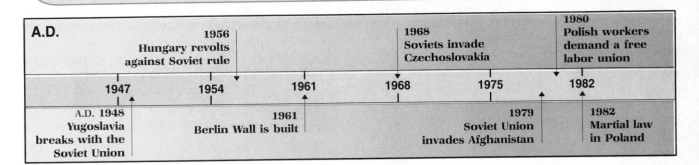

The Soviet Union gained much because of its role in World War II. It was the leader of the communist nations set up after the war. In Eastern Europe these nations included East Germany, Poland, Czechoslovakia, Hungary, Romania, Bulgaria, Yugoslavia, and Albania. In Asia it included North Korea. By surrounding itself with satellites, the Soviet Union had friendly nations to the east and also to the west.

Rebuilding Industry After the War

Of all the Allies that fought in World War II, the Soviet Union suffered the most. Many Russian soldiers died in the fighting. Men, women, and children also suffered. Farms and factories were destroyed. The people faced the hard problem of rebuilding their nation. The Soviet leader during the war was Joseph Stalin. He was powerful and ruthless. Stalin decided to put all the Soviet Union's energies into rebuilding its industries. Labor camps were built. Workers from all over the Soviet Union were forced to supply their labor. They built roads, dams, and whole cities. Scientists from the satellite nations were brought to the Soviet Union to start up new technology.

Rebuilding Soviet industries was not easy. The Soviet people had to work long and hard. Consumer goods were scarce. There were hardly any products made for personal use. It was more important to build steel mills, for example. The economy had to be made stronger to compete in world markets.

The growth of industry in the Soviet Union can be seen in the chart on page 138. It shows production for 1940, 1965, 1979, and 1982.

Changes in Farming

Under Stalin, farming in the Soviet Union changed. All peasants were forced to give up their land and farm animals. They had to join together in **collective farms.** These farms were run by the government. Collective farms were thought to produce food more efficiently.

Soviet agriculture has not grown at the same rate as industry. The collective farm system was not popular. The peasants did not want to give up their farms. Bad weather hurt crop harvests. There have been food shortages in the Soviet Union. This is a big problem for the government as it tries to meet the food needs of the people.

Output of Industry in the Soviet Union

	1940	1965	1979	1982
Coal (in millions of tons)	166	578	719	480
Steel (in millions of tons)	18	91	149	147
Oil (in millions of tons)	31	243	586	613
Electricity (in millions of kilowatt hours)	48	507	1,239 (trillion kilowatt hours)	1,366 (trillion kilowatt hours)

Workers harvesting grapes on a Soviet collective farm. This collective is in Azerbaijan, one of the republics that make up the Soviet Union.

The Soviet Union's Power is Tested

The Soviet Union set up new governments in its satellite nations. The Soviet Union wanted them to be dependent. Some countries went their own way, however. Yugoslavia asked for aid through the Marshall Plan after World War II. The Yugoslav leader, Marshal Tito, did not want to be a puppet of the Soviets. In 1948, Yugoslavia declared that it would be free of Soviet control. Yugoslavia kept its communist government, however. This was the first time that the leadership of the Soviet Union had been challenged by another communist nation. The split between the two nations has never healed. Relations have improved, though, in recent years.

Other differences of opinion took place after the death of Joseph Stalin in 1953. A workers' strike broke out in East Berlin in 1953. The Soviet Union feared another break in their iron curtain. Soviet troops were sent in to put down the workers' strike. The Soviets would not allow any other satellite nation to go its own way.

A New Leader

In 1958, Nikita Khrushchev (KROOS-chehv) became the new Soviet leader. He said that Stalin had been responsible for the arrest, exile, and death of many Soviet citizens. Those arrested and killed included leading communists. Khrushchev's statements shook the Soviet system and world communism. It seemed to be a sign of reform in the government. Under Khrushchev, a number of reforms came about. Writers and artists in the Soviet Union gained some freedom. The government still kept strict control over most parts of life, however.

Unrest in Eastern Europe

The changes in the Soviet Union after Stalin's death affected Eastern Europe. Some countries saw it as a good time to try to break away from Soviet rule.

Nikita Khrushchev led the Soviet Union from 1958 to 1964. He is shown here speaking before the United Nations in 1960.

In Hungary, nationalist leaders tried to overthrow Soviet control. This was in 1956. A more liberal communist government came into power. The Soviet Union moved troops into Hungary. The Hungarian reform movement was crushed.

In 1968, Soviet troops were used again to put down a liberal communist government, this time in Czechoslovakia. The Soviet actions in Hungary and Czechoslovakia were criticized by many other nations. Even some communist parties in Western Europe did not like the Soviet use of force. There had not been any criticism by communist parties up to this time.

Poland

The Soviet Union faced another challenge to its power. This time the challenge came from Poland. Workers there wanted higher pay and better working conditions. In 1956, riots in Poland led to a change in communist leaders. Some reforms took place. In 1970, there was another change in leadership. This resulted from new riots caused by the workers. They wanted more goods. They also wanted better goods. For the next ten years,

the Polish workers grew more and more unhappy. In 1980, there were riots in the shipyards of Gdansk (guh-DANSK). The workers wanted to form a free labor union. There had never been anything like it in any communist country before.

The Polish government agreed to the workers' demands. They could form a free trade union. The new trade union was called Solidarity.

Solidarity asked the Polish government to change its economic policies. The government was pressured to reform. Solidarity then began to question whether or not the communist government should continue to rule Poland. The communist leaders felt that this was asking too much. In 1982, the government responded. It declared a state of **martial law** in Poland. Solidarity was ended. Its leaders were arrested. After several months martial law was lifted. It was clear to many that the Soviet Union forced Poland's government to crack down on Solidarity. Today the situation in Poland is still a problem for both the Soviets and the communist government of Poland.

Lech Walesa being carried on the shoulders of his fellow workers, 1980. Walesa led the fight to set up a free trade union in Poland.

The Spread of Communism

Communism spread to other parts of the world after World War II. In China, a communist government was set up in 1949. This gave the Soviet Union a giant ally in Asia. In 1954, Vietnamese communists drove the French out of Vietnam. This action set the stage for much conflict in that country. It also helped spread communism in Southeast Asia.

In 1959, the dictator of Cuba, Batista, was overthrown. A young Cuban named Fidel Castro became prime minister. Castro made Cuba into a communist country. It was the first communist country in the Western Hemisphere. Cuba is only 90 miles from the United States. With a communist country so close to the United States, relations between the Soviet Union and the United States became very tense.

New Governments Are Set Up

Several African nations have become communist. Sometimes that has happened with the help of Soviet advisors. Cuban troops helped set up a communist government in Angola. Afghanistan became a communist state in 1979. Afghanistan is a country in western Asia. The government was overthrown and a new, communist government was set up. The people of Afghanistan rebelled. The new communist government then asked the Soviet Union for help. The Soviet Union sent troops to support the government. Central America is presently the site of conflict. There, pro- and anti-communist forces fight for power.

China and the Soviet Union Disagree

A major split in world communism took place in 1963. It involved the Soviet Union and the People's Republic of China. Mao Zedong and other Chinese communists had long felt that the Soviet Union was trying to rule China. Mao had changed communism to better meet the needs of China. China had a huge population, a culture different than that of the Soviet Union, and few natural resources. Soviet ways did not work in China. The Chinese leaders felt that the Soviet Union did not speak for all the world's communists. This led to a split between the two countries.

After the split, China had developed atomic weapons. This worried many Soviet leaders. They feared the possibility of war between China and the Soviet Union. Fighting took place between Soviet and Chinese troops in some border areas in the late 1960s. This showed the seriousness of the split between the two countries. Soviet-Chinese tensions have eased somewhat since 1969. The two countries still follow their own paths of communism, however.

Soviet-American Relations

Relations between the United States and the Soviet Union have not been friendly since World War II. The two nations are both superpowers. Neither one trusts the aims of the other. During Khrushchev's leadership there was an easing of tensions. Each superpower had its own sphere of influence. Both countries maintained a policy of **peaceful coexistence.** This situation was upset in 1954. That was when the French were driven out of Vietnam. The Soviet Union wanted to set up communist governments in Southeast Asia. The United States wanted to set up democracies. This led to war in Southeast Asia.

The 1960s—A Time of Crises

During the 1960s, several events upset peaceful coexistence. In 1960, an American spy plane was shot down over the Soviet Union. The pilot, Gary Powers, was captured. This was a great embarrassment to the United States. An apology was made to the Soviet Union.

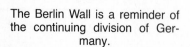

The Berlin Wall is a reminder of the continuing division of Germany.

In 1961, Germany became a trouble spot. Many East Germans were escaping communism by fleeing into West Berlin. The East German government took strong action. It built a wall between East and West Berlin. The United States was very angry. War seemed possible. The crisis passed, however.

The most serious test to peaceful coexistence came in 1962. The Soviets tried to put missile bases in Cuba. President John F. Kennedy of the United States set up a blockade around Cuba. The United States hoped to stop Soviet ships from entering with their missiles. The Cuban Missile Crisis brought the United States and the Soviet Union close to war. The Soviets backed down. They removed the missile bases from Cuba.

Changing Relations

In 1970, President Nixon of the United States tried to ease tensions between the United States and the Soviet Union. Soviet and American officials began to talk about more cooperation between the two countries. The new arrangement was called **détente** (day-TAHNT). The United States and the Soviet Union began to cooperate in science and space exploration. Cultural exchanges were arranged. There was also a steady rise in trade relations.

For a time, it seemed that cold war attitudes might disappear. At the height of détente the United States and the Soviet Union signed a human rights agreement in Helsinki, Finland. They also held Strategic Arms Limitation Talks (SALT). The purpose of SALT is to limit nuclear arms.

Détente Is Upset

By 1980 détente was over. The United States was angered by the way the Soviet Union treated its **dissidents.** These Soviet scientists, artists, and thinkers want more personal freedom within the communist society. Their views are not popular with the Soviet leaders. Most dissidents in the Soviet Union are put in jail. Some are sent to mental institutions for "re-education." The Soviet government uses similar treatment for Soviet Jews who want to leave the country.

The Soviets, on the other hand, are upset by the worldwide military presence of the United States. The United States has military bases in allied countries. These countries surround the Soviet Union.

The U.S. and the Soviet Union Move Farther Apart

Several events have caused the United States and the Soviet Union to move even farther apart. In 1979, the Soviet Union feared a rise in Islamic religious and political action on its southern borders. Communists took over the government of Afghanistan. The people of Afghanistan are Muslim. Soviet troops were called in to help when the people rebelled. Most of the world was angered by the Soviet invasion. Many countries said the Soviet Union was wrong.

Because of the invasion of Afghanistan, the U.S. Congress would not approve a new SALT II agreement on arms control. Instead, the United States decided to send new and more powerful missiles to Europe. The first missiles arrived in 1983. This brought threats from the Soviets. They said they would rearm their satellite countries.

Also, in 1983, a Korean Air Lines jumbo jet was shot down over Soviet territory. More than 200 people from different parts of the world were killed. The Soviet Union accused the plane of spying. The world reacted strongly to the loss of so many innocent lives. Late in 1983, the United States sent a force of Marines to the island of Grenada. The government of this small nation in the Caribbean Sea had been overthrown by a communist group. U.S. troops were ordered in to protect U.S. citizens. The Soviets said the United States was invading a free country.

The cold war and the tensions it brings are a global problem. Every conflict in the world is seen as a possible showdown between the superpowers. Many small countries are forming alliances of their own. They want to keep out of the cold war.

Exercises

A. Finding the Main Ideas:
Put a check next to the sentences that give the main ideas of what you have just read.

_____ **1.** Relations between the Soviet Union and the People's Republic of China changed after 1963.

_____ **2.** The Berlin Wall was built to keep East Germans from escaping into West Berlin.

_____ **3.** The Soviet Union's role as the leader of world communism has changed.

_____ **4.** Nikita Khrushchev brought some changes to the Soviet Union.

_____ **5.** Soviet control has been challenged by Yugoslavia, Hungary, Czechoslovakia, and Poland.

_____ **6.** The relations between the United States and the Soviet Union have changed since World War II.

B. What Did You Read?
Choose the answer that best completes each sentence. Write the letter of your answer in the space provided.

_____ **1.** Soviet actions in Afghanistan were criticized by
   a. China.
   b. the United States.
   c. several European communist parties.
   d. all of the above.

_____ **2.** Marshall Plan aid was sought by
   a. the United States.
   b. Yugoslavia.
   c. the Soviet Union.
   d. all the Soviet satellite nations.

_____ **3.** At the end of World War II, the Soviet Union was the leader of
   a. Europe.
   b. Asia.
   c. the world.
   d. world communism.

_____ **4.** In 1959, communism entered the Western Hemisphere when a revolution took place in
   a. Nicaragua.
   b. Argentina.
   c. Cuba.
   d. Brazil.

C. Checking for Details

Read each statement. Put a T in the space next to each statement if it is true. Put an F in that space if it is false. Put an N if you cannot tell from the reading if it is true or false.

_____ **1.** The Chinese wanted to build their industries.

_____ **2.** The Marshall Plan offered economic aid to European nations.

_____ **3.** Soviet leaders are chosen from the Communist party.

_____ **4.** Many communist nations asked for Marshall Plan aid.

_____ **5.** Yugoslavia has stayed free of the Soviet Union.

_____ **6.** Soviet production of coal and steel in 1965 was greater than U.S. production.

_____ **7.** Consumer goods production lagged behind industrial production in the Soviet Union.

_____ **8.** Khruschev spoke out against Stalin.

_____ **9.** The People's Republic of China turned away from the communist form of government.

_____ **10.** The introduction of missiles in Europe angered the Soviet Union.

D. Thinking it Over:

Answer the following question in at least 75 words. Use a separate sheet of paper.

How would you describe relations between the Soviet Union and the United States today? Base your answer on what you have read in the newspapers or heard on television or radio.

E. Understanding Global History:

On page 136 you read about four factors in global history. Which of these factors applies to each statement listed below? Fill in the number of the correct statement on page 136 in the space provided.

_____ **1.** The Chinese Communists wanted to use their own form of communism. They did not want to copy the kind of communism that the Soviet Union had.

_____ **2.** The United States and the Soviet Union were separated by economic and cultural differences that made understanding difficult.

_____ **3.** In Poland, the people wanted more goods. They wanted the government to change so that the basic needs of the people were met.

_____ **4.** Yugoslavia said it would be a communist nation free of the Soviet Union.

Chapter 6

The United States Since World War II

Understanding Global History

Think about the following statements as you read about the United States after World War II.

1. Location, topography, and resources affect interaction among people.
2. Nations are sometimes dependent upon other nations for economic and political survival.
3. Events occurring in one part of the world have influenced developments in other parts of the world.
4. Nations are economically interdependent.

President and Mrs. Reagan visited China in 1984. They are shown here with China's Minister of Culture. The United States and China have started talks about building trade and cultural contacts with each other.

Learning New Words and Terms

The following words are used in this chapter. Think about the meaning of each one.

cartel: a group that tries to control the production of a good or item in order to drive up the price

shah: the title of the ruler of Iran

jihad: a Muslim holy war

Think As You Read

1. How did the United States change its policy of isolationism after World War II?
2. What was the Marshall Plan? NATO?
3. Why did the United States fight a war in Vietnam? What was the outcome of this war?
4. Why is the Middle East important to the United States?
5. How did the United States react to events in Nicaragua in 1979?

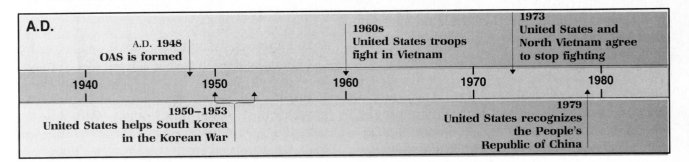

A.D.

A.D. 1948
OAS is formed

1960s
United States troops
fight in Vietnam

1973
United States and
North Vietnam agree
to stop fighting

1940　　1950　　1960　　1970　　1980

1950–1953
United States helps South Korea
in the Korean War

1979
United States recognizes
the People's
Republic of China

At the end of World War II, the United States was the world's strongest nation. It had not been damaged by the war. It was also the only nation with atomic weapons. The geography of the United States had long influenced its view of the world. The United States was rich in natural resources. It was also separated from most of the world by two great oceans. These factors led to a policy of isolationism in U.S. foreign affairs. This policy was very strong during most of the nation's history.

World War II changed the outlook of the United States in foreign affairs. By 1945 the United States had moved away from isolationism. It began to take a more active role in world affairs. It was the first nation to join the United Nations. Since 1945, the United States has spread its influence to all parts of the world.

United States Influence in Europe

The United States and the Soviet Union fought on the same side during World War II. Their alliance broke up at the end of the war. After 1945, the United States spoke out against communism.

Americans saw communism as a threat to everything they valued. Many saw Soviet power in Eastern Europe as only the start of a Communist takeover of the world.

In 1947, President Harry Truman acted to stop the spread of communism. He formed what came to be known as the Truman Doctrine. It stated that the United States would offer military and economic aid to any country fighting communism. Under the Truman Doctrine, military aid was given to Greece and Turkey. These nations seemed likely to fall to communism.

The Marshall Plan and NATO

The United States also tried to stop the spread of communism through the Marshall Plan. In 1947, the United States gave economic aid to the nations of Europe. The United States wanted to strengthen the economies of Europe. It also wanted to stop a possible Soviet takeover of Europe. The nations of Europe were very dependent upon the United States for their economic survival.

145

The North Atlantic Treaty Organization (NATO) was another way of holding back the Soviet Union. The United States organized NATO in 1949. The purpose of NATO is to check Soviet power in Europe. NATO has a military force of over one million troops. It also has much military equipment and weapons. Europe still depends on the United States for protection, even though the nations there have become a strong force in the world themselves.

United States Influence in Asia

The United States has also taken a very active part in Asian affairs since 1945. The United States was the main armed force in the Pacific during World War II. U.S. influence continued in several countries after the war. Rebuilding Japan was one of the main goals of the United States after the war. A strong Japan would help control the spread of communism in Asia.

Two Chinas

During World War II, the United States gave military and economic aid to China. When the war ended, fighting broke out again between the Nationalists and Communists. The Chinese Communists won control of the Chinese mainland in 1949. They forced Chiang Kai-shek and the Nationalists onto the island of Taiwan. There, the Republic of China was set up. The two Chinas are still enemies. For many years, the United States had very little to do with mainland China. The United States did not fully recognize the People's Republic of China until 1979.

The United States Fights in Korea and Vietnam

One test of U.S. strength in Asia came in 1950. The United States fought to stop the spread of communism. The Korean War lasted from 1950 to 1953.

Another test of the United States in Asia took place in Southeast Asia. At the end of World War II, many people in French Indochina wanted freedom from France. The Vietminh League was the most important nationalist group. It was led by Ho Chi Minh. In 1945, the Vietminh set up a new nation. It was called the Democratic Republic of Vietnam. The French would not give up their colony, however. A war broke out in 1946. It lasted until 1954. The French were defeated by the Vietminh at Dien Bien Phu. The French agreed to a treaty.

——	Boundary of French Indochina before 1954
DMZ	Demilitarized zone set by 1954 truce
☐ Communist in 1954	☐ Communist today
☐ Non-communist today	→ Communist supply route

CHINA

CHINA

•Dien Bien Phu

•Hanoi

GULF OF TONKIN

NORTH VIETNAM

LAOS

THAILAND

Vietnam War

0 — 200 Miles
0 — 200 Kilometers

Ho Chi Minh Trail

DMZ (1954)

SOUTH CHINA SEA

CAMBODIA

SOUTH VIETNAM

GULF OF THAILAND

•Saigon

Ho Chi Minh at a meeting of French communists in the 1920s. Ho later returned to Vietnam and became the leader of a freedom movement there.

In 1954, the Geneva Conference divided Vietnam into two zones. The Vietminh ruled the north, the non-communist Vietnamese the south. The North Vietnamese wanted total control of Vietnam. The United States sent money and advisors to South Vietnam. The United States was helping the South Vietnamese fight the North Vietnamese. The United States began to take part in a war against North Vietnam.

The war in Vietnam became very unpopular in the United States. Many Americans felt that too many lives were being lost. They felt that too much money was being spent. They wanted the United States to get out of the war. In 1973, President Richard Nixon set up a peace conference. Both sides agreed to stop fighting. In 1975, the North Vietnamese overran South Vietnam. In 1976, the two Vietnams were joined together. The Vietnam War showed that the United States could lose wars as well as win them.

The Middle East is Important

The Middle East became very important after 1945. One reason was oil. The world needed cheap oil for growing industries and economies. The Middle East had huge amounts of oil. This part of the world was often the scene of some conflict, however. The United States wanted to protect its ability to get oil from the Middle East. The Middle East became important to the economy and safety of the United States as well as to other nations.

The Price of Oil Rises

Most of the oil-rich nations of the world are found in the Middle East. By the 1960s they joined together in a **cartel**. This cartel was the Organization of Petroleum Exporting Countries (OPEC). OPEC had one purpose—to drive up the price of oil. Since the countries of the Middle East produced most of the world's oil, they could control its supply. They could also control its price. Soon the world was suffering from a shortage of oil. Prices rose sharply. By the late 1970s and early 1980s, however, the price of oil dropped. The oil crisis had passed.

Revolution in Iran

One of the United States' closest friends in the Middle East was Iran. There were several reasons for this. Iran shares a border with the Soviet Union. Iran has an outlet to the oil-rich Persian Gulf. Iran is also very rich in oil.

The **shah** of Iran wanted to make Iran a modern nation. He spent a great deal of money on new projects. He brought many reforms to Iran. He also used harsh methods to get his way.

Many people in Iran did not like the shah's changes, however. Iran is a Muslim nation. The Muslim religious leaders of Iran were not happy with the shah. The most powerful religious leader was Ayatollah Khomeini (eye-uh-TOH-luh koh MAY-nee). He led a revolt against the shah in 1979.

In November 1979, young Iranians took over the United States embassy in Teheran, the capital of Iran. They were angry over the fact that the shah had been allowed into the United States. The Iranians held 62 Americans captive inside the embassy. Talks between the United States and Iran went on for a long time. The hostages were finally set free in 1981. Iran still held the United States responsible for the shah's actions. Iran declared a **jihad**, or holy war, to punish the United States.

A worker at an oil refinery in Iraq. The oil of the Middle East is needed by many countries.

Israel is an Important Ally of the United States

An important ally of the United States in the Middle East is Israel. The Jewish state of Israel was created in 1948. It was formed out of the British mandate called Palestine. Jewish newcomers quickly moved into Israel. This made Israel's Arab neighbors uneasy. War broke out between Israel and some Arab nations. Israel survived the war, however.

The United States built close ties to Israel. This support has led to anti-American feelings in some Arab lands. Arab nations waged war on Israel in 1956, 1967, and 1973. These wars did little to change the position of Israel. In 1979, Egypt signed a peace treaty with Israel. It was the first time an Arab state had done so.

The Egypt-Israel peace treaty was a step toward peace in the Middle East. Tensions in the region are still high, however. The United States continues to support Israel. The Arab nations are still hostile toward Israel.

United States Influence in Latin America

After World War II the United States began to take greater interest in Latin America. The United States hoped to keep communism out of the Western Hemisphere. The Good Neighbor Policy of the 1930s continued into the 1940s. The United States was trying to build a partnership with Latin American nations. In 1948, the United States formed the Organization of American States (OAS). The purpose of the OAS was to promote interdependence among member states.

Cuba

The island nation of Cuba became a trouble spot for the United States in 1959. A communist government came into power in Cuba at that time. The United States does not recognize the Cuban government. Relations between the two countries have been strained. Cuba has helped revolutionary groups in other Latin American countries.

Central America

The policies of the United States have sometimes led to conflicts with other Latin American nations. In 1979, the dictator of Nicaragua, Anastasio Somoza, was overthrown. He was replaced by a group called the Sandinistas. The new government favored communism. It became involved in fights with the United States. The United States had supported Somoza. The United States accused Nicaragua of helping rebel groups enter neighboring El Salvador. Nicaragua denied this. They said the United States was helping to arm groups trying to overthrow the Nicaraguan government. The situation in this area is still troubled.

Panama

In 1979, the United States and Panama signed a new treaty. It stated that Panama would take over full ownership of the Panama Canal in 1999. This is one example of good relations between the United States and a Latin American country. In spite of such agreements, many Latin Americans still view the United States as an imperialist power. They do not fully understand U.S. attitudes toward revolutionary movements within Latin America. Many of these movements are supported by many Latin Americans.

The Panama Canal joins the Atlantic and Pacific oceans.

Exercises

A. Finding the Main Ideas:
Put a check next to the sentences that give the main ideas of what you have just read.

_____ **1.** The NATO alliance is important to the safety of Europe.

_____ **2.** American foreign policy changed after 1945.

_____ **3.** The Arab-Israeli wars were important to world affairs.

_____ **4.** OPEC had an important effect on U.S. foreign policy.

_____ **5.** After 1945 the United States tried to hold back Soviet influence in Europe.

_____ **6.** The Truman Doctrine helped Greece and Turkey.

_____ **7.** The United States played a role in Asia after World War II.

B. What Did You Read?
Choose the answer that best completes each sentence. Write the letter of your answer in the space provided.

_____ **1.** The United States foreign policy after 1945 was
  a. isolationist.
  b. friendly to the Soviet Union.
  c. against communism.
  d. all of the above.

_____ **2.** In the fighting between the Nationalists and Communists in China, the United States was
  a. neutral.
  b. in favor of the Nationalists.
  c. in favor of the Communists.
  d. against both groups.

_____ **3.** In the Middle East, the United States has supported
  a. Arab nations.
  b. oil-producing nations.
  c. British interests.
  d. Israel.

_____ **4.** Which of the following were tests of U.S. strength and influence?
  a. Korea.
  b. Panama.
  c. Canada.
  d. Israel.

C. Map Skills

Look at the map on this page. Match the places on the map with the statements below. Then write in the name of the place in the spaces on the left. Some letters have already been written in to help you.

E _ S _ _ V _ _ _ _   San Salvador is the capital

_ _ _ R _ _ R _ _ O   U.S. island east of the Dominican Republic

_ _ _ _ N _ D _   Small nation southwest of Barbados

_ _ C _ _ _ G _ _   Managua is the capital

_ _ B _ _   Became Communist in 1959

_ _ _ _ T _ R _ _ A   Bordered by Nicaragua and Panama

_ _ _ _ _ C _   About 100 miles south of Cuba

_ _ H _ M _ _   Nation closest to Florida

_ _ Y _ _ _   Nation east of Venezuela

_ _ L _ _ _   Fronts Mexico and the Caribbean Sea

_ _ _ T _   Shares island with the Dominican Republic

Central America and the Caribbean Today
✪ Capital

D. Checking for Details:

Read each statement. Put an F in the space next to each statement if it is a fact. Put an O in that space if it is an opinion. Remember that facts can be proved, but opinions cannot.

_____ **1.** The United States does not have enough oil resources for the future.

_____ **2.** OPEC nations raised the price of oil after 1960.

150

_____ **3.** Muslim religious leaders took control of Iran after the shah was overthrown.

_____ **4.** Oil is important to the economies of most nations.

_____ **5.** Isolationism was a good policy.

_____ **6.** The United States changed its foreign policy after World War II.

_____ **7.** The Organization of American States (OAS) was created to build interdependence.

_____ **8.** The war in Vietnam was unpopular in the United States.

_____ **9.** OPEC oil profits were greater than they should have been.

_____ **10.** OPEC will regain its power in the future.

E. Word Meanings:

Match each word in Column A with the correct meaning in Column B. Write the letter of each answer in the space provided.

Column A

_____ **1.** cartel
_____ **2.** jihad
_____ **3.** shah

Column B

a. the title of the ruler of Iran
b. a group that tries to control the production of a good or item in order to drive up the price
c. a Muslim holy war
d. a Muslim religious leader

F. Understanding Global History:

On page 144 you read about four factors in global history. Which of these factors applies to each statement listed below? Fill in the numbers of the correct statement on page 144 in the space provided.

_____ **1.** OPEC's attempt to control oil supplies affected many economies throughout the world.

_____ **2.** Iranians took Americans captive in Teheran 1979 after they learned that the shah of Iran had been allowed into the United States.

_____ **3.** U.S. isolationism before 1945 was related to the nation's geography.

_____ **4.** Europe was able to rebuild rapidly after World War II. This was made possible largely by Marshall Plan aid from the United States.

Chapter 7

India Since World War II

Understanding Global History

Think about the following statements as you read about India after World War II.

1. Location, topography, and resources affect interaction among people.

2. Nations borrow and adapt ideas and institutions from other nations.

3. Providing for individual and group needs in a common goal of all peoples and cultures.

4. The culture in which we live influences our view of other people.

New Delhi is the capital of India. Government offices are located here.

Learning New Words and Terms

The following words are used in this chapter. Think about the meaning of each one.

passive resistance: a form of civil disobedience using nonviolent methods

British Commonwealth: an association of more than 40 former British colonies and the United Kingdom; now known as the Commonwealth of Nations

self-sufficient: able to take care of one's own needs

Think As You Read

1. Why was India divided into two nations after World War II?
2. What problems has India faced since it won its freedom?
3. Why was Bangladesh created? How did this affect Pakistan?

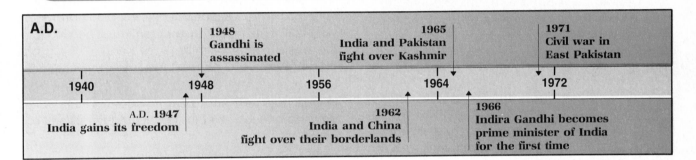

A.D.					
	1948 Gandhi is assassinated		**1965** India and Pakistan fight over Kashmir		**1971** Civil war in East Pakistan
1940	1948	1956	1964		1972
A.D. 1947 India gains its freedom		**1962** India and China fight over their borderlands		**1966** Indira Gandhi becomes prime minister of India for the first time	

India asked for its freedom from Britain in 1918. Indians felt that their country should be free because of the part it played in World War I. India had supported Britain during the war. The British government was not ready to let go of India, however. It did give India some limited self-rule. This caused unrest among many Indians. A freedom movement began.

By the 1920s, the Indian National Congress had become India's major political group. It was led by Mohandas K. Gandhi. Gandhi was the greatest leader of the freedom movement. He used **passive resistance** as a way to win freedom. Gandhi asked Indians not to pay taxes, use any British goods, or serve in the British armed forces. Gandhi and the Indian nationalists did not use force. Because of this, Gandhi and his followers won many supporters throughout the world.

During World War II, the British promised India its freedom if India would supply soldiers to help in the fighting. Gandhi and his followers would not help. Because of this, Gandhi and many others were jailed for most of the war. Many Indians did serve in the British armed forces, however. Indian soldiers fought in Asia and Europe during World War II.

Gandhi led the fight for Indian independence. He taught non-violence as a way of meeting this goal.

India Wins Its Freedom

After World War II, the British kept their promise. They gave India its freedom in 1947. There were some problems to solve, however. India's people were not joined. Hindus and Muslims did not like one another. They were the two main religious groups living in India. When India became free, riots broke out between Hindus and Muslims. The British turned political power over to two governments. The central part of India was put under the control of Gandhi and other Hindus. Muslims were given control over parts of India where they were a majority. The Muslim parts were found in northeastern and northwestern India. These areas became known as East Pakistan and West Pakistan. The Muslims were led by Muhammad Ali Jinnah.

Troubled Times

Differences in religion and geography caused the division of India. The division of India did not bring peace, however. More than 10 million people left their homes. They feared their religion would cause trouble. They moved either to Hindu or Muslim lands. Riots broke out between Hindus and Muslims. Thousands were killed. Gandhi called upon Indians to live and let live. He promised to go without eating until the violence stopped. The leaders of the fighting groups agreed to stop the bloodshed. Gandhi gave up his fast. In 1948, Gandhi was killed by a Hindu who did not agree with his ideas.

Jawaharlal Nehru led India after Gandhi's death.

Gandhi's death did not destroy India. In 1947, Jawaharlal Nehru (jah-WAH-har-lal NAY-roo) became India's first prime minister. India took over many of the British legal, political, and educational systems. India also changed these systems to meet the special needs of the Indian people. After it won its freedom, India became part of the **British Commonwealth**. India worked with Britain and other Commonwealth nations in areas such as trade and defense.

India After Independence

India has faced many problems since winning its freedom. A major problem has been its number of people. India's population has been growing very fast. The Indian government must provide for the basic needs of millions of people. Many of these people are poor. Sometimes they cannot grow enough food for themselves. Today, India is still far from **self-sufficient** in food. It has trouble growing enough food to feed its many millions of people.

India has also tried to build up its industry. India has modern factories and good transportation. In 1970, India built its first nuclear power plant. The United States helped India with this project. By 1974, India had also built an atomic bomb. The United States did not approve of this action. It feared that Pakistan would try to build its own nuclear weapon to match India. This might hurt chances for peace in the area.

India Has Problems With its Neighbors

India has tried to be a neutral nation in its relations with other nations. It has not always agreed with some of its neighbors, however. A serious dispute arose with the People's Republic of China in 1962. Chinese troops occupied and held part of the land on the India-China border. Both India and China wanted to have this land. Neither side was willing to consider the view of the other. Relations with China were strained.

A border problem also arose with Pakistan. In 1965, India and Pakistan fought a three-week war over Kashmir. Both countries claim parts of the land in northern India.

Most problems between India and Pakistan are based on religious differences. However, India and Pakistan often find it hard to understand one another in other matters as well. A civil war broke out in East Pakistan in 1971. The people of East Pakistan felt that they were not treated fairly by the central government. The government was based in West Pakistan. The people in East Pakistan wanted their own country. They received strong support from India. A war broke out between India and Pakistan in 1971. Because of the war, Pakistan lost its eastern lands. East Pakistan became the nation of Bangladesh. India has survived its border wars. Relations with its neighbors are still a matter of concern, however.

Problems Within India

India has also had problems at home. Prime Minister Nehru led India from 1947 until his death in 1964. In 1966, his daughter, Indira Gandhi, was elected prime minister. She led the Congress party. This party had led Indian politics since India won its freedom. In the 1970s, food shortages, strikes, and riots troubled India. To deal with these problems, Mrs. Gandhi took over more powers in 1975. She started press censorship. Newspapers were not given the freedom to write what they wanted. Those who were against Mrs. Gandhi were arrested and jailed. In spite of these measures, India did not move away from the democratic system. Elections were held in 1977. Mrs. Gandhi and the Congress party lost. However,

Indira Gandhi led India until 1984.

India's new leaders did not win the confidence of the people. So Mrs. Gandhi's party was returned to power in 1979. She became prime minister for a second time. In 1984, Mrs. Gandhi was assassinated by opponents of her rule.

Freedom has not solved the problems of India, Pakistan, and Bangladesh. New leaders will have to deal with this region's problems in the future.

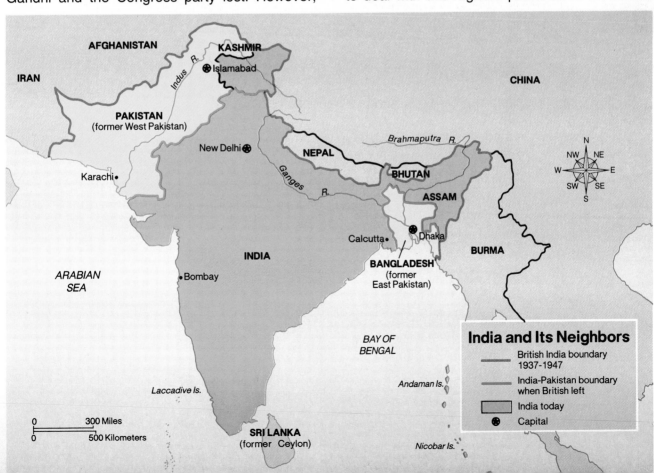

India and Its Neighbors

— British India boundary 1937-1947
— India-Pakistan boundary when British left
▨ India today
⊕ Capital

Exercises

A. Finding the Main Ideas:

Put a check next to the sentences that give the main ideas of what you have just read.

_____ **1.** The division of India in 1947 led to the creation of free India and Pakistan.

_____ **2.** Indira Gandhi first became prime minister of India in 1966.

_____ **3.** Bangladesh was once East Pakistan.

_____ **4.** Providing for the basic needs of its large population is a major problem for India.

_____ **5.** Border fights with China and Pakistan have led India into conflicts.

_____ **6.** Military leaders have taken control of governments in Bangladesh and Pakistan.

B. What Did You Read?

Choose the answer that best completes each sentence. Write the letter of your answer in the space provided.

_____ **1.** Pakistan was the part of India where the majority of the people were
  a. Hindus.
  b. Muslims.
  c. Chinese.
  d. all of the above.

_____ **2.** Who led India right after Mohandas Gandhi's death?
  a. Indira Gandhi
  b. Muhammad Ali Jinnah
  c. the British
  d. Jawaharlal Nehru

_____ **3.** In foreign affairs, India has
  a. favored the Soviet Union.
  b. favored the United States.
  c. favored the Chinese.
  d. tried to stay neutral.

_____ **4.** India has
  a. built an atomic bomb.
  b. built its industries.
  c. helped Bangladesh in its revolt against Pakistan.
  d. done all of the above.

C. Checking for Details:

Read each statement. Put an F in the space next to each statement if it is a fact. Put an O in that space if it is an opinion. Remember that facts can be proved, but opinions cannot.

_____ **1.** Indira Gandhi was not a good leader for India.

_____ **2.** Bangladesh did not have to revolt against Pakistan.

_____ **3.** India agreed with many British ideas.

_____ **4.** India and Pakistan fought over Kashmir.

_____ **5.** China took hold of parts of its border with India.

_____ **6.** Gandhi was wrong in not helping Britain in World War II.

_____ **7.** Pakistan was right in its 1971 war with India.

_____ **8.** Nuclear weapons have made India stronger in its relations with other nations.

_____ **9.** Many Indians fought in the British armed forces in World War II.

_____ **10.** Those in the Congress party have been the best leaders of India.

D. Word Meanings:

Look up the following words in the glossary. Write the meaning next to each word.

SELF-SUFFICIENT _____

_____

PASSIVE RESISTANCE _____

_____

E. Understanding Global History:

On page 152 you read about four factors in global history. Which of these factors applies to each statement listed below? Fill in the numbers of the correct statements on page 152 in the space provided.

_____ **1.** One of India's largest problems is making sure its people get enough to eat.

_____ **2.** The separation of East and West Pakistan created a situation that led to distrust, suspicion, and violence.

_____ **3.** Indian nationalists worked to free India from British rule. India's leaders adopted many British ideas after winning their freedom, however.

_____ **4.** Indians, Pakistanis, and Chinese each viewed the world in a different way. Each failed to understand the other.

Chapter 8

China Since World War II

Understanding Global History

Think about the following statements as you read about China after World War II.
1 Nations are sometimes dependent upon other nations for economic and political survival.
2 Basic human needs—food, clothing, and shelter—are influenced by our physical environment and our culture.
3 Nations are linked by a network of economic interdependence.
4 Location, topography, and resources affect interaction among people.

There are over 1 billion Chinese. To make sure there is enough food for the people, the government of China is trying to convince couples to have only one child.

Learning New Words and Terms

The following words are used in this chapter. Think about the meaning of each one.

reform: to try to make things better by change
morale: a sense of common purpose or common goals
cooperatives: organized groups sharing in work and costs
communes: organized groups of people working together for a common purpose

Think As You Read

1. How have the farm policies of the Chinese Communists changed since 1949?
2. What have the relations been between the Chinese government and the Soviet Union?
3. What have the relations been between the Chinese government and the United States?

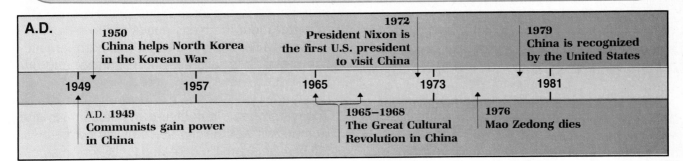

A.D.

| 1950 China helps North Korea in the Korean War | 1972 President Nixon is the first U.S. president to visit China | 1979 China is recognized by the United States |

1949 — 1957 — 1965 — 1973 — 1981

A.D. 1949 Communists gain power in China

1965–1968 The Great Cultural Revolution in China

1976 Mao Zedong dies

The war between Japan and China ended in 1945. During the war, the Chinese Nationalists and Communists ended their own civil war. However, neither side really trusted the other. Each side seemed to be waiting for the end of World War II to begin the fighting again.

The Communists

During World War II the Chinese Communists gained strong support in northern China. Their leader was Mao Zedong. The Communists defended many peasant villages against the Japanese. They also stopped landlords from charging rents that were too high. Their promises of land **reform** won the Communists many followers among Chinese peasants.

When World War II ended, Mao and the Communists were given military aid from the Soviet Union. The Soviet Union had declared war on Japan just before the Japanese surrender. This made it possible for Soviet troops to enter Manchuria at the end of the war. They took over Japanese military supplies. The Soviets gave these to the nearby Chinese Communists. The military supplies helped Mao and his Communist troops a great deal.

The Nationalists

During the war, the Chinese Nationalists had been much better supplied than the Chinese Communists. The Nationalists received arms from the United States to fight the Japanese. Nationalist troops had done little, however. Their **morale** was low. The Nationalists were also corrupt. Their leader was Chiang Kai-shek. He seemed to be saving his energies for a new battle with the Communists once the Japanese were defeated.

Civil War Breaks Out Again

Civil war broke out again between the Communists and the Nationalists soon after the surrender of Japan. By 1948, the Communists had won major victories. Chiang Kai-shek and the Nationalists were forced to leave mainland China in 1949. They went to the island of Taiwan. On Taiwan, the Nationalists set up a new government. It was called the Republic of China. The Republic of China was recognized by the United States. Taiwan was protected by an American naval force. Taiwan was also given economic help from the United States. It was able to build its industries.

The Communists Take Hold of China

The Chinese Communists took over mainland China in 1949. Their new government was called the People's Republic of China. It was soon recognized by the Soviet Union. Later, it was recognized by Britain and many other nations, too. The United States did not recognize the new government, however. Instead, the United States helped the Nationalist government on Taiwan. The government on Taiwan also kept its seat at the United Nations. Because the United States favored Taiwan, the People's Republic of China (mainland China) was kept out of the United Nations until 1971.

Land Reform in China

China's Communist leaders began to try to improve the lives of the people soon after they came to power. In 1949, most Chinese were peasant farmers. They had suffered for centuries at the hands of landlords, bandits, and the government. Land reform had been one of the earliest promises of the Communists.

By the early 1950s, the promise of land reform was carried out. Land was taken from rich landlords. Most farm families got no more than two to three acres. The land reform policy was still very popular, however.

More Changes

For a time, the government allowed the peasants to run their land. These small farms, however, were thought to be inefficient. The Communists next tried to improve production. They put an end to all private ownership of land. Farmers were encouraged to join **cooperatives.** They were asked to give their tools to the cooperatives. With their neighbors, the farmers formed teams to work the land. Food shortages were still China's biggest problem.

In the late 1950s the government acted again. It joined small farms and cooperatives into huge farm **communes.** Some of the communes were home to 10,000 people or more. Men, women, and children lived in separate houses. Men and women worked in the fields and were watched over by commune leaders. The commune lands were owned by the government. Commune members worked for wages. In this way, the Communists hoped to organize China's land and people to better meet the basic needs of the nation.

For a while, this system worked. Farm production grew. Crop failures, poor planning, and unhappiness over living conditions, however, brought an end to the plan in the early 1960s. Today, families live in their own homes. Men and women still work in the fields of the communes. Many have a small plot of land for their own crops, however. Small industries have also been built on the communes.

Industrial Reform

The Chinese Communist government also started changes in industry. The government took over factories, mines, and small businesses. The government tried to improve industrial output. There were good results. There were increases in many parts of production. Today, China is a major industrial force in Asia. It has also become one of

Chinese peasants at work on a commune.

160

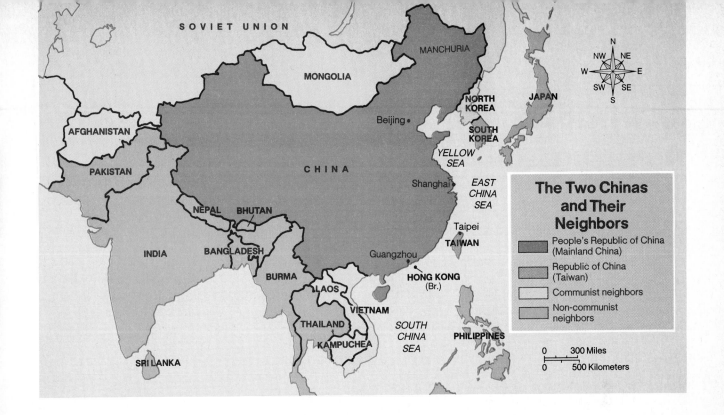

The Two Chinas and Their Neighbors

People's Republic of China (Mainland China)

Republic of China (Taiwan)

Communist neighbors

Non-communist neighbors

0   300 Miles
0   500 Kilometers

the world's nuclear powers. China is still behind the United States and the Soviet Union in industrial production, however.

The Great Cultural Revolution

In the 1960s, Mao Zedong worried that life in China might go back to the way it was before the Communists took over. He led a movement to make his ideas new again. Millions of young people joined together in units called Red Guards. They helped Mao's plan. Life in China was turned upside down. Those who did not agree with Mao's ideas were punished hard. Factory production fell. Schools and universities closed. The entire nation was thrown into chaos from 1965 to 1968. China's economic, educational, and political systems grew weak during this period. This time is known as The Great Cultural Revolution.

China's Foreign Policy

Mao Zedong tried to make China a major world power after World War II. He encouraged other nations to follow China's example. When war broke out in Korea in 1950, China sent 200,000 troops to help North Korea. During the Vietnam War, China sent aid to the North Vietnam forces.

Relations between China and the Soviet Union fell apart in the late 1950s. Each claimed to be better in communist belief than the other. There were also several small fights along the Soviet-Chinese border. This created a fear of war between the two communist nations. The Soviet Union was upset when China built nuclear weapons. The Chinese accused the Soviets of trying to force Soviet rule upon other lands.

Soviet-Chinese relations grew worse in the 1970s. Relations between China and the United States did improve, however. President Richard M. Nixon visited China in 1972. The People's Republic of China was given a seat in the UN. It took the place of Taiwan. The United States was in favor of these changes in the United Nations. However, the United States has also kept up its friendly relations with Taiwan.

New Ties With the World

The death of Mao Zedong in 1976 has led to changes in Chinese Communist policies. New leaders have come into power since Mao's death. They have moved China away from Mao's rigid ideas. They have taken steps to make China more modern. China's leaders are building up trade and economic relations with other nations. China has many people. The United States and other capitalist nations want to build up markets for their goods in China. In 1979, the United States gave full recognition to the People's Republic of China. It still kept up friendly relations with the Taiwan Nationalists.

Exercises

A. Finding the Main Ideas:

Put a check next to the sentences that give the main ideas of what you have just read.

_____ **1.** Communists and Nationalists fought a civil war in China.

_____ **2.** President Nixon visited China in 1972.

_____ **3.** The two Chinas have disagreed about which one should have a seat in the United Nations.

_____ **4.** China has built nuclear weapons.

_____ **5.** The economic life of China changed when the Communists took over.

_____ **6.** Mao Zedong had a great influence upon China.

_____ **7.** China's relations with the Soviet Union have suffered.

B. What Did You Read?

Choose the answer that best completes each sentence. Write the letter of your answer in the space provided.

_____ **1.** Cooperatives in China were set up by the
  a. Nationalists.
  b. Japanese.
  c. Communists.
  d. Europeans.

_____ **2.** The People's Republic of China has been recognized by
  a. the Soviet Union.
  b. Britain.
  c. the United States
  d. all of the above.

_____ **3.** The Red Guards tried to
  a. take over Vietnam.
  b. help North Korea.
  c. make Mao's ideas new again in China.
  d. move China away from the rigid ideas of Mao.

_____ **4.** Today, China is represented in the United Nations by
  a. the Taiwan government.
  b. both Taiwan and the People's Republic of China.
  c. the People's Republic of China.
  d. neither Taiwan nor the People's Republic of China.

C. Understanding What You Have Read:

Tell whether each of the following involves (P) political, (E) economic, or (M) military issues. Place the correct answer in the space provided.

_____ **1.** China built its industrial output after 1949.

_____ **2.** Mao Zedong led the Chinese Communists.

_____ **3.** China's farmers were organized into cooperatives.

_____ **4.** Small industries have been built on the communes.

_____ **5.** Chinese troops fought in the Korean War.

_____ **6.** The United States recognized the People's Republic of China in 1979.

_____ **7.** China has nuclear weapons.

D. Behind the Headlines:

Each headline has a story behind it. Write two or three sentences that support or tell about each headline. Use a separate sheet of paper.

COMMUNISTS AND NATIONALISTS IN CHINA RECEIVE MILITARY SUPPLIES

MAINLAND CHINA FALLS TO COMMUNISTS

MAO'S DEATH BRINGS CHANGES TO CHINA

E. On Your Own:

Write a 100-word essay about the topic below. Base your answer on what you have read in the newspapers or heard on television and radio. Use a separate sheet of paper.

Describe the relations between the People's Republic of China and the United States.

F. Understanding Global History:

On page 158 you read about four factors in global history. Which of these factors applies to each statement listed below? Fill in the number of the correct statement on page 158 in the space provided.

_____ **1.** China has many people. This factor has made capitalist nations interested in trading with China.

_____ **2.** Chinese Communist leaders tried to use communes to meet the needs of the people.

_____ **3.** Today, China is building trade and economic relations with other nations.

_____ **4.** Taiwan was protected by an American naval force. It was also given economic help by the United States.

Chapter 9

Southeast Asia Since World War II

Understanding Global History

Think about the following statements as you read about Southeast Asia after World War II.

1 Events occurring in one part of the world have influenced developments in other parts of the world.

2 The culture in which we live influences our view of other people.

3 People should learn to understand and appreciate cultures different from their own.

4 Contact among peoples can lead to cultural diffusion.

5 Nations are sometimes dependent upon other nations for economic and political survival.

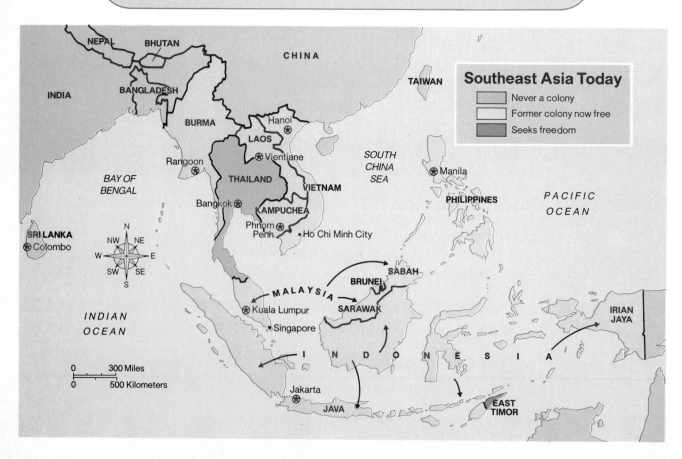

Southeast Asia Today

- Never a colony
- Former colony now free
- Seeks freedom

Learning New Words and Terms

The following words are used in this chapter. Think about the meaning of each one.

guerrillas: military troops who carry out war on an irregular basis

discrimination: a difference in treatment of a person or group

Think As You Read

1. What factors helped freedom movements in Southeast Asia?
2. What happened to Southeast Asia after the end of World War II?
3. How was the United States involved in Southeast Asia after World War II?

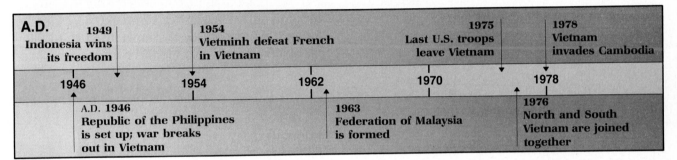

A.D.	1949 Indonesia wins its freedom	1954 Vietminh defeat French in Vietnam		1975 Last U.S. troops leave Vietnam	1978 Vietnam invades Cambodia
1946	1954	1962	1970	1978	
	A.D. 1946 Republic of the Philippines is set up; war breaks out in Vietnam		1963 Federation of Malaysia is formed	1976 North and South Vietnam are joined together	

The Road to Independence

With the exception of Thailand, all of the nations of Southeast Asia were once European or American colonies. Japanese troops took over much of Southeast Asia early in World War II. The Japanese had trouble with nationalist groups, however. When the war ended, Britain, France, and the Netherlands tried to rule their colonies again. Nationalist groups had become very strong. They wanted their freedom. This could not be ignored.

Freedom came more quickly for some nations than others in Southeast Asia. Thailand got back its freedom as soon as Japanese troops withdrew. Other nations also got their freedom quickly and peacefully. Some countries had to fight for their freedom. Some got help from the Soviet Union and the People's Republic of China. All were helped by the strong anti-colonialist feeling in the world after World War II.

The Philippines

The Philippines had been a colony of the United States since 1898. In 1934, the U.S. Congress gave the Philippines its freedom. Full freedom was delayed by World War II. The Japanese occupied the Philippine islands during the war. On July 4, 1946 the free Republic of the Philippines was set up.

In the 1970s communist **guerrillas** and some Muslims led an uprising in the Philippines. They wanted to overthrow the government of President Ferdinand Marcos. To deal with the unrest, President Marcos declared martial law. He arrested hundreds of people who were against him.

In January 1981 Marcos ended martial law. He freed hundreds of prisoners. However, Marcos still rules the Philippines. He has kept many of the laws that were set up under martial law.

Indonesia

Indonesia is a chain of some 3,000 islands. These islands were once known as the Dutch East Indies. After winning their freedom from the Dutch, the new leaders called their land Indonesia. Most Indonesians are Muslims.

Indonesians had long disliked Dutch rule. When the Japanese took hold of the islands during World War II nationalist feelings grew among the people. Some Indonesians saw Japan as an ally against the Dutch. Most felt few ties with either the Japanese or the Dutch, however. Indonesia's culture was not understood by either foreign power.

The Dutch tried to rule the islands after World War II. Indonesian nationalists led a revolt against the Dutch. They were led by Achmed Sukarno. After bitter fighting, Indonesia won its freedom in 1949.

165

Sukarno ruled Indonesia for 15 years. In 1963 he made himself president for life. The country's problems grew during Sukarno's rule. The economy grew worse and worse.

In 1966 General Suharto led a revolt. He took over as acting president of Indonesia. Suharto has tried to rebuild the country. He was given aid from Western countries. In the 1978 elections he was reelected for his third five-year term.

Indonesia is rich in oil. Money from the state-owned oil company has been used to build up industry. In 1976 the company failed. Much of the oil money now goes to pay off foreign debts. Because of this, the growth of industry in Indonesia has slowed down.

Burma

Burma won some self-government from the British in 1937. It was taken over by the Japanese in 1942. Japan held Burma until the end of the war. Burma became free in 1948.

Burma has tried to stay neutral in its relations with the world's powers. In 1974, a new constitution was written. Burma became a socialist democratic republic.

Many Chinese and Indians have lived in Burma for hundreds of years. The government of Burma has allowed **discrimination** against these two groups. Many Chinese and Indians have been pushed out of jobs and businesses.

Malaysia and Singapore

In 1963, Malaya, Singapore, Sarawak (Northwest Borneo), and Sabah (North Borneo) joined together to form the Federation of Malaysia. They had all been British colonies.

The new Federation of Malaysia faced many problems. Tensions grew between the Malays and the Chinese living in Singapore. Most Malays had no education. They were farmers. The Chinese were highly educated. They lived in the city. The Malays ran the government of Malaysia. The Chinese ruled most of the business and wealth.

In 1965 the Malays forced Singapore to leave the Federation. Singapore formed its own nation. It was called the Republic of Singapore. Even today there is much tension between the Malays and the Indians and Chinese who still live in Malaysia. The Malaysian government has tried to improve education for the majority of the Malay population. It has also tried to improve their economic status. Some progress has been made. The situation is still tense, however.

Indochina

Indochina included the nations known today as Vietnam, Kampuchea (Cambodia), and Laos. These areas had been under French rule since the late 1800s. The French language and culture had blended with the original languages and cultures of the area.

Japan took over Indochina during World War II. The Japanese pushed out the French. After the defeat of Japan, the French returned to Indochina. They found Japan had divided Indochina into Vietnam, Laos, and Cambodia. The French kept these divisions. They also granted some self-rule to the colonies. Nationalists and Communists in Indochina did not want to go back to French colonial rule. Conflict broke out almost at once.

Singapore is a major banking and commercial center in Asia.

South Vietnamese troops fighting the North Vietnamese, 1969. United States troops soon took over most of the fighting.

Vietnam

In 1946, a war broke out in Vietnam between the French and the Vietnamese Communists. The Communists were called the Vietminh. A year earlier, in 1945, the French had set up a government in the south. The Vietminh had set up a government in the north. Their leader was Ho Chi Minh. In 1954, the Vietminh finally defeated the French. A conference was held in Geneva, Switzerland, to discuss how to settle the situation.

France, the Vietminh, Cambodia, Laos, China, Britain, the United States, and the Soviet Union tried to work out a plan for Indochina. Vietnam was divided into two zones. Ho Chi Minh was to rule in the north. Non-communist Vietnamese were to rule in the south. An election was to be held in 1956 to choose a new government. Many people hoped this new government would unite the country.

The election never took place. North Vietnam stayed communist. South Vietnam became strongly anti-communist. North Vietnam rebuilt its industry. China and the Soviet Union helped North Vietnam. South Vietnam had to face many problems. Its new government had to rebuild its economy and reorganize the army. The head of the government was Ngo Dinh Diem. He would not hold elections.

In 1959, communist guerrillas tried to take over the South Vietnamese government. The guerrillas were called the Vietcong. They used persuasion or terror to win the support of the peasants in South Vietnam. In 1963, Diem was assassinated. Over the next three years, nine different military groups ruled South Vietnam.

The United States Enters the Conflict

In the 1960s the United States gave more military aid to South Vietnam. That aid soon included units of the United States armed forces. Hundreds of thousands of American soldiers fought against the Vietcong. Billions of dollars in military supplies and economic aid were given to South Vietnam. South Vietnam still could not win, however. The Vietcong fought on.

Americans Protest

A strong protest movement began in the United States against the Vietnam War. By 1972, most American troops were taken out of Vietnam. The United States took out its last troops in 1975. Nearly 50,000 Americans had been killed and 300,000 had been wounded in the Vietnam War.

In 1975, the Vietcong and North Vietnamese attacked South Vietnam. They were able to take over the country. In July 1976, the two Vietnams were joined together. The Socialist Republic of Vietnam was formed. Hanoi became the capital.

After the Fall of South Vietnam

After the fall of South Vietnam, large numbers of South Vietnamese left their country. They did not want to live under communist rule. Many of these people fled by boat. They came to be known as "boat people." Many of the refugees died attempting to get away. Others spent long months in camps trying to get permission to live elsewhere. Several hundred thousand of these "boat people" settled in the United States.

Cambodia

Cambodia won its freedom from France in 1953. The new government was led by Prince

167

The government of Pol Pot brought chaos to Cambodia. Perhaps as many as one million people died in Cambodia between 1975 and 1979. Thousands of refugees fled to Thailand. They lived in camps like the one shown here.

Norodom Sihanouk (SEE-ah-nuhk). He tried to keep Cambodia neutral during the Vietnam War. This was hard, however. North Vietnamese and Vietcong troops tried to escape South Vietnamese and American troops by entering Cambodia.

In 1970, a new government overthrew Sihanouk. Lon Nol took over. He demanded that North Vietnamese troops leave Cambodia. He allowed American and South Vietnamese troops to chase the North Vietnamese and Vietcong forces into Cambodia.

The North Vietnamese answered by encouraging a communist takeover of Cambodia. This took place in 1975. The Communists were led by Pol Pot. Under the new government, all cities in Cambodia were emptied. City people were sent to the country. They were forced to learn farming. Many were not able to and died of hunger. At the same time, government officials, teachers, and other leaders were killed.

Problems continued between Vietnam and Cambodia after 1975. In 1978, Vietnam invaded Cambodia. Pol Pot was forced out. A new government was set up. Cambodia was renamed the People's Republic of Kampuchea.

Laos

In 1953, civil war broke out in Laos. France gave Laos its freedom in 1954. The French arranged for peace in the civil war. From 1954 to 1975 a royal government headed by the king ruled Laos.

Laos became involved in the Vietnam War. A supply route from North Vietnam to South Viet-

nam and Cambodia ran through Laos. In 1975, a communist government was set up. It was called the Lao People's Democratic Republic. The government tried to stay neutral in the war going on around it. This was impossible, however. Laos wanted to rule anti-communist forces in the northern part of the country. To do this, Laos needed help from Vietnam. Vietnam and Laos continue to be close allies. They are against their northern neighbor, China.

Thailand

Since World War II, Thailand has suffered greatly because of the problems of its neighbors. In 1958, the army took control of the Thai government. The new government was very pro-Western. It received help from the United States. The Thai government allowed the United States to set up bases for its troops and aircraft.

Communist takeovers in Vietnam, Cambodia, and Laos in 1975 forced Thailand to think about its policies. It asked the United States to remove its bases. The Thai government became more friendly with China, the Soviet Union, Laos, and Vietnam.

The invasion of Cambodia by Vietnam brought new problems to Thailand. Thousands of Cambodian refugees fled to Thailand. They joined hundreds of thousands of Vietnamese refugees already in Thailand. This put a great strain on relations between Vietnam and Thailand. It also put a great strain on the Thai economy. Thailand finally had to close its border with Cambodia. Thailand called for stronger international efforts to solve the refugee crisis in Southeast Asia.

Exercises

A. Finding the Main Ideas:

Put a check next to the sentences that give the main ideas of what you have just read.

_____ **1.** Nationalism has had a great influence upon Southeast Asia.

_____ **2.** Communism has influenced events in Indochina.

_____ **3.** Indonesia was once ruled by the Netherlands.

_____ **4.** Japan's World War II victories influenced nationalism in Southeast Asia.

_____ **5.** Indians and Chinese suffer from discrimination in Burma.

_____ **6.** The United States fought a war in Vietnam.

B. What Did You Read?

Choose the answer that best completes each sentence. Write the letter of your answer in the space provided.

_____ **1.** The government of the Philippines is headed by
   a. Ho Chi Minh.
   b. Pol Pot.
   c. Ferdinand Marcos.
   d. General Suharto.

_____ **2.** The areas that now make up the Federation of Malaysia had been colonies of
   a. the Netherlands.
   b. France.
   c. Japan.
   d. Britain.

_____ **3.** The region once called Indochina does *not* include
   a. Laos.
   b. Malaysia.
   c. Cambodia.
   d. Vietnam.

_____ **4.** Kampuchea is the new name given to
   a. Laos.
   b. Cambodia.
   c. Vietnam.
   d. all of Indochina.

C. Map Skills:

Look at the map on this page. Identify the areas shown by the letters on the map. Place the correct letter in the space provided. You may use the map on page 164 for help.

_____ **1.** Burma

_____ **2.** Indonesia

_____ **3.** Vietnam

_____ **4.** Kampuchea (Cambodia)

_____ **5.** Malaysia

_____ **6.** Laos

_____ **7.** Thailand

_____ **8.** India

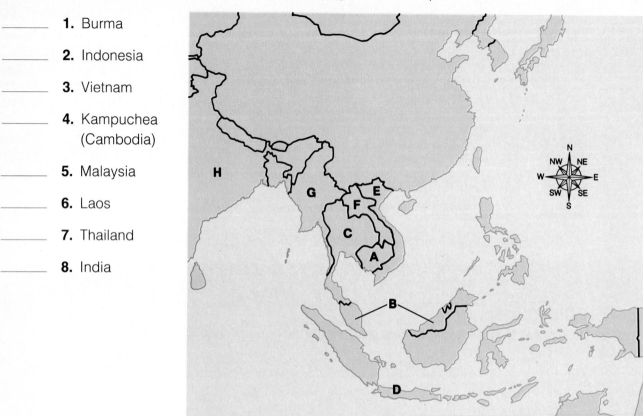

D. Matching:

Match each colony in Column A with the country that ruled it in Column B. The countries in Column B will be used more than once. Write the letter of each answer in the space provided.

Column A

_____ **1.** Malaysia

_____ **2.** Laos

_____ **3.** Burma

_____ **4.** Vietnam

_____ **5.** Kampuchea (Cambodia)

_____ **6.** Indonesia

Column B

a. France

b. the Netherlands

c. Britain

E. Checking for Details:

Read each statement. Put a T in the space next to each statement if it is true. Put an F in that space if it is false.

_____ **1.** The Vietcong tried to take over the North Vietnamese government.

_____ **2.** Indochina was once called the Dutch East Indies.

_____ **3.** Indonesia is made up of a number of islands.

_____ **4.** Singapore is no longer a part of Malaysia.

_____ **5.** Indonesia is rich in oil.

_____ **6.** Japan took hold of Indonesia, Malaya, Burma, and Vietnam in World War II.

_____ **7.** Islam is the religion of most people in Vietnam.

_____ **8.** Japan divided Indochina into Vietnam, Laos, and Cambodia.

F. Behind the Headlines:

Each headline has a story behind it. Write two or three sentences that support or tell about each headline. Use a separate sheet of paper.

DUTCH AGREE TO GIVE FREEDOM TO INDONESIA
SINGAPORE LEAVES FEDERATION OF MALAYSIA
U.S. TROOPS LEAVE VIETNAM
COMMUNISTS FIGHT COMMUNISTS IN CAMBODIA

G. Understanding Global History:

On page 164 you read about five factors in global history. Which of these factors applies to each statement listed below? Fill in the number of the correct statement on page 164 in the space provided.

_____ **1.** Contacts between the French and the people of Indochina led to a blending of the languages and cultures of France and Indochina.

_____ **2.** Large amounts of economic and military aid from the United States helped South Vietnam survive.

_____ **3.** The defeat of the Europeans by the Japanese and the growth of anti-colonial feelings in the world helped nationalism grow in Southeast Asia.

_____ **4.** The Malay and Chinese people of Malaysia failed to understand each other's culture.

_____ **5.** The European culture of the Dutch colonists made it hard for them to look upon the Indonesian culture as equal to their own.

171

Chapter 10

Africa Since World War II

Understanding Global History

Think about the following statements as you read about African freedom movements.
1 Events occurring in one part of the world have influenced developments in other parts of the world.
2 Present culture is shaped by the past.
3 Nations borrow and adapt ideas and institutions from other nations.
4 Basic human needs—food, clothing, and shelter—are influenced by our environment and our culture.
5 Nations choose what they borrow and adapt from other nations.

Dar es Salaam. This city is the capital of Tanzania, a large country in eastern Africa.

Learning New Words and Terms

The following words are used in this chapter. Think about the meaning of each one.

sanctions: actions taken by one country against another; limits placed on the trade or actions of another country
embargo: a government order that does not allow trade between countries
apartheid: the Afrikaner word for separateness; in South Africa, a policy of separation of races

Think As You Read

1. How did freedom affect Uganda, Kenya, and Tanzania?
2. How did freedom come to Zimbabwe?
3. What special problems are there in South Africa?
4. What happened to the colonies once held by Portugal and Belgium in Africa?

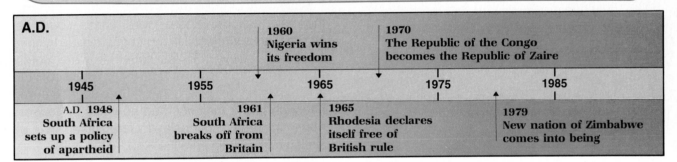

A.D.

| 1945 | 1955 | 1965 | 1975 | 1985 |

1960 Nigeria wins its freedom

1970 The Republic of the Congo becomes the Republic of Zaire

A.D. 1948 South Africa sets up a policy of apartheid

1961 South Africa breaks off from Britain

1965 Rhodesia declares itself free of British rule

1979 New nation of Zimbabwe comes into being

Nearly all of Africa was once held as colonies by European countries. World War II brought an end to European colonialism. Feelings of nationalism that swept the world also came to Africa. The desire for freedom grew rapidly among Africans after 1945. The map on page 175 shows each African country and the date of its independence.

African colonies gained their freedom by both peaceful and violent means. In many cases, violence was caused by efforts to crush African nationalism. Sometimes, violence came from conflicts within the nationalist and freedom movements themselves.

British Colonies Win Their Freedom in Sub-Saharan Africa

In the years after 1945 many changes took place in Britain's African colonies south of the Sahara.

- The Sudan won its freedom from Great Britain. Sudan is the largest country in Africa. Recently, Sudan's freedom has been threatened by its neighbor, Libya.

- The Gold Coast won its freedom. It became the free country of Ghana. Kwame Nkrumah (en-KROO-muh) led Ghana through its first years of freedom. His government policies, however, were not liked. Nkrumah jailed all those who spoke out against his programs. In 1966, army officers took over the government. Elections were held in 1969. Four different governments have held power since then, however.

- Nigeria won its freedom. Ethnic and regional differences caused problems, however. A civil war broke out in 1967. The people of the eastern region broke off from Nigeria. They formed a new country called Biafra. The war ended in 1970. That is when Biafra gave up. The people of Biafra suffered terribly during the war. Nearly two million died from hunger and sickness.

- Tanganyika won its freedom.

- Uganda won its freedom. General Idi Amin took over in 1971. Amin carried out a policy of terror toward those who were against him. Thousands of Ugandans were killed. General Amin became "President for Life" in 1976. He soon faced local revolts, however. In 1979, Ugandan rebels drove Amin from power. The rebels were helped by soldiers from Uganda's neighbor, Tanzania. Since 1979, rival political leaders have competed for rule of Uganda.

• Zanzibar won its freedom. Zanzibar and Tanganyika joined to form the new country of Tanzania (TAN-zuh-NEE uh). The president of Tanzania was Julius Nyerere (ny-RER-ay). He was one of the best-known black nationalist leaders of Africa. He started a system of communal agriculture. The goal of the new system was to supply the basic needs of the people. At the same time, it tried to use the environment in a way that did not upset the region's culture. The system was not successful. Tanzania's economy has grown weaker and more disorganized in recent years.

Jomo Kenyatta led Kenya's fight for independence.

• Kenya also won its freedom. Some white settlers in Kenya were against a free black government. Black nationalists struck back with violence and terrorism. They were helped by a secret society called the Mau Mau. Jomo Kenyatta was the leader of the black nationalists. He was jailed by the British. They accused Kenyatta of helping the Mau Mau. Kenyatta was finally let go. Kenyatta led the nation until his death in 1978. Daniel Arap Moi then became

the new leader. Kenya has been one of the most stable African countries.

• Northern Rhodesia became the new nation of Zambia. Nyasaland became the new nation of Malawi.

• Bechuanaland became free. It changed its name to Botswana. This nation had once been a British protectorate.

The new black African nations had been against British rule for many years. They still kept many things that were British, however. Some of these were systems of law, government, and education. The Africans adapted, or changed, the British systems to fit their own special needs.

Rhodesia

Black Africans led the governments in most of the new nations. There were some countries where blacks were still trying to get a voice in government, however. These countries were South Africa and Rhodesia. In the British colony of Rhodesia, whites held all the political power. Blacks, although in the majority, had no voice in government. In 1965, Rhodesia declared itself free of British rule. Britain said the Rhodesian action was against the law. Britain wanted blacks to be given voting rights so that one day they could run the government. Rhodesia ignored the British. Britain asked the United Nations to place **sanctions** and an **embargo** on Rhodesia. In Rhodesia, black nationalists rose up against the government. They were led by Joshua Nkomo (en-KOH-moh) and Robert Mugabe (moo-GAH-bay). They wanted a government led by blacks.

Zimbabwe

Countries of the world put pressure on the government of Rhodesia to change. Elections were finally held. Robert Mugabe and his followers won. He became the first prime minister of the new nation of Zimbabwe (zihm-BAH-bweh). This was the ancient name for the land that was once Rhodesia. Mugabe promised fair treatment for whites as well as blacks. There was fear of a new civil war, however. Some whites still fear for their future in Zimbabwe. There is also fear among the supporters of Joshua Nkomo. He left Zimbabwe and later came back. His power has been sharply reduced by the government of Prime Minister Mugabe.

174

South Africa

South Africa is the only country in sub-Saharan Africa where the white minority holds all the political power. In 1961, South Africa broke off from Britain. It called itself the Republic of South Africa. Today, the government of South Africa is ruled by the Afrikaners. They are the descendants of the Dutch colonists who settled in South Africa. In the past, Afrikaners did not trust the British and black Africans. This attitude continues today. It has played a large part in the Afrikaner policy of separation of the races.

In 1948, the Afrikaner government of South Africa set up a policy of **apartheid** (uh-PAHRT-hayt). Apartheid is the Afrikaner word for "separateness." In South Africa, apartheid means a strict separation of the races in all parts of daily life. The rights of black Africans and Asians are very limited. They are not allowed to live in the same parts of town as white people. They cannot

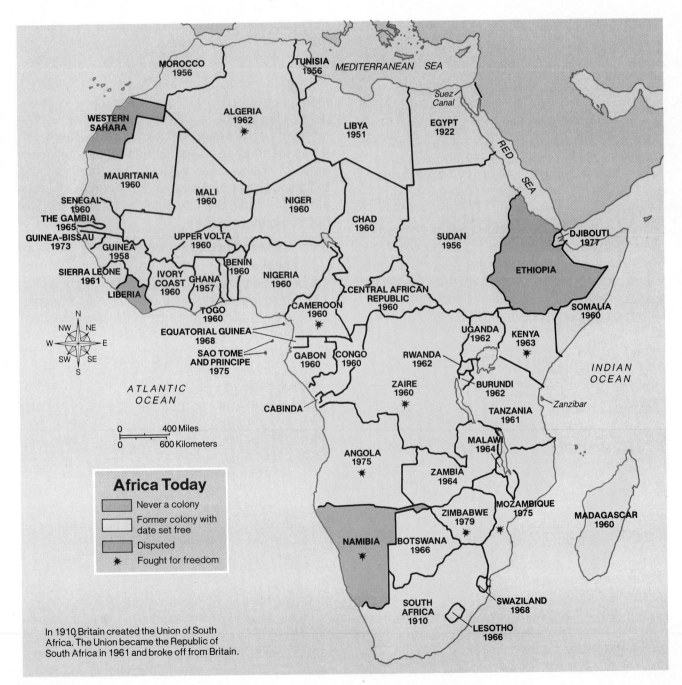

Africa Today

- Never a colony
- Former colony with date set free
- Disputed
- ✳ Fought for freedom

In 1910, Britain created the Union of South Africa. The Union became the Republic of South Africa in 1961 and broke off from Britain.

Factories, restaurants, and other places in South Africa have separate entrances for whites, black Africans, and Asians.

go to the same schools. Their chances of getting certain jobs are limited.

Some rules of apartheid have been lifted over the years. The basic policy of apartheid is still the same in South Africa, however. Most countries of the world do not approve of South Africa's racial policies. World opinion has not yet forced the leaders of South Africa to change. South Africa still holds to a policy of rule by the white minority.

Namibia

South Africa has also tried to rule Namibia (nah-MIB-ee-uh). This land was once known as Southwest Africa. It was a German protectorate. South Africa took over Namibia in 1915. It has ruled Namibia since then. South Africa has refused to turn Namibia over to UN rule. Black nationalists in Namibia have fought a guerrilla war against South African rule.

Freedom for Belgium's Colony

Britain was not the only country to lose its colonies in Africa. Belgium also lost its only African colony. In 1960, the Belgian Congo won its freedom. It became the Republic of the Congo. Soon after freedom was won, a civil war broke out. The rich mining province of Katanga left the Republic

of the Congo. UN troops from other African countries were sent in to bring back order.

When the UN troops were taken out in mid-1964, fighting broke out again. Many people were killed. General Joseph Mobutu became president in 1965. He tried to "Africanize" the Congo. The Belgian names of many cities were changed. The new names were taken from African history and culture. Leopoldville (named for a Belgian king) became Kinshasa. Stanleyville (named for the British explorer, Henry Stanley) became Kisangani. Joseph Mobutu took the African name, Mobutu Sese Seko.

Zaire

There was no clear leader in the Congo for many years. In 1970, Mobutu was elected president. The Republic of the Congo had a new name. It was now the Republic of Zaire (zah-IHR). It has taken Zaire a long time to recover from the years of civil war. Since 1977, Zaire has also had to fight groups from its neighbor, Angola. The rebels from Angola are interested in Katanga and its rich mineral resources.

Freedom for Portugal's Colonies

Portugal kept its African colonies until 1975. These colonies were Angola and Mozambique. In 1975, a revolt overthrew the dictator of Portugal. The new Portuguese government gave freedom to Mozambique and Angola. At first, there was some conflict in Mozambique. The new country overcame its problems. Mozambique set up a socialist government.

Angola also had its problems. Civil war broke out soon after Angola gained its freedom. Two main groups fought for power. One group was backed by the Soviet Union and Cuba. The other group was helped by the United States and South Africa. In 1975 several thousand Cuban troops were in Angola. Their job was to help the Soviet-backed Angolans. This group won out and took complete control of Angola in 1976. Today, Angola gets much aid from the Soviet Union and Cuba.

France's African Colonies Win Their Freedom

In 1960, France gave freedom to its sub-Saharan colonies. These colonies were Cameroon, Chad, Gabon, Mali, Mauritania, Niger, and Senegal. In 1956, France had granted freedom to its colonies of Morocco and Tunisia in North Africa. Only Algeria in North Africa was still a colony.

France did not want to let go of Algeria. It thought of Algeria as a part of France. In the 1950s, there were about ten million Algerians. One million of these were mainly the descendants of French settlers. They owned most of the best land in Algeria. They also owned most of the businesses. The rest of the Algerians were mostly Arabs. They shared little in the wealth of the country.

Conflict in Algeria

In 1954, civil war broke out in Algeria. Algerian nationalists wanted freedom. The French settlers wanted to stay with France. The two sides fought a bitter struggle. Both sides used terrorism and torture. The fighting lasted four years. In 1958, President Charles de Gaulle of France made peace with nationalist leaders. Algeria won its freedom in 1962.

Countries in North Africa

The new countries in North Africa faced some problems. Morocco is ruled by a king who has very wide powers. Since 1976, Morocco has tried to bring its rule into Western Sahara. It has been opposed by a guerrilla movement called the Polisario. The Polisario has been helped by Algeria. Morocco has been helped by France and the United States. The fighting in Western Sahara has created tensions between Morocco and Algeria. It has also created foreign relations problems for the United States.

Algeria became a military state soon after winning its freedom. Its leaders were members of the armed forces. Relations with the United States have been poor. Algeria is an enemy of Israel. Although it does not have a communist government, Algeria's strongest ties have been with the Soviet Union. In 1980, Algeria helped in the release of the American hostages held in Iran.

Tunisia won its freedom in 1956. It became a republic in 1957. An effort was made to join Tunisia and Libya together in 1974. That effort failed. Tunisia has remained independent.

Libya

When World War II ended, in 1945, Italy had to give up its colony of Libya. In 1951, Libya became a free nation. It was ruled by a king. In 1969, the king was overthrown by a military leader. This was Muammar el-Qaddafi (guht-DAH-fee). Qaddafi ended Libya's ties with Western countries. He set up close ties with the Soviet Union. In 1972, Libya and Egypt tried to join together. They soon separated, however. Two years later, an effort to join Libya and Tunisia also failed. Recently, Libya has discussed a union with Syria. These actions show Qaddafi's desire to spread Libya's strength and influence.

Libya is rich in oil. This has made Libya powerful. Much of its money from oil has been spent on the latest military weapons. Libya has also tried to take over leadership of the Arab nationalist movement. Libya is an enemy of Israel. It helps terrorist groups in Europe and the Middle East. The Libyan government has also threatened its Islamic neighbors. These include Egypt, Chad, and the Sudan. Libya's leaders describe their government as Islamic and socialist. However, the socialism of Libya has little in common with European ideas of socialism.

Father and son in the Algerian rebel army, 1957. They were fighting the French.

Exercises

A. Finding the Main Ideas:

Put a check next to the sentences that give the main ideas of what you have just read.

_____ **1.** Many new rulers came into power in the new nations of sub-Saharan Africa.

_____ **2.** The new African nations faced many problems.

_____ **3.** Most of Britain's colonies in Africa south of the Sahara became free after 1945.

_____ **4.** Libya is rich in oil.

_____ **5.** White minority governments held power in some nations of sub-Saharan Africa.

B. What Did You Read?

Choose the answer that best completes each sentence. Write the letter of your answer in the space provided.

_____ **1.** After World War II, Britain gave freedom to
  a. Nigeria.
  b. Tanganyika.
  c. the Gold Coast.
  d. all of the above.

_____ **2.** Afrikaners are the
  a. black leaders of Uganda.
  b. Belgian colonists who once ruled the Congo.
  c. white minority rulers of South Africa.
  d. black nationalists in Africa.

_____ **3.** Mozambique had been a colony of
  a. France.
  b. Britain.
  c. Portugal.
  d. Belgium.

_____ **4.** In 1975 Cuban troops were fighting in
  a. Mozambique.
  b. Angola.
  c. Uganda.
  d. the Sudan.

C. Checking for Details:

Match the names of the nations in Column A with the descriptions in Column B.

Column A   Column B

_____ **1.** Zimbabwe   **a.** terrorized by General Idi Amin

_____ **2.** Kenya   **b.** once known as Southwest Africa

_____ **3.** Tanzania   **c.** follows a policy of apartheid toward black Africans and Asians

_____ **4.** South Africa   **d.** Cuban troops support this new nation

_____ **5.** Namibia   **e.** led to freedom by Jomo Kenyatta

_____ **6.** Zaire   **f.** chose Robert Mugabe as its first black prime minister

_____ **7.** Uganda   **g.** had an agricultural plan formed by Julius Nyerere

_____ **8.** Angola   **h.** was once known as the Belgian Congo

D. Behind the Headlines:

Each headline has a story behind it. Write two or three sentences that support or tell about each headline. Use a separate sheet of paper.

AMIN DRIVEN FROM POWER
NYERERE SEEKS AFRICAN SOLUTION TO PROBLEMS
UNITED NATIONS ACTS AGAINST RHODESIA
CUBANS IN ANGOLA
ALGERIA WINS FREEDOM

E. Understanding Global History:

On page 172 you read about five factors in global history. Which of these factors applies to each statement listed below? Fill in the number of the correct statement on page 172 in the space provided.

_____ **1.** The agricultural system of Tanzania tried to use the local environment and local culture to meet the basic needs of the people.

_____ **2.** Many countries in Africa have changed the British systems of law, government, and education to meet their own needs.

_____ **3.** Afrikaners have a history of fear and distrust of the British and black Africans. The attitudes of the past have influenced Afrikaner actions today.

_____ **4.** Feelings of nationalism swept the world after World War II. Feelings of nationalism influenced events in sub-Saharan Africa.

_____ **5.** Many countries in Africa have kept parts of the British system of law, government, and education.

Chapter 11

The Middle East Since World War II

Understanding Global History

Think about the following statements as you read about events in the Middle East.
1 Contact among peoples and nations can lead to cultural diffusion.
2 Present culture is shaped by the past.
3 The culture in which we live influences our view of other people.
4 Events occurring in one part of the world have influenced developments in other parts of the world.

Jerusalem is the capital of Israel. It is holy to Jews, Christians, and Muslims.

Learning New Words and Terms

The following words are used in this chapter. Think about the meaning of each one.

partition: divided into two or more parts
stalemate: a condition in which little or no action is taken

Think As You Read

1. How have oil, nationalism, and religion affected the Middle East?
2. How have Arab countries reacted to the state of Israel?

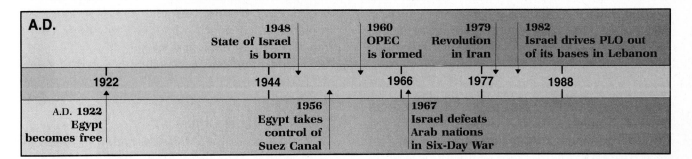

A.D.		1948 State of Israel is born		1960 OPEC is formed	1979 Revolution in Iran	1982 Israel drives PLO out of its bases in Lebanon
1922		1944		1966	1977	1988
A.D. 1922 Egypt becomes free		1956 Egypt takes control of Suez Canal		1967 Israel defeats Arab nations in Six-Day War		

National movements in the Middle East have many goals. Arab nationalists want to return to the glories of the days of the Islamic Empire. Muslim armies had swept out of Arabia after A.D. 650. They brought their Arabic language and Islamic religion to all of the Middle East, North Africa, and southern Spain. They even spread as far east as India. Arab nationalists remember those days. They want the Arabs to be as powerful today as they were in the past.

The Rise of Arab Nationalism

Nationalism in the Middle East first came into being in the early 1900s. Most of the Middle East was then part of the Ottoman Empire. After World War I, the Ottoman lands were ruled by France and Great Britain. Syria and Lebanon became French mandates. Iraq and Palestine (present-day Israel and Jordan) became British mandates. Egypt was a British protectorate from 1914 to 1922. It then became free. Egypt stayed under indirect British rule until 1953, however. The Arabian peninsula was joined together as Saudi Arabia in the 1920s. Rich oil deposits were found in Saudi Arabia in the 1930s. European and American oil companies quickly began to explore more of the Middle East. They found large deposits of oil. The foreign oil companies controlled the oil

deposits. The oil-producing nations—Saudi Arabia, Iran, and Iraq—received little income from their rich oil fields.

The mandates of the Middle East became free before World War II. During the war, most of the Middle East and North Africa tried to stay neutral. Some of the heaviest fighting of the early part of the war, however, took place in North Africa.

Arab nationalism grew stronger after World War II. Arab nationalists often came into conflict with the European powers, the United States, and Jews. Jews were coming to Palestine in search of a homeland. Some areas of conflict were resolved, however. The Middle Eastern countries took over their oil fields after World War II. Other questions remained unsolved.

Jews Want a Homeland in Palestine

Palestine had been the homeland of the Hebrews, or Jews, in early times. That homeland was lost when the Romans crushed a Jewish revolt in A.D. 69. The Jews were forced out of Palestine. Their holiest city, Jerusalem, was destroyed. The idea of a return to Palestine and Jerusalem remained a part of Jewish life. In the 1890s a Jewish nationalist movement was started. It was called Zionism. Zionism wanted a homeland for Jews in Palestine.

At first, there were very few Jews in Palestine. They had few contacts with the Arabs living there. The Zionist movement soon changed that. In the late 1800s and early 1900s, several thousand Jews moved to Palestine. They came mainly from Europe. The Arabs in Palestine viewed the newcomers with suspicion. Almost at once, fights arose between Arabs and Jews.

Zionism became more popular after World War II. Six million European Jews had died in Nazi death camps during the war. Many of those who lived through the Holocaust wanted to go to Palestine. The idea of Palestine as a Jewish homeland won support from Jews and others throughout the world.

Israel is Born

In 1947 the British gave up their Palestine mandate. The same year the United Nations **partitioned** Palestine into Arab and Jewish states. The Jews accepted the partition. The Arabs did not. The Jewish state declared itself to be the state of Israel in 1948. It was quickly recognized by the United States, the Soviet Union, and many other countries. However, Israel was invaded by the armies of its Arab neighbors. Israeli troops defeated the Arabs. Israel was able to spread out its borders. Meanwhile, Arabs took over the rest of Palestine. This became the state of Jordan. Other Arabs were against this move.

David Ben-Gurion was the first prime minister of Israel.

Thousands of Arabs from Palestine fled Israel during the 1948 war. That war left about 600,000 Palestinian Arabs homeless. Many lived in refugee camps in neighboring Arab states. Today, great numbers of Palestinian Arabs still live in these camps. They live under very poor conditions. Palestinian Arabs have joined together to try to win back what they consider to be their homeland. Fighters for this cause have formed the Palestine Liberation Organization (PLO).

Soon after the 1948 war, several Arab countries forced Jews to leave. Jews had lived for centuries in North Africa and the Middle East. After 1948, they were forced to leave Yemen, Iraq, Libya, Tunisia, and other lands. More than 500,000 Jews left their homes in Arab countries. Most settled in Israel.

The Suez Canal Crisis

The defeat of the Arab countries by Israel, in 1948, was a disaster for Egypt. This country was the leader of Arab nationalism. Egypt's monarch, King Farouk, was blamed for the Arab loss. Farouk's government was corrupt. In 1952, a group of young military officers forced Farouk to give up power. Egypt became a republic. Gamal Abdel Nasser was elected president in 1956. Nasser held power until his death in 1970.

In 1955, the Soviet Union decided to challenge Western influence in the Middle East. The Soviets offered to sell weapons to Egypt. The United States and its allies took action. They offered to build a much-needed dam in Egypt. This was a costly project. The dam was to be built at Aswan on the Nile River. The United States and its allies withdrew the offer when Nasser seemed to be moving closer towards the Soviets. Nasser then took over the Suez Canal. This was in July 1956.

Egypt's takeover of the Suez Canal upset Britain, France, and Israel. They saw the takeover as a possible threat to Europe's oil supply. Most of Europe's oil was shipped through the Suez Canal. Egypt also would not allow Israeli ships and ships headed for Israel to go through the canal.

Israel was the first to take action. In a swift move, Israeli troops moved into the Gaza Strip and the Sinai Peninsula. They began to move toward the canal (see map, p. 183). Britain and France made a secret agreement with Israel. They took over the other end of the canal. They threw back the Egyptian army.

World opinion was against the invasion. The United States spoke out against the action. The British, French, and Israelis were forced to withdraw. The Suez Canal stayed in Egyptian hands. Arab fear and distrust of Israel grew.

The Six-Day War

The Suez Canal dispute led to a buildup of Arab nationalism. Arab nations now felt the need for stronger leadership and more military power. Their desire for military strength was helped by tensions between the Soviet Union and the United States. The Soviet Union soon gave economic and military aid to Arab countries. The United States gave much aid to Israel.

In May 1967, Egypt again put pressure on Israel. Nasser wanted UN troops to leave the area. They had been policing the border between Egypt and Israel since the end of the Suez Crisis in 1956. Nasser also closed the Gulf of Aqaba (AHK-uh-buh). This blocked Israel's sea route to Africa and Asia. Egypt and other Arab nations said they would destroy Israel.

Israel took action by entering into another war. On June 5, 1967, Israel moved into Arab territory. Six days later it had taken over the Sinai Peninsula and Gaza Strip. Israel then took the Golan Heights from Syria. From Jordan it took the entire west bank of the Jordan River. Israel also took control of Jerusalem. The UN had declared Jerusalem an international city. It only took six days for Israel to capture this much land. The action became known as the Six-Day War.

The Formation of OPEC

In 1960, the Latin American country of Venezuela and the oil-producing countries of the Middle East formed the Organization of Petroleum Exporting Countries (OPEC). OPEC members meet to set up a common price on oil. OPEC represents the oil-producing countries to the oil-consuming industrial countries. In the 1960s, OPEC began to raise the price of unrefined oil. In the early 1970s, oil prices took a big jump. OPEC began to use their oil as a way to get the most money for themselves. They wanted to run oil supplies and prices. These efforts caused energy

problems in Japan, Europe, and the United States. But it brought profits and power to the Middle East.

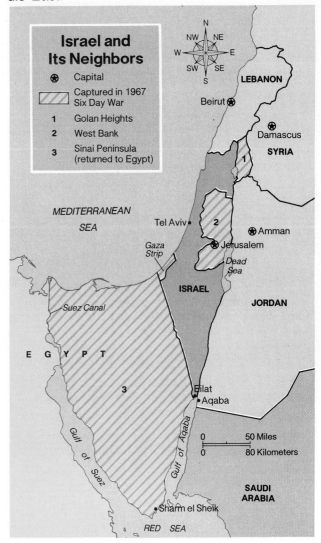

Israel and Its Neighbors

⊛ Capital

▨ Captured in 1967 Six Day War

1 Golan Heights

2 West Bank

3 Sinai Peninsula (returned to Egypt)

The Yom Kippur War

In 1973, Egypt, Syria, Jordan, and Iraq attacked Israel. The attack began on the holiest of Jewish holidays, Yom Kippur. This has become known as the Yom Kippur War. Israel was nearly conquered. It was able to beat back the attacks, however. A cease-fire was set up by the UN. Soon after that, Israel and Egypt came to an agreement.

During the war with Israel, OPEC countries said they would cut back their production of oil. They did this to pressure Israel and its supporters. Their action caused world oil prices to skyrocket. The cutbacks were later eased. The power of OPEC was established, however.

183

Golda Meir was one of the founders of the state of Israel. She was prime minister during the Yom Kippur War.

Peace Between Egypt and Israel

In 1977, President Anwar Sadat of Egypt visited Israel. It was the first time any Arab leader had visited Israel. In 1979, Egypt and Israel signed a peace treaty. They were helped toward peace by President Jimmy Carter of the United States.

The improved Israeli-Egyptian relations upset the Arab nationalists. They accused Egypt of letting down the Arab cause. Israel said that Arab nationalists wanted to destroy the Jewish state.

Recent Conflicts in the Middle East

Middle East conflicts have not been limited to fighting between the Arabs and Israelis. Wars and civil strife have also broken out within the Arab world. The PLO set itself up in Jordan during the 1960s. King Hussein (hoo-SAYN) of Jordan saw the PLO as a threat. He drove the PLO out of Jordan in 1970. The PLO next set up its main bases in Lebanon. It was soon heavily involved in the civil war that tore Lebanon apart after 1975.

Lebanon

The fighting in Lebanon continues. Muslim and Christian armies there are battling for political power. Syrian troops entered Lebanon. They said they were going to help the Muslims. They also wanted to set up Syrian influence in Lebanon. Christian groups in southern Lebanon were getting aid from Israel.

In 1982, Israel accused the PLO of using Lebanon as a base for attacks upon border towns in Israel. A huge Israeli invasion of Lebanon drove the PLO out of Lebanon. Even though Israel won, Israeli action caused public opinion to be divided. Many people feared that Israel would be trapped in the political fights between Christians and Muslims in Lebanon.

The United States has also become involved in this conflict. In 1983, troops from the United States, France, Italy, and Britain were sent to Lebanon to help keep the peace. By the end of the year, most of the troops had been removed. Many

Beirut, Lebanon in 1983.

soldiers had been killed by acts of terrorism from Muslim groups. They found it hard to protect themselves and still be peace keepers. Meanwhile, fighting has made Lebanon a wasteland. Many people have been killed by the different sides. Towns and cities have been destroyed.

Iran, 1979. Supporters of the Ayatollah Khomeini.

Revolution in Iran

During the 1960s and 1970s the shah of Iran, Mohammad Reza Pahlavi, tried to modernize his nation. He used the wealth from Iran's oil. Land was given to the peasants. Industries grew up. Schools were opened. Women were given more freedom to attend school and to work. Iran also tried to become a major military power in the Persian Gulf.

Quick change caused problems, however. There were economic problems. Millions moved into Iran's cities. They had few skills. They had trouble finding jobs. These unhappy peasants

began to follow new leaders. The new leaders began to call for a revolution in Iran.

Other people did not like the shah because of his ways of doing things. The shah had his secret police, Savak, quiet anyone who spoke out against his rule. Savak was accused of many beatings, shootings, and unsolved murders in Iran. The shah also tried to keep all the power in Iran in his own hands.

In 1978, riots and demonstrations broke out against the shah. By this time the Ayatollah Khomeini had become the leader of the revolution. Khomeini was a 76-year-old Muslim religious leader.

In 1979, the shah tried to make changes that would stop the revolution. It was too late, however. He left the country. Khomeini and his followers set up an Islamic republic. They wanted to run the country according to the religious teachings of Islam.

In November 1979, Iranians captured the American embassy in Teheran, the capital of Iran. Americans were taken hostage. In return for the hostages, the Iranians wanted the shah to be returned to Iran to stand trial.

The shah died in Egypt in July 1980. The hostages were finally set free in January 1981. Many countries spoke out against Iran. This had little effect on Khomeini and his government. Political and economic conditions in Iran are still not settled today.

The Iraq-Iran War

Iran's problems grew in 1980. Iraq started a war with Iran then. By 1983, that war had become a **stalemate.** Each side suffered heavy loss of life and great damage to oil fields. Neither side would give in, though. Efforts to get the two sides to end the war failed. The war showed how strongly two Islamic nations could oppose one another. The Muslim world was split as it took sides over the Iraq-Iran war.

The Middle East Today

Today, tens of billions of dollars are spent on wars and military equipment in the Middle East. Very little of the wealth from oil has been used to help the people in the Middle East. Most of them are poor. Poverty and the threat of war are the major problems of the Middle East.

Exercises

A. Finding the Main Ideas:

Put a check next to the sentences that give the main ideas of what you have just read.

_____ **1.** Oil prices have been rising steadily since the 1970s.

_____ **2.** Religion and nationalism have had a strong effect upon the Middle East.

_____ **3.** There have been changes among the rulers and leaders of the Middle East.

_____ **4.** There has been a clash between Zionism and Arab nationalism.

_____ **5.** There have been many causes for conflict in the Middle East.

B. What Did You Read?

Choose the answer that best completes each sentence. Write the letter of your answer in the space provided.

_____ **1.** Before 1945, the oil of the Middle East
  a. had not yet been discovered.
  b. was ruled by Israel.
  c. was ruled by foreign companies.
  d. was ruled by Arab nations.

_____ **2.** Since 1945, fighting in the Middle East has involved
  a. Israel.
  b. Lebanon.
  c. Iraq.
  d. all of the above.

_____ **3.** After World War II, the Middle East oil fields were
  a. taken over by Europeans.
  b. taken over by the countries of the Middle East.
  c. taken over by Israel.
  d. ruled by Egypt.

_____ **4.** The fighting in the Middle East, in 1948, resulted in
  a. Israel spreading its borders.
  b. many Arabs leaving Palestine.
  c. the defeat of Arab forces.
  d. all of the above.

C. Checking for Details:

Read each statement. Put a T in the space next to each statement if it is true. Put an F in that space if it is false. Put an N if you cannot tell from the reading if it is true or false.

_____ **1.** The Arabs ran the oil fields of the Middle East during the 1930s.

_____ **2.** OPEC members did not try to control the prices and production of oil.

_____ **3.** Most Arab refugees from Palestine returned to their homes after a time.

_____ **4.** Britain did not want to give up the Suez Canal to Egypt.

_____ **5.** After 1948, many Jews were forced to leave their homes in North Africa and the Middle East.

_____ **6.** The actions of OPEC caused energy problems in many parts of the world.

_____ **7.** The Soviet Union has given military aid to Arab nations.

_____ **8.** Christian groups in southern Lebanon have received aid from Syria.

D. On Your Own:

Write short essays of at least 50 words each to answer any one of the following questions. Use what you have read in magazines and newspapers or seen on television to help you. Write your answers on a separate sheet of paper.

1. What are the present-day relations between Israel and its Arab neighbors?

2. What, if anything, has happened to the Arab refugees from Palestine in the past year?

E. Understanding Global History:

On page 180 you read about four factors in global history. Which of these factors applies to each statement listed below? Fill in the number of the correct statement on page 180 in the space provided.

_____ **1.** OPEC cut oil production and raised prices. This action caused energy problems in many parts of the world.

_____ **2.** Arabs understand little of the cultural background of Zionism. Supporters of Zionism understand little of the Arab culture.

_____ **3.** Cold War politics played a role in the Middle East. The Soviets gave aid to Arab nations. The United States gave aid to Israel.

_____ **4.** The nationalist feelings of many Arabs are based upon the Islamic culture that grew up centuries ago.

_____ **5.** The Arab culture was brought to all parts of the Middle East by Islamic armies hundreds of years ago.

Unit 3
Economic, Technologic, and Cultural Changes in the World Today

There have been many economic changes in the world since 1945. In those years Germany and Japan replaced Great Britain, France, and Italy as major producers of economic goods. The Soviet Union greatly increased its economic production. In the 1950s, the United States was the leading economic nation. Its position was steadily reduced by competition from other countries. One of the big competitors was Japan.

In Unit 3, you will read about the interdependence of the economies of all the countries of the world. You will learn how economics unites countries. You will also learn about the factors that keep developed and less developed countries apart. Interdependence also extends to the environment. In Unit 3, you will learn how problems in the environment can affect countries thousands of miles apart. Technology is also discussed in this unit. You will learn how technology has changed our lives. At one time, computers were used only in offices and in industry. Today, students are using computers in their schools. Computers are also used in the home for a variety of purposes. This is just one example of the changes brought about by technology. Finally, you will look at the ways in which traditional ways of living and thinking have changed.

In Unit 3, you will read the following chapters:

Chapter 1

The Economies of the World Are Interdependent

Understanding Global History

Think about the following statements as you read how nations depend on each other.

1. Nations are linked by a network of economic interdependence.
2. Events occurring in one part of the world have influenced developments in other parts of the world.
3. People use the environment to achieve economic goals.
4. Providing for individual and group needs is a common goal of all peoples and cultures.

An outdoor market in Mali, a country in western Africa. Buyers and sellers meet in the marketplace to exchange goods. This is one of the earliest forms of economic interdependence.

Learning New Words and Terms

The following words are used in this chapter. Think about the meaning of each one.

interdependent: depending upon one another; in global terms, the idea that nations are bound to one another

client-states: nations or states that are completely dependent on another nation or state

market economy: an economy in which individuals own the means of production

command economy: an economy in which the government owns the means of production

Think As You Read

1. What is meant by specialization? How did it affect interdependence in early times?
2. Explorations and changes in industry led to world trade. They also caused nations to depend on each other economically. How did these things happen?
3. What are the differences between developed market economies and centrally planned economies?
4. Which nations have market economies? Which nations have command economies?

Human Beings Have Always Depended on Each Other

From our birth we are always near or with other people. We depend on them for food, love, and much more. People are **interdependent** by nature. They have always needed other people. In early times, people had their own family members to take care of them. They also needed other family groups, however. People began to work together in groups. They built shelters and looked for food. People worked together to take care of all their needs.

In time, some people became experts in just one job. They became what we now call specialists. People in the villages and cities depended on the specialists. City people did not grow their own food. This was left to the farmers, hunters, and fishers. These specialists also needed the people in villages and cities. The people in cities made tools, weapons, cloth, and other goods. People were joined together in a network of economic interdependence.

Trade Leads to Greater Interdependence

The growth of trade in early times led to more economic ties among people. Early Egypt, Sumer, Phoenicia (fuh NEESH uh), and Greece all carried on large-scale trade. Goods were traded among people in different parts of the world. The networks of economic interdependence became larger and larger.

Later, these networks grew even more. Trade was important in the economic life of early Rome. Romans ruled over most of western Europe, Britain, North Africa, and the Middle East. These places sent slaves, metals, silks, spices, and foods to Rome. For more than five hundred years, Rome depended upon these places. Their products were necessary for Roman economic life.

During the 400s A.D., warlike groups took over much of the Roman Empire. These were the Goths, Huns, and others. Trade to Rome was cut off. The networks of trade within the Roman Empire were upset. This helped speed up the fall of the Roman Empire in western Europe.

After the fall of Rome, there was still trade in Europe. The many small European kingdoms of the Middle Ages traded with one another. There was much less trade and interdependence, however. The trade networks were small. After A.D. 1400, world trade and economic interdependence began to grow again.

A Growing Worldwide Interdependence

The mid-1400s to the 1600s was a time of explorations. Europeans explored lands in Africa, Asia, and the Americas. These lands had large amounts of raw materials. Some of these were food, timber, furs, and minerals. These were important trade items. People wanted them. Nations that controlled raw materials became strong.

An important event helped build economic ties. This was the change in industry that took place in the 1700s and 1800s. The Industrial Revolution brought about great changes in the world's economic ties. Networks of trade spread around the world. Industrial countries got raw materials from faraway lands.

By the early 1900s, there were five major industrial countries. They were the United States, Britain, Germany, France, and Japan. These were also the major imperialist countries. Either directly or not, they ruled over much of Africa, Asia, and Latin America. Some of these places were colonies. Other places were ruled indirectly as **client-states.**

Imperialism Caused a Special Kind of Interdependence

Many industrial countries needed colonies and client-states. The colonies supplied cheap raw materials. Some of these were wool, palm oil, rubber, tin, and a number of foods. These raw goods were shipped to the industrial countries. There they were used to make many things. The finished goods were then sold at home and throughout the world. Some were even sold in the colonies and client-states.

Many colonies and non-industrial lands grew dependent upon industrial countries. In return for cheap raw materials they got costly machine-made goods. These machine-made goods helped wipe out small handcraft industries in many non-industrial places. Industrial and non-industrial countries grew more dependent on each other.

The 1900s brought greater economic interdependence to the world. That interdependence was based upon the economic power of the industrial imperialist countries. This power lasted even after the end of the colonial empires.

Kinds of Economic Systems

There are two main kinds of economic systems in the world today. They are **market economies** and **command economies.**

A Market Economy

In a market economy, the means of production are owned mainly by individuals. These individuals are producers. They use their resources to make goods for other individuals. The people who buy the goods are consumers. In a market econ-

A fruit seller in New York City. In a market economy, individuals own the businesses and the means of production.

omy, the producers and consumers influence one another. They decide what goods or services to produce.

In a market economy, consumers decide what they want to buy. This causes the producers to make those goods. The producers hope to make a profit by giving consumers the goods they want. Producers try to sell their goods for more than they cost to make. When producers and consumers influence one another, they control the production of goods and services. They decide what will be produced, how it will be produced, and how it will be shared.

The United States, Britain, France, Japan, Canada, and West Germany are some of the countries that have market economies. Another name for a market economy is a free-enterprise economy.

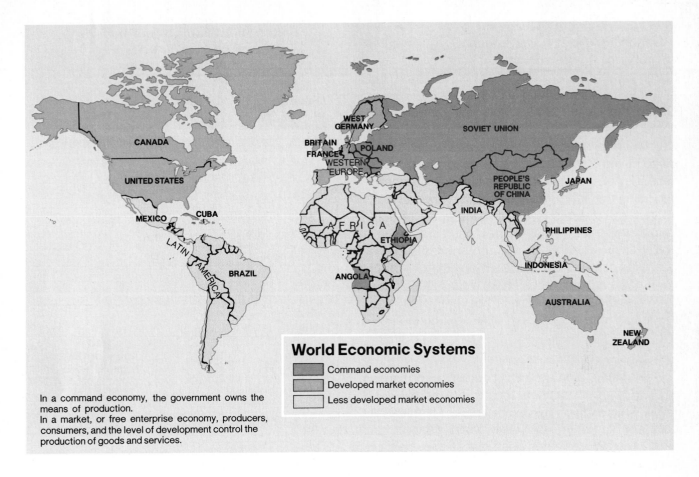

In a command economy, the government owns the means of production.
In a market, or free enterprise economy, producers, consumers, and the level of development control the production of goods and services.

World Economic Systems
- Command economies
- Developed market economies
- Less developed market economies

A Command Economy

In a command economy, the government owns and runs the means of production. The political leaders of the country decide what will be produced. They also set prices for all goods and services. In a command economy, the consumers' demands are not listened to very much. There may not be enough of the goods and services that the people want. For example, the government may think it is more important to make tractors than television sets.

A command economy may offer consumers fewer choices of goods or services. It may be able to provide for peoples' basic needs, however. These basic needs are food, shelter, and clothing.

The Soviet Union, the People's Republic of China, Cuba, and the communist countries in Eastern Europe have command economies.

Shoppers in Moscow, the capital of the Soviet Union. Because the government decides what will be produced in a command economy, there are often shortages of certain foods and other consumer goods.

Economic Systems Overlap

No country today has either a pure market economy or a pure command economy. All economic systems are mixed. That is, all economic systems have something of both kinds. For example, in the United States, the government runs some industries. One of these is the postal service. The government also influences other industries. In the Soviet Union, the government runs almost all the industries. Some kinds of economic decisions are left up to individuals, however.

Societies, therefore, differ in the kinds of economic systems they have. They also differ in their ability to give people goods and services. Some countries can give consumers many things. Other countries can give consumers very little. These countries differ in their level of development. You will learn more about this in the next chapter.

Economic Interdependence

One of the major facts about today's economies is their interdependence. There is a global network of economic interdependence. This ties all countries together. It makes them depend on each other. All countries need places to export, or sell, goods they make. And all countries need to import, or buy, goods to supply some of their basic needs. The following chart shows the economic interdependence of the United States. The chart compares the goods the U.S. sells (exports) with the goods it buys (imports).

United States exports and imports have grown a great deal. The economic interdependence of the United States and other countries has grown. The United States has one of the world's strongest economies. Even so, it depends upon other countries. It is very much a part of our economically interdependent world.

United States Exports and Imports— 1965, 1975, 1981 (in millions of dollars)		
1965 Value of U.S. Exports to		1965 Value of U.S. Imports from
$9.9	Western Hemisphere	$9.2
$9.3	Europe	$6.2
$7.1	Asia and Oceania (Australia and New Zealand)	$4.9
$1.0	Africa	$.867
1975 Value of U.S. Exports to		1975 Value of U.S. Imports from
$38.8	Western Hemisphere	$37.7
$32.7	Europe	$21.4
$31.2	Asia and Oceania	$28.5
$4.2	Africa	$8.2
1981 Value of U.S. Exports to		1981 Value of U.S. Imports from
$81.6	Western Hemisphere	$85.4
$69.7	Europe	$53.4
$70.3	Asia and Oceania	$95.3
$11.0	Africa	$27.0

Source: *U.S. Commerce Department*

Exercises

A. Finding the Main Idea:

Put a check next to the sentence that gives the main idea of what you have just read.

_____ **1.** Industrial countries need raw materials.

_____ **2.** There was trade in the Middle Ages.

_____ **3.** All economies today are interdependent.

_____ **4.** The United States, Britain, France, Germany, and Japan were major industrial countries in the early 1900s.

B. What Did You Read?

Choose the answer that best completes each sentence. Write the letter of your answer in the space provided.

_____ **1.** Village and city people depended upon
   a. fishing groups.
   b. farmers.
   c. hunters.
   d. all of the above.

_____ **2.** Industrial countries got raw goods from
   a. industrial countries.
   b. imperialist countries.
   c. colonies and client-states.
   d. all of the above.

_____ **3.** In countries with market economies, most decisions are made by
   a. skilled workers.
   b. individuals.
   c. government leaders.
   d. landowners.

_____ **4.** In countries with command economies, most decisions are made by
   a. individuals.
   b. government leaders.
   c. landowners.
   d. business owners.

C. Matching:

Match each country in Column A with the kind of economy listed in Column B. Write the letter of each answer in the space provided. You may use the map on page 193 for help.

Column A

_____ **1.** Japan
_____ **2.** Cuba
_____ **3.** Soviet Union
_____ **4.** People's Republic of China

_____ **5.** Britain
_____ **6.** France
_____ **7.** Canada
_____ **8.** Poland
_____ **9.** West Germany

Column B

a. market economy
b. command economy

D. Graph Skills:

Use the two graphs shown here and the chart on page 194 to answer the questions that follow. Write the letter of your answer in the space provided.

United States Exports and Imports
(in millions of dollars)
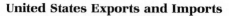

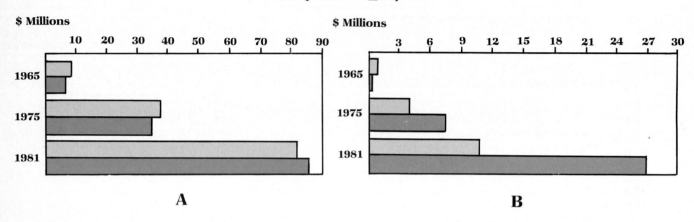

A   B

_____ **1.** Graph A shows United States exports to
  a. Europe
  b. the Western Hemisphere
  c. Asia and Oceania
  d. Africa

_____ **2.** Graph B shows United States exports to
  a. Europe
  b. Asia and Oceania
  c. Africa
  d. the Western Hemisphere

E. Understanding Global History:

On page 190 you read about four factors in global history. Which of these factors applies to each statement listed below? Fill in the number of the correct statement on page 190 in the space provided. If no factor applies, fill in the word NONE.

_____ **1.** Village and city people were interdependent in early times. They worked together to meet individual and group needs.

_____ **2.** Industrial countries used the raw materials of colonies and other less developed places to provide for their own economic goals.

_____ **3.** The United States, like all countries, is economically interdependent with other countries.

_____ **4.** The fall of Rome cut off trade and interdependence in parts of the world far removed from Rome.

Enrichment:
Japan's Economy

One hundred years ago, Japan was one of the less developed countries of the world. Today, it has one of the leading developed economies. Japan is a world leader in the production of steel, ships, automobiles, and electronic goods. Japan is also one of the most economically interdependent countries in the world. Its economic health depends upon a proper balance between imports and exports.

Japan is made up of four main islands and a number of smaller islands. They stretch for about 1,300 miles (2,092 kilometers) and include an area of about 143,574 square miles (371,856 square kilometers). More than 120 million people live in Japan. That is about one-half the number of people living in the United States. The United States has more than 3,600,000 square miles (9,324,000 square kilometers) of land, however. This comparison gives you some idea of how small and crowded Japan is. It also gives an idea of what some of its problems are likely to be.

Japan's economy depends upon its imports and exports. Only about 15 percent of Japan's land is useful for farming. Japan must import at least 30 percent of its food. Wheat, corn, sugar, wool, and cotton are Japan's major farm imports.

In 1983, Japan imported almost 114 billion dollars' worth of food and raw materials. That same year it exported 145 billion dollars worth of goods. These were mostly industrial goods. Japan has a high level of industrial production even though it lacks many natural resources.

Japan has only enough coal to meet about 45 percent of its needs. Its iron ore is of very poor quality. Japan must, therefore, import coal and iron ore. Much of this is used to make steel. In 1981, Japan made about 100 million metric tons of steel. To produce steel, Japan must import iron ore from the United States, the

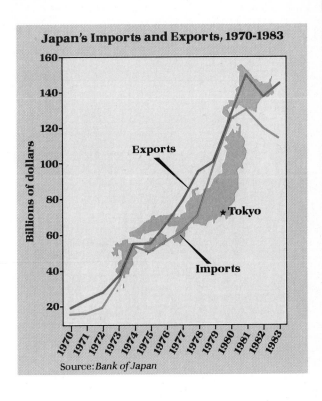

Japan's Imports and Exports, 1970-1983

Billions of dollars

Exports

★Tokyo

Imports

Source: *Bank of Japan*

Soviet Union, Brazil, Canada, China, India, Sweden, and South Africa. It must import coal from the United States, the Soviet Union, Britain, India, South Africa, Poland, Austria, Czechoslovakia, and East and West Germany.

Steel is only one example of Japan's economic interdependence. Another example is petroleum. Many of Japan's industries are completely dependent upon oil. Much of the oil comes from the Persian Gulf area. It is brought 6,500 miles (10,460.7 kilometers) to Japan by supertankers. This imported oil supplies over 99 percent of Japan's oil needs. It supplies over 70 percent of Japan's total energy needs. Japan must also import 90 percent of the natural gas that it needs. Japan is one of the world's most striking examples of economic interdependence.

Chapter 2

Developed and Less Developed Countries

Understanding Global History

Think about the following statements as you read about developed and less developed countries.
1 People use the environment to achieve economic goals.
2 Nations are sometimes dependent on other nations for economic and political survival.
3 Events occurring in one part of the world have influenced developments in other parts of the world.
4 Nations borrow and adapt ideas and institutions from other nations.

The presidents and prime ministers of the United States, Britain, West Germany, France, Italy, Japan, and Canada met in June 1984 for an economic summit meeting. They discussed issues that unite and divide world economies. Some of these issues are growth, trade, world debt, and unemployment.

Learning New Words and Terms

The following words are used in this chapter. Think about the meaning of each one.

literacy: the percentage of the people in a country who can read and write

gross national product: the total value of goods and services produced in a country in a year

per capita income: a number found by dividing the total amount of money earned in a year in a country by the number of people in that country

capital: money used to start a business

cash crops: crops raised to be sold instead of to be eaten or used; single crops that are a country's main source of export income

recession: a drop in business activity that lasts for a limited time

Think As You Read

1. How do developed and less developed countries differ in terms of literacy, gross national product, and per capita income?
2. What are some of the special problems affecting less developed countries?

People everywhere try to use their resources to improve their lives. The world's resources are not divided evenly, however. Some countries don't have the rich soil needed for good farming. Others don't have the resources needed to start up industries. Other countries may have the resources but these resources may be controlled by industrial countries.

The countries of the world differ in their level of economic development. One group is called developed countries. Another group is called less developed countries, or developing countries.

Developed Countries

The developed countries of the world are the United States, the Soviet Union, Great Britain, Japan, France, Australia, New Zealand, Canada, West Germany, and other countries of Western Europe. Some of these countries have been developed for a long time. Others, like the Soviet Union, have become developed more recently.

Developed countries have advanced economies. Their industries are very complex. They can produce almost everything they want. They have enough money to buy goods from other countries. In developed countries, few people need to farm the land. The country either produces enough food or is able to buy it.

Most people in developed countries work in industries. Many work in jobs that give services. Secretaries, doctors, teachers, and postal workers are examples of people who give services. Most people can read and write in developed countries. They have skills that help them in their daily lives. People in developed countries have many economic choices. They also have more time for themselves. Their standard of living is generally high.

Less Developed Countries

Most countries in the world today are less developed. People in these countries are often quite poor. Farming is the way of life for most people. They must farm to get enough food just to keep the country's people alive. Less developed countries usually don't have the resources needed to produce other goods and services. They have few economic choices. Saudi Arabia, Bahrain (ba RAYN) and the United Arab Emirates (eh MIR ayts) are exceptions. They are less developed countries. They are very rich in oil, however. Their economies can give the people better lives.

Most people in less developed countries cannot read or write. They have few skills. There are few industries. The standard of living for the people is generally quite low.

The chart on page 200 and the map on page 201 look at some developed and less developed countries in three areas. These are **literacy, gross national product,** and **per capita income.** Literacy refers to the percentage of the people in a country who can read and write. The gross na-

199

Some Developed and Less Developed Countries (approximate figures for 1981)			
Developed Countries	Literacy	Gross National Product (in trillions and billions of dollars)	Per capita income (in dollars)
United States	99%	2,937 trillion	$12,820
Great Britain	99%	503 billion	$9,110
West Germany	99%	683 billion	$13,450
Japan	99%	1,128 trillion	$10,080
France	99%	569 billion	$12,190
Less Developed Countries	Literacy	Gross National Product (in billions of dollars)	Per capita income (in dollars)
Afghanistan	10%	3.4	not available
Argentina	85%	72.1	$2,560
Bangladesh	23%	not available	$140
Brazil	45%	250	$2,220
Egypt	44%	28.1	$650
India	29%	176.6	$260
Libya*	35%	26.0	$8,450
Indonesia*	60%	78.7	$530
Saudi Arabia*	20%	117.2	$12,600
Mexico*	65%	160.2	$2,250
Venezuela*	70%	65.0	$4,220
Nigeria*	25%	76.1	$870
Peru	45%	19.9	$1,170

*countries with rich oil deposits

Source: *World Bank Atlas*

tional product (GNP) is the total value of all goods and services produced in a country in a year. Per capita income is a number found by dividing the total amount of money earned in a year in a country by the number of people in that country.

To understand what these figures mean, think about these examples. In Bangladesh the per capita income in 1981 was $140. This means that an average person only earned $140 per year. Think what your life would be like if you made only $140 a year.

Differences Between Developed and Less Developed Countries

There are many differences between developed and less developed countries. The less developed countries don't have **capital** for investment in industry. They don't have good schools, good roads, skilled workers, or the transportation systems needed for industry. These things are all found in developed countries. They help to make countries rich. They also help to make people's lives better.

The gross national product (GNP) is generally much lower in less developed countries than it is in developed countries. This is because less developed countries produce much less. Look at the example of Japan, a developed country. The total GNP of Japan in 1981 was $1.1 trillion. This was greater than the total GNP of all less developed countries for that same year. This means that the value of things made in Japan was greater than the value of things made in less developed countries together.

The per capita income of Japan was $10,080 in 1981. This was greater than that of every less

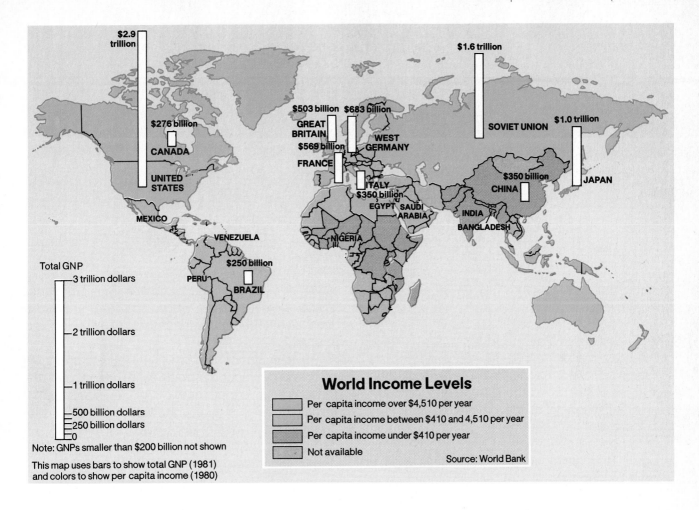

$2.9 trillion

$276 billion
CANADA

UNITED STATES

MEXICO

VENEZUELA

PERU

$250 billion
BRAZIL

$503 billion
GREAT BRITAIN

$569 billion
FRANCE

$683 billion
WEST GERMANY

ITALY
$350 billion
EGYPT SAUDI ARABIA

NIGERIA

$1.6 trillion
SOVIET UNION

$1.0 trillion

$350 billion
CHINA

JAPAN

INDIA
BANGLADESH

Total GNP

—3 trillion dollars

—2 trillion dollars

—1 trillion dollars

—500 billion dollars
—250 billion dollars
—0

Note: GNPs smaller than $200 billion not shown

This map uses bars to show total GNP (1981)
and colors to show per capita income (1980)

World Income Levels

Per capita income over $4,510 per year

Per capita income between $410 and 4,510 per year

Per capita income under $410 per year

Not available

Source: World Bank

developed country, except oil-rich Saudi Arabia. Finally, the level of literacy in each developed country is 99 percent. This is much higher than the literacy level of any of the less developed countries. This also means that less developed countries lack skilled people to work in industry or other jobs.

Factors Affecting Less Developed Countries

Many less developed countries depend economically on a single crop or mineral resource. They depend upon certain developed countries that buy this crop or mineral. For example, in 1961 the United States stopped buying sugar and tobacco from Cuba. That nation's new leaders were Communists. The United States did not want to buy from a communist nation. Sugar and tobacco are the two major **cash crops** of Cuba. Its main source of income was from sugar and tobacco. Its

main customer for these goods was the United States. Cuba turned to the Soviet Union for economic and political help.

Less developed countries can be harmed by many things. Bad weather can harm the major crops that they sell. Wars can also harm the production and the shipment of important goods. New discoveries can lessen the desire for their goods. All of these things can hurt the economies of less developed countries. This is because they depend upon only a few crops or goods.

All countries can be harmed by some actions. For example, the raising of prices by oil-producing countries can bring economic problems to everyone. Less developed countries suffer the most. They have very little money to buy oil. Developed countries can try to save energy. By doing this, they can force down the price of oil. This can help many of the less developed countries. It can also

A banana plantation in Ecuador. Many developing countries such as those in Latin America are trying to break out of dependence on one crop.

weaken the oil-producing less developed countries, however.

The Problems of Less Developed Countries in an Interdependent World

We live in an economically interdependent world. In such a world the less developed countries need the help of the developed countries. But there are disagreements about how much help is needed and how that help is to be given.

Some less developed countries have tried to use the economic ways of the developed countries. These less developed countries borrow billions of dollars from banks and other international groups. They use this money to build roads, factories, airports, and railroads. These are all things needed for economic development. They are needed in an industrial economy. The less developed countries hope these things will raise the economic level of their country. Mexico, Venezuela, Nigeria, Brazil, Chile, and Peru are some less developed countries that have borrowed money.

Borrowing money has not solved the problems of less developed countries. These countries have come near economic disaster. They cannot repay their debts. The worldwide **recession,** poor planning, and rising costs have all hurt their attempts to make their economies stronger. Now these countries owe huge debts to banks and international groups.

The problem of how to improve the economic level of the less developed countries is still unsolved. An answer must be found, however. Since the world is economically interdependent, all countries are affected. And without an answer, the anger, fear, and mistrust of less developed countries can only increase tensions in the world.

Debts Owed by Some Less Developed Countries

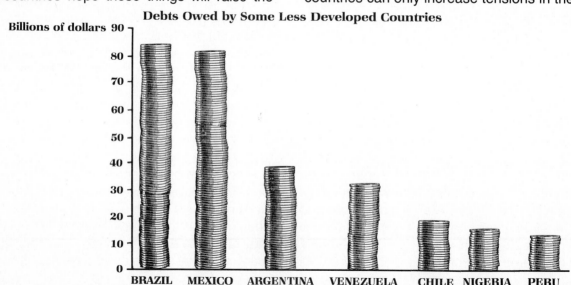

Billions of dollars

BRAZIL MEXICO ARGENTINA VENEZUELA CHILE NIGERIA PERU

Exercises

A. Finding the Main Ideas:

Put a check next to the sentences that give the main ideas of what you have just read.

_____ **1.** The gross national product (GNP) is important to a country.

_____ **2.** There are many differences between the economies of developed and less developed countries.

_____ **3.** Per capita income is important to a country.

_____ **4.** There are many differences between developed and less developed countries.

_____ **5.** Different factors affect the less developed countries of the world.

B. What Did You Read?

Choose the answer that best completes each sentence. Write the letter of your answer in the space provided.

_____ **1.** The typical less developed countries do *not* include
    a. Peru.
    b. India.
    c. Saudi Arabia.
    d. Bangladesh.

_____ **2.** The rich, developed countries have
    a. high literacy rates.
    b. industrial development.
    c. high living standards.
    d. all of the above.

_____ **3.** A list of developed countries would include
    a. France, Japan, and Peru.
    b. West Germany, the United States, and France.
    c. the United States, West Germany, and Brazil.
    d. Mexico, Great Britain, and Japan.

_____ **4.** Saving energy can result in
    a. benefits to less developed countries.
    b. lower oil prices.
    c. the weakening of oil-producing, less developed countries.
    d. all of the above

C. Chart and Map Skills:

Use the chart on page 200 and the map on page 201 to answer the following questions. Write your answers in the space provided.

1. The three less developed countries on the chart that have the highest rates of literacy are:
    a. _____   **b.** _____   **c.** _____

2. The less developed country on the chart with the *lowest* GNP is _____.

3. The less developed country on the chart with the *highest* GNP is _____.

4. The country on the map with the highest *total* GNP is _____.

5. The countries on the map with per capita incomes under $410 per year are found in _____ and _____.

D. Matching:

Match each country in Column A with the descriptions in Column B. Write the letter of each answer in the space provided.

Column A

_____ **1.** Saudi Arabia
_____ **2.** France
_____ **3.** Bahrain
_____ **4.** Egypt
_____ **5.** Soviet Union
_____ **6.** Mexico
_____ **7.** Great Britain
_____ **8.** Canada
_____ **9.** Brazil
_____ **10.** India

Column B

a. Developed country
b. Less developed country
c. Less developed country rich in oil

E. Thinking It Over:

Answer the following question in about 100 words. Use a separate piece of paper.

Why is it important for developed countries to try to improve the conditions of life in the less developed countries?

F. Understanding Global History:

On page 198 you read about four factors in global history. Which of these factors applies to each statement listed below? Fill in the number of the correct statement on page 198 in the space provided. If no factor applies, fill in the word NONE.

_____ **1.** When the United States stopped buying Cuban goods, Cuba became more dependent upon the Soviet Union for economic and political help.

_____ **2.** Increasing oil prices by Middle East producers have hurt the economies of many less developed countries in Africa and South America.

_____ **3.** Some less developed countries borrowed money to try to use the economic ways of the developed countries.

_____ **4.** A country must make use of its resources to improve the peoples' way of living.

Enrichment:
World Population Growth

For thousands of years, the world's population grew slowly. But within the past 150 years, world population has increased steadily. It increased from 1 billion people in 1850 to 4.7 billion in 1983. It is estimated that there will be 6.1 billion people in the world by the year 2000.

The increase in world population has both good and bad aspects. On the good side it proves that we have overcome problems that limited our early ancestors—disease, the elements, and lack of food. Improved agriculture, medicine, and better housing have made our lives longer. On the bad side, there may not be enough food for all the people alive now. And there may not be enough food for those yet to be born.

For now, rich, developed countries can buy the food they need. But poor, less developed countries will have a problem. They may not be able to get enough food. Most of the less developed countries are in Africa, Asia, and Latin America. These are the areas where population is growing fast. The threat of hunger is also greatest here. The following chart shows the increase of population in Africa, Asia, and Latin America.

Population Growth 1920–1960
Latin America   135% increase
India   85% increase
Africa   70% increase (approximate)
Far East   45% increase

For the future, the population pattern shows a decline in the rate of increase for developed countries. For example, the expected increase in population for 1980–1990 is only 6% for Europe and 10% for the United States. The expected rate of increase for 1980–1990 for Latin America, Asia, and Africa will range from 22% to 31%.

The increasing number of people, especially in the less developed countries, presents many economic and social problems. Population growth slows down the growth of per capita income. Most people must spend their time growing food. It becomes difficult to raise the people's standard of living if a government must spend all its money providing basic necessities. Population growth can cause a strain on a country's resources. Food is not the only problem, however. It also becomes difficult to supply energy needs, goods and services, and many other things. Population growth strains the water supply of many countries. It is also a strain on other parts of the environment such as the forests. Many people in less developed countries cut down forests to get firewood and materials to build houses.

Since we live in an interdependent world, the problems of one country affect all of us. Feeding the world's growing population is a problem we must all try to solve.

Chapter 3

Nuclear Power

Understanding Global History

Think about the following statements as you read about nuclear power.
1 The culture in which we live influences our view of other people.
2 Contact among peoples and nations can lead to cultural diffusion.
3 Nations are sometimes dependent upon other nations for economic and political survival.
4 Nations are linked by a network of economic interdependence.

A nuclear bomb being exploded.

Results of the First Atomic Bomb Blast

In August 1945, the world's first atomic bombs were dropped. The United States bombed two cities in Japan to try to end World War II. The first result was that Japan gave up the war. The terrible power of atomic, or nuclear, weapons had other results, too.

The United States came out of World War II as the strongest country in the world. It had a strong economy. In 1945 the United States was also the only country that knew how to make atomic bombs. The United States had a power that no other country had. This caused problems, especially with the Soviet Union.

Other Countries Want Atomic Bombs

There were great differences between the ways of thinking of the Soviet Union and the United States. Neither side tried to understand the other. The Soviet Union was suspicious of the United States. The Soviet leaders also felt threatened. They did not know what the United States was going to do with its atomic bombs. The Soviets wanted to get atomic bombs of their own.

Ideas About Warfare Change

Ideas about warfare changed because of the atomic bomb. With atomic bombs, war could be much more destructive. More people could be killed. More land could be wiped out. Atomic bombs had terrible power. Many people felt that atom bombs should never be used again. Otherwise, the whole world might come to an end.

The atomic bomb also changed ideas about sources of energy. Atomic bombs gave off huge amounts of energy. This **nuclear energy** might be used in industry. It might take the place of oil, coal, and other sources of energy.

Limiting the Spread of Atomic Bombs

After World War II, American scientists pointed out that there were no real atomic secrets. Scientists had always shared ideas and knowledge. Therefore, it was only a matter of time before other countries would use atomic energy. The question was whether it would be used for war or peace.

The United Nations Atomic Energy Commission was formed to think about nuclear matters. In 1946 the United States put forth a plan to the commission. This plan would set up an International Atomic Development Authority. The Authority would control almost all atomic materials. It would also control the factories that made those materials. This plan said that atomic research would be carried on only for peaceful reasons. The Authority would watch over atomic production in any country. It was hoped that this plan would stop the growth of atomic weapons.

The US and the Soviet Union Disagree

The United States said it would destroy its atomic bombs if this plan was followed. It also promised to share what it knew of atomic energy with other countries. The Soviet Union would not accept the American plan. The Soviets wanted a treaty outlawing the atomic bomb. They also wanted all existing atomic bombs to be destroyed. The Soviets wanted to set limits on inspections. Efforts to reach a compromise on the plan failed. The first attempt to limit the growth of nuclear weapons failed.

The Nuclear Arms Race Begins

By the mid-1950s, other countries were making atomic bombs. The Soviet Union exploded its first atomic bomb in 1949. Great Britain had an atomic bomb in 1952. Within a few years the United States replaced the atomic bomb with a more powerful bomb. This was the hydrogen bomb.

The atomic race continued into the 1960s. Great Britain, France, and the Soviet Union all tested hydrogen bombs by 1961. The People's Republic of China tested its first atomic bomb in 1964. India tested its first atomic bomb in 1974. Many of the new bombs had a power of 60 megatons. This was equal to 60 million tons of TNT. By comparison, the bombs dropped on Hiroshima and Nagasaki had the power of about 20,000 tons of TNT. Bombs made later had even greater power. Their destructive power was huge. The thought of such weapons used in war filled the world with fear.

The Dangers of Nuclear Radiation

Nuclear weapons are feared for more than just their destructive power. Nuclear weapons give off **radiation.** Atomic and hydrogen bomb blasts send clouds of dust particles into the air. These particles give off deadly rays. These particles settle to the earth as **radioactive fallout.** Such fallout pollutes the air, soil, plants, foods, and water on earth. The fallout can remain dangerous for years.

Radioactive fallout is given off in every bomb blast. Even the testing of nuclear weapons is a great danger. This danger led countries to agree to limit the testing of bombs. A limited test ban agreement was signed in 1963. The United States, Great Britain, and the Soviet Union were the signers. They agreed to stop testing bombs in the air. They still tested under the ground, however. These are less dangerous because less radiation is given off below the ground. France and China did not accept the agreements on testing. Even so, the level of nuclear testing in the atmosphere fell off sharply.

Limits on Arms

In 1968, the United States and the Soviet Union signed a treaty. This treaty banned the spread of nuclear weapons to countries that did not already have such weapons.

Other efforts have been made to lessen the chance of nuclear war. Countries have agreed to limit the number of nuclear weapons built. In 1972, the United States and the Soviet Union signed the Strategic Arms Limitation Talks (SALT I) agreement. This agreement set limits on long-range offensive nuclear weapons. It also set limits on short-range defensive nuclear weapons. A second round of talks (SALT II) led to further agreements about limiting weapons. However, many Americans were against the second agreement. They felt it gave a nuclear weapons advantage to the Soviet Union. The SALT II treaty has not been approved by the U.S. Senate. Many of its provisions are honored by both the United States and the Soviet Union, however.

A nuclear power plant in the United States.

U.S.—Soviet Relations Worsen

Relations between the United States and the Soviet Union became worse during the early 1980s. The United States wanted to spread its nuclear weapons systems in Western Europe. The Western European countries depended upon the United States for survival in the event of war. The Europeans were afraid to let the United States put more weapons on their land, however. They feared that they would then become a main target in a war. Strong anti-nuclear movements began in Western Europe. They wanted both the United States and the Soviet Union to freeze nuclear weapons.

The United States turned down a nuclear weapons freeze. It warned that a freeze would only help the Soviet Union. The United States and the Soviet Union agreed to hold new talks anyway. The Strategic Arms Reduction Talks (START) began in 1982. The United States and the Soviet Union could not reach an agreement, however. Little progress was made after a year of talks. So late in 1983 the United States began putting new missile systems in Western Europe. This upset the Soviet Union. It warned that it would spread its nuclear weapons systems. The world seemed to be heading toward a new nuclear arms race. Tensions between the United States and the Soviet Union grew. Relations between the two countries did not stop, however. The Soviet Union still had large-scale trade with the United States and Western Europe. The nuclear arms disputes did not cause a breakdown in international trade relations. The economic interdependence of the world prevented such a breakdown.

Peacetime Use of Nuclear Energy

Most people know about the use of nuclear energy as weapons. Nuclear power also has important peacetime uses. One of the most important uses is for energy. The energy problems of the 1970s made people think more about nuclear power as an energy source.

The world still faces a serious energy problem. Oil, coal, and natural gas are being used up rapidly. These are **non-renewable resources.** They cannot be replaced once they have been used up. What will happen when the world uses up its non-renewable resources?

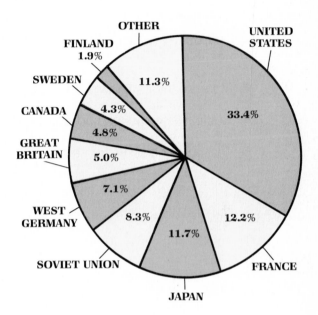

Major Producers of Nuclear Energy, 1982

OTHER 11.3%
UNITED STATES 33.4%
FINLAND 1.9%
SWEDEN 4.3%
CANADA 4.8%
GREAT BRITAIN 5.0%
WEST GERMANY 7.1%
SOVIET UNION 8.3%
JAPAN 11.7%
FRANCE 12.2%

Source: *International Energy Annual*

Many scientists believe that nuclear energy can meet the energy needs of the future. By 1982 there were 189 nuclear power plants in the world. Seventy-one of these were in the United States. Nuclear power plants are expensive. Many people also fear an accident at a nuclear power plant. Such an accident could release deadly radiation. An accident did take place at a nuclear power plant in 1979. It happened at Three Mile Island in Pennsylvania. This accident did not cause any serious damage that we know of. It did increase some people's fears about nuclear energy.

People also fear the nuclear waste materials that are left over when energy is made. What should be done with this dangerous material? Where can it be put so it will not harm people or the environment? Many people have spoken out against the use of nuclear power plants. Because of this, fewer plants are being built in the United States and in other parts of the world.

Exercises

A. Finding the Main Ideas:

Put a check next to the sentences that give the main ideas of what you have just read.

_____ **1.** The energy crisis has had a big effect on the peaceful uses of nuclear power.

_____ **2.** The United States and the Soviet Union have different ideas about nuclear weapons controls.

_____ **3.** More countries know about nuclear energy today.

_____ **4.** Nuclear energy has had a big effect on the countries of the world.

_____ **5.** Testing nuclear weapons is a problem for the world.

B. What Did You Read?

Choose the answer that best completes each sentence. Write the letter of your answer in the space provided.

_____ **1.** Until 1949 the secret of making atomic bombs was
  a. shared by the United States and Great Britain.
  b. known to many countries.
  c. known only to the United States.
  d. known only to the Soviet Union.

_____ **2.** The United States plan, given to the United Nations Atomic Energy Commission in 1946, did *not* include
  a. an international atomic development authority.
  b. immediate sharing of atomic secrets with the world.
  c. unlimited international inspection of atomic production.
  d. elimination of UN veto power in atomic matters.

_____ **3.** The country that does *not* have atomic weapons today is
  a. India.
  b. China.
  c. Japan.
  d. France.

_____ **4.** Radioactive fallout is a major problem because
  a. it pollutes the air, plants, and water.
  b. it is expensive.
  c. it destroys property.
  d. no one really knows what it does.

C. Checking For Details:

Read each statement. Put a T in the space next to each statement if it is true. Put an F in that space if it is false. Put an N if you cannot tell from the reading if it is true or false.

_____ **1.** In 1945 the Soviet leaders felt threatened by the atom bomb.

_____ **2.** It is possible to build safer nuclear power plants.

_____ **3.** The United States and the Soviet Union could not agree in 1946 on how to limit the growth of nuclear weapons.

_____ **4.** The first atomic bombs were dropped in 1945.

_____ **5.** Nuclear bomb explosions can produce radioactive fallout that lasts for years.

_____ **6.** Great Britain and France did not build hydrogen bombs.

_____ **7.** All countries with atomic bombs agreed to ban the spread of nuclear weapons to countries that did not already have such weapons.

_____ **8.** Many people in Western Europe are worried about having American missiles placed on their land.

_____ **9.** The SALT II agreement has not been approved.

_____ **10.** The peaceful use of nuclear power is the only hope for solving the future energy crisis.

D. Thinking It Over:

Read the following statement. Write your answer in seven or eight sentences. Use a separate sheet of paper.

The world faces a serious energy crisis. In your opinion, are nuclear energy plants the best way to solve this problem?

E. Understanding Global History:

On page 206 you read about four factors in global history. Which of these factors applies to each statement listed below? Fill in the number of the correct statement on page 206 in the space provided. If no factor applies, fill in the word NONE.

_____ **1.** Contacts among scientists from many different countries led to the spread of knowledge about atomic energy.

_____ **2.** The economic interdependence of the world has caused trade to go on in countries that are on different sides in nuclear arms disputes.

_____ **3.** Cultural and political differences kept the United States and the Soviet Union from understanding their differing views on atomic energy.

_____ **4.** Western Europe depends upon the United States for political survival in the event of a non-nuclear war.

211

Chapter 4

Changes in Technology

Understanding Global History

Think about the following statements as you read about changes in technology.
1 People use the environment to achieve economic goals.
2 Nations borrow and adapt ideas and institutions from other nations.
3 Contact among peoples and nations can lead to cultural diffusion.

Robots at work in an automobile assembly plant.

On July 20, 1969, people first stepped on the moon. This first step was important for many reasons. Most of all, it showed what people could do. It also showed what could be done with **technology.**

Technology is the use of science and machines in everyday life to solve practical problems. As people build upon what they already know, they make their technology better. In the 1700s and 1800s, people learned more about the way things worked. They used this knowledge to improve their lives. Great advances were made in technology. Inventions appeared in great numbers. Some of these were the steam engine, dynamo, locomotive, steamship, telegraph, telephone, and electric light. These inventions were part of the first and second Industrial Revolutions. These revolutions in industry greatly changed the way people lived.

How Technology Spreads

Technology does not come from any one person or country. It comes from contacts between and among peoples. New ways of doing things spread from place to place. New ideas take time to travel, however. Think about this example. In 1769, a French engineer built a carriage run by steam. During the next 40 years, British inventors improved the steam carriage. Then, in 1815, George Stephenson built the first locomotive to use the steam blast. The steam locomotive also ran on iron wheels and rails. These wheels and rails were designed especially for the locomotive.

German inventors were among the first to think about the idea of iron wheels and rails. This was in the 1550s, however.

British railway engineers of the early 1800s found new ways of doing things. They used some methods that were very old. They joined these with new methods. Then, after 1830, many British engineers and railway workers carried their new skills and know-how to other lands. They built and ran railroads in many countries. Some of these were the United States, Canada, Russia, Egypt, Australia, India, and South America. Methods first developed in Britain found their way to faraway places. British ways were adapted to meet the special needs of each place, however.

Contacts among people have helped spread knowledge and new ways of doing things around the world. This is an example of cultural interaction. Contacts among people have helped technology spread quickly. They have also helped speed up technological change.

Technology in the 1900s

Many changes in ways of doing things came about in the 1700s and 1800s. Change did not end at that time, however. Changes in technology have continued. The inventions of the 1900s have changed life in many ways. They have also spread quickly from country to country. People's lives all over the world have been changed by technology. For example, think about changes in transportation, communication, and industry.

Changes in Transportation

The automobile has changed the way people and goods move about. This change has taken place in the 1900s. Inventors used their know-how to build the **internal-combustion engine.** This engine was used for motor vehicles. The assembly line made it possible to produce hundreds and thousands of motor vehicles. The process of making large numbers of goods that are all the same is called mass production. At one time, the United States led the way in the mass production of automobiles. Soon other nations also used the new technologies. Tens of millions of cars, trucks, and buses were built in Japan, Canada, Great Britain, France, and Italy.

The motor vehicle industry grew very quickly in the United States. In 1900, the United States had only 8,000 automobiles. By 1983, there were 130 million automobiles in the United States.

The great rise in the use of motor vehicles was helped by other things. One of these was paved roads. By 1984, there were millions of miles of paved roads and highways in the world. The transportation revolution of the twentieth century was made possible by other kinds of technology. One kind was that needed to build roads and highways. This example shows how many technologies are united to improve ways of living.

Airplanes

The change in transportation included more than just cars, trucks, and buses. It also included the growth of the airplane industry. The use of gasoline-motor, propeller airplanes had grown steadily after World War I. In 1950 the United States made 3,500 commercial airplanes and 2,700 military airplanes. These planes were all of the propeller type. Jet aircraft replaced many propeller airplanes after 1960. In 1978, the United States made 17,000 commercial planes. Many of these were jet-propelled. Also, thousands of other jet-propelled military planes were made.

The United States was not alone in building planes. Other major industrial countries such as Great Britain, France, West Germany, and the Soviet Union also made many aircraft. All the advances made in air transportation were helped by new kinds of engines and other inventions.

Robert H. Goddard and one of his rockets.

Computers are a part of everyday life in most developed countries. They are slowly being introduced into developing countries.

Rockets and Space Exploration

New ways of doing things led to space exploration. Robert H. Goddard, an American, was a leader in the study of rockets in the 1920s. The Germans built powerful rockets during World War II. After the war, the United States and the Soviet Union built newer and more powerful types of rockets. These efforts made possible many space projects during the 1960s and 1970s. One of these projects put the first people on the moon in 1969.

Changes in transportation, then, have changed people's lives. The world seemed to become a smaller place. Distances could be covered in short spans of time. It also became easier to move from place to place.

Changes in Communication

Another important area of change has been in communication. The telephone and telegraph brought great changes in communication in the 1800s. The electric telegraph was invented in 1837. Telegraph lines soon linked the cities of the United States. People no longer had to wait days or weeks to hear important news. By 1866, a telegraph cable across the Atlantic Ocean joined the United States and Europe.

Then, in 1876, the telephone was invented. This invention soon became one of the necessities of life. By 1920, there were already about 13 million telephones in the United States. By 1895, the wireless telegraph, or radio, was invented. This made communication faster than ever.

Electronics brought changes to communications in the 1900s. Electronics is the use of electrical energy in vacuum tubes and transistors (devices used for greater electrical power). Electronics has made radios and television sets a part of everyday life. Electronics had led to the use of robots in industry. Communication by means of space satellites is made possible by advanced electronics.

The Computer

The rate of technological change became faster after World War II. One reason for this is the **computer.** The computer is an electronic machine that solves and answers questions with great speed. There have been great changes in computers over the years. They are getting smaller and smaller. This has come about because of changes in the way of making transistors. Today, computers and microcomputers (very small computers) are used by millions of people in all parts of the world. Computers have taken over much of people's work. They are giving people more freedom to do other jobs.

Electronics and computers have been joined together in outer space. Together, they run satellite communication stations in space. These satellites beam radio, television, telephone, and computer signals to all parts of the world. They have made worldwide communication quicker and easier. They have helped to shrink our world even more.

215

Changes in Industry

Inventions in industry have made possible the mass production of all kinds of goods. These goods have raised people's standard of living throughout the world. Today, many people are better housed, fed, and clothed than at any time in the past. In many countries, goods once thought to be luxuries are now thought of as necessities.

The ability to mass-produce goods has made the United States one of the greatest industrial countries in the world. New methods in industry have been used by many other countries as well. Since the 1960s, there has been a great rise in the use of industrial technology throughout the world. West Germany, Japan, South Korea, and other countries have taken over many markets once held by American industries. The United States is no longer the world leader in the production of motor vehicles, television sets, radios, electronic equipment, and textiles. American industries now have to learn new methods from other countries. The United States must join with other countries to improve its industrial know-how.

Japan uses many of the newest industrial technologies. Japan has led the world in using computers and robots in industry. This is especially true in the mass production of motor vehicles. Japanese engineers learned much about mass production and quality control from Americans during the mid-1900s. By 1980, Japan had moved far ahead of the United States in many areas of mass production. American engineers are now learning about the newest technologies of industrial production from the Japanese.

The Importance of Technological Change

From these examples, we can see the importance of technology and the changes it brings. Technology helps people make their lives better. It helps people do things more quickly and easily.

Technology has made it possible for the handicapped to work and lead independent lives.

We can also see that improvements in technology often depend upon cultural contacts. Different cultures borrow, change, and use technologies from other cultures. This not only helps them. It also helps in the development of other, newer technologies.

Technology is not always good, however. Nuclear power can provide energy for everyday needs. It can also be used to make weapons that have the power to destroy the world. There is also the danger that people can become slaves to their machines. The careless use of technology can also harm the environment. People must learn how to use technology wisely.

Exercises

A. Finding the Main Ideas:

Put a check next to the sentences that give the main ideas of what you have just read.

_____ **1.** Ideas about new technologies have been passed from country to country.

_____ **2.** Japan has played a big role in developing new technologies.

_____ **3.** Jet-propelled aircraft are made by many countries.

_____ **4.** New technologies were part of the first and second Industrial Revolutions.

_____ **5.** Industrial technology has helped raise the standards of living of people.

_____ **6.** New technologies brought about great changes in transportation, communication, and industry.

B. What Did You Read?

Choose the answer that best completes each sentence. Write the letter of your answer in the space provided.

_____ **1.** Today, many American markets have been taken over by
   a. Japan.
   b. South Korea.
   c. West Germany.
   d. all of the above.

_____ **2.** The country that leads in the use of robots in industry is
   a. the United States.
   b. Japan.
   c. West Germany.
   d. Great Britain.

_____ **3.** Recent technologies have included
   a. robots, locomotives, television sets.
   b. transistors, motor vehicles, steam engines.
   c. computers, robots, space satellites.
   d. rockets, the telegraph, the telephone.

_____ **4.** In which area is electronic technology *least* involved?
   a. the use of robots
   b. the use of computers
   c. the building of space satellites
   d. the building of highways

C. Checking for Details:

Read each statement. Put an F in the space next to each statement if it is a fact. Put an O in that space if it is an opinion. Remember that facts can be proved, but opinions cannot.

_____ **1.** Motor vehicles changed transportation in the 1900s.

_____ **2.** British railroad workers brought their know-how to many other lands.

_____ **3.** The United States has too many motor vehicles in use today.

_____ **4.** The internal-combustion engine is used in motor vehicles.

_____ **5.** American planes are the best in the world.

_____ **6.** The electric light was a more important invention than the steam engine.

_____ **7.** The United States will soon regain its industrial lead over Japan.

_____ **8.** Robot technology is useful in industrial production.

_____ **9.** Transistor technology makes it possible to build very small computers.

_____ **10.** Rocket technology is used in space projects.

D. Graph Skills:

Pictographs use picture symbols to stand for numbers. Look at the information on automobile use given below. Then draw in the correct number of picture symbols for each country in the space provided in the graph.

AUTOMOBILES IN USE—1980

France	19 million
Great Britain	15 million
the United States	120 million

= 10 million ⬤⬤⬤ = 5 million ⬤⬤⬤ = 1 million

France	
Great Britain	
United States	

E. Thinking It Over:

Choose any two topics listed below. Write at least eight sentences for each of the topics you choose. Use a separate sheet of paper.

1. How many new technologies affected industry in the 1900s?

2. Which parts of your own life are most affected by the newest technologies?

3. How do you think technologies will affect your life in the future? in the world's future?

F. Understanding Global History:

On page 212 you read about three factors in global history. Which of these factors applies to each statement listed below? Fill in the number of the correct statement on page 212 in the space provided.

_____ **1.** British know-how in building railroads was used in many countries.

_____ **2.** Technology makes it possible for people to make better use of their environment. By doing this, people can improve their country's economic life.

_____ **3.** Facts about technology spread throughout the world because of the contacts among people and countries.

Enrichment:
Robotics

Robot is a word from the Czechoslovak language. It was first used in a Czech play in 1921. It means dull, boring work. The play told of human-like machines that did the work of people.

Many people still think of robots as machines that look and act like people. Actually, a robot is any electronically operated device that is programmed. This means it is set up to do a certain type of work. Today, the most important use of robots is as computer-controlled machine tools. Robots are programmed to do specific jobs. This can include welding, assembling, and moving and storing products.

The use of robots is known as **robotics.** Robotics is a product of electronic technology. Robots have many advantages over human labor. Robots can work without becoming tired or bored. Robots also make very few errors after they are programmed to do a task. Finally, the cost of using robots is less than the cost of using human labor in the long run. Robots can work a twenty-four-hour shift without stopping.

There are no costs for extra workers or overtime. There are also no problems with labor unions or strikes. This is one part of robotics that worries many workers. They fear that they will be put out of work by machines.

Robotics does present some problems to industry. Robots are expensive to buy. They must be maintained from time to time. This is also expensive. For these reasons, robots are more practical for large industrial companies than for small ones. If many large companies use robots, there is also a danger to smaller companies. Small companies may find it hard to compete with efficient, robot-run industries. The small companies may be forced out of business.

In 1983, Japan was the most advanced user of robotics. In that country, more than 15,000 robots were in use. The United States was far behind—in second place. West Germany, Sweden, and Great Britain were next. Robots are being used mainly in the automobile and steel industries.

Chapter 5

The Environment and the Future of the World's Economies

Think about the following statements as you read about the environment and the world's economies.
1 People use the environment to achieve economic goals.
2 Environmental problems can affect people who live miles apart.
3 Events occurring in one part of the world have influenced developments in other parts of the world.

This picture shows Switzerland, a country in western Europe. Which things shown in the picture are part of the environment?

Learning New Words and Terms

The following words are used in this chapter. Think about the meaning of each one.

aquifer: an underground layer of rock and sand containing water

conservation: protecting resources from loss or waste

nutrients: substances that aid growth and life in humans, plants, and animals

Think As You Read

1. What is the environment? What elements make up the environment?
2. How have people used technology to change the environment?
3. Why is the world called a "system"?
4. How can what we do to the environment affect the future of our economy?

The environment is everything around us that touches our lives. The environment is made up of the climate and the seasons. It is air, water, soil, plants, forests, minerals, and animals. The environment is also customs, languages, and other parts of culture.

All of these things play a large part in our lives. They affect us as separate persons. They also affect us as societies. The environment can affect how we think, eat, act, and dress. It can also affect how our society meets its political, social, and economic goals.

People Use Technology to Change the Environment

Throughout history, people have used technology to change their environment. Sometimes technology has helped people live better in their environment. For example, people invented irrigation to grow food in dry climates. People made different kinds of clothing to help them live in hot or cold climates. Later, they invented air conditioning or heating systems. People have used technology to change the environment or use it for their own needs. For example, people cut trees for firewood or lumber for building. They dig minerals out of mines and use the minerals to make goods. People have built near rivers to get energy from the running water.

Some Worries About the Environment

Many people are worried about the environment. They fear that technology may be destroying the environment. Instead of improving people's lives, it may be making their lives worse.

Irrigation is one example of how humans have changed the environment. Irrigating the land started in very early times.

How we use our environment not only affects our own lives. It may also affect the lives of people who are not even born yet.

The World Is a System

People now know that what happens to the environment in one part of the world affects the environment in other parts of the world. They have found out that the world is a system. Everything in that system is joined together. Let us look at some parts of our environment and see how they are changing and affecting our lives.

221

Air and Water—The Most Important Parts of the Environment

Air and water are the two most important parts of the environment. People cannot live without them. Keeping our air and water clean and safe is very important. Inventions have harmed the air and water in many places. Automobiles, airplanes, and factories give off pollution. This causes smog. Sickness, discomfort, or even death can come from too much pollution in the air.

Pollution in the air is sometimes trapped in rain. This is called acid rain. Acid rain has fallen in some parts of the world. The plants and animals that are in or near many lakes have died because of acid rain. The acid rain often falls hundreds or thousands of miles from where the pollution came. For example, lakes in eastern Canada have been affected by acid rain pollution from the midwestern United States.

Farmers in Tanzania, Africa. They are plowing their fields with a tractor. Improved farming methods can help people of developing countries grow more food.

Changes in the Climate

Air pollution has also harmed other parts of the environment. Pollution can cause plants and crops to die. It can harm animals. It may even be affecting the climate. Some people think air pollution may be causing the climate to become hotter. This process is called the greenhouse effect. A greenhouse effect may turn more land to deserts. Or it may melt the polar ice caps and raise the level of the oceans.

Polluted Water

Streams, rivers, lakes, and even the oceans are being polluted by technology. Industries pour waste materials into water. This often kills fish and plant life. Oil spilled in the oceans has washed ashore. It has killed fish and birds. Beaches have also been damaged. Drinking water is affected by pollution, too. Polluted water seeps through the ground to underground **aquifers.** These aquifers provide drinking water in many places.

Air and water pollution are important problems. Solving these problems takes time. The solutions can cost a lot of money, too. Important economic decisions have to be made. Governments could put limits on the activities that cause pollution. Ways could also be found to use technology to clean up the air and water.

Soil, Plants, and Forests

Soil, plants, and forests are important parts of the environment. They can usually be replaced after they have been used. If soil, plants, and forests are not cared for properly, however, they can be destroyed. A large part of saving these resources involves **conservation.**

Topsoil is important to farming. It takes millions of years to produce an inch of topsoil. Winds, rain, and poor farming methods can wear away topsoil. Thousands of acres of topsoil are blown or washed away each year throughout the world. Topsoil is also damaged by crops that take away chemical **nutrients.**

It is important that steps be taken to save the soil. Otherwise, farmers will not be able to grow many crops. They will lose money, too. There is also the danger of shortages of food because of the loss of farmlands. This could hurt many people. Many countries have to buy food. Therefore,

Forest workers in Honduras, Central America. They are putting out a fire.

a loss of crops in one country can affect people in other countries.

Finding Better Ways

It is important that the soil be saved. People must plan better. They must also change their ways of doing things. Farmlands must be plowed and planted in new ways. New crops must be planted. People should replace nutrients. Or they should take fewer nutrients from the soil. Chemical nutrients can also be used in the soil. They will make the soil richer. These new ways cost money. People also have to change.

Saving the Forests

Forests are another important resource. Trees have to be cut properly. New trees have to be planted. Then forests can grow back. There were once huge forests on earth. They have disappeared over the centuries, however. Fires and careless cutting ruined these forests. In some places, forests are cleared to get new farmland. In some parts of the world, people burn the wood from the forests as fuel. They cut the trees in the forest and never plant new ones. Soon there are no more trees and no more firewood. If there are no trees growing, serious erosion can take place. This is especially likely to happen on hillsides.

The world's forests can be saved. This also involves economic decisions. Short-term needs have to be weighed against long-term gains. The policies that are made will greatly affect the economic futures of many countries.

Mineral Resources

Mineral resources do not grow back. When oil, iron ore, coal, and other minerals are taken from the earth, they are gone forever. Many countries have already used up their minerals. Minerals are needed for industry. Without them, the economies of many countries will be hurt. This will not only affect the countries that run out of the minerals. Since many industrial countries import minerals, their economies will be hurt as well. The situation will get worse unless people learn how to protect mineral resources. Mineral resources can be recycled. That is, they could be used more than once. Used metal can be turned into scrap metal and used again. Certain minerals can take the place of those that are too few or too costly. Artificial materials can be used instead of minerals. For example, plastics can be used in place of certain metals. Making better use of the mineral resources will greatly help the economic future of all countries.

Animal Resources

Animal resources are wild animals as well as animals that are raised for food. Many kinds of birds, animals, and insects are in danger of dying out. In some cases they have been killed. In other cases, their environments have been destroyed. In some places, special animal reserves have been set up to help protect wild animals. Special laws have also been passed to protect wildlife. Such protection costs a great deal. The environment is richer for this protection, however.

Cattle, pigs, fish, and poultry are important sources of food. More of these kinds of animals are needed to feed the growing numbers of people. Scientists are finding new ways of providing animal resources.

Human Resources

The people of a country are its greatest source of strength. Human resources are the people and their culture. All countries must provide for the needs of their people. These needs include health, education, safety, and economic well-being.

Providing for human needs is an important job. It can be done in many ways. The ways chosen often deal with hard political and economic decisions. The steps that are taken, or not taken, can greatly influence the future of human life on this planet.

A Global Responsibility

Economics plays an important part in dealing with the environment. The technology needed to solve environmental problems is sometimes costly. Politics also plays an important part in environmental matters. Countries must decide how they will deal with environmental problems. Will they use conservation or technology? Or will they use some of both? Political decisions are also needed about how to pay for the solutions that are chosen.

Environmental problems often go beyond national boundaries. For this reason, different countries must work together to control global pollution. They must work together to solve global environmental problems. Countries must cooperate with one another. In our interdependent world, this working together will help secure the lives of all people living now. It will make life better for people yet to be born.

Women planting rice, Thailand. Human beings are a country's most valuable resource.

Exercises

A. Finding the Main Idea:
Put a check next to the sentence that gives the main idea of what you have just read.

_____ **1.** The environment is made up of many parts.

_____ **2.** Pollution is a serious problem.

_____ **3.** Conservation is important for some parts of the environment.

_____ **4.** How people treat their environment will affect their lives and economic future.

B. What Did You Read?
Choose the answer that best completes each sentence. Write the letter of your answer in the space provided.

_____ **1.** Pollution of aquifers affects our
    a. mineral resources.
    b. water resources.
    c. soil resources.
    d. forest resources.

_____ **2.** An example of technology that people have used to adapt to the environment is
    a. air conditioning.
    b. irrigation.
    c. heating.
    d. all of the above.

_____ **3.** Recycling is a way of saving our
    a. technology.
    b. mineral resources.
    c. animal resources.
    d. vegetation.

_____ **4.** Human resources include all of the following *except*
    a. culture.
    b. people.
    c. minerals.
    d. customs.

C. Checking For Details:
Read each statement. Put a T in the space next to each statement if it is true. Put an F in that space if it is false. Put an N if you cannot tell from the reading if it is true or false.

_____ **1.** Climates have a greater effect than seasons upon the environment.

_____ **2.** Pollution affects our air and water.

_____ **3.** Aquifers are the most important source of our drinking water.

_____ **4.** Topsoil is never lost.

_____ **5.** Crops can be planted that will replace nutrients in the soil.

_____ **6.** Forests are renewable if trees are cut and replaced with care.

_____ **7.** Recycling helps conserve mineral resources.

_____ **8.** Many wildlife reserves are located in Africa.

_____ **9.** Human cultures are not part of our environment.

_____ **10.** Science and technology have little effect upon overcoming environmental problems.

D. Thinking It Over:

Write an essay of at least 65 words telling how the environment and our economic future are affected by any _two_ of the factors listed below. Use a separate piece of paper.

1. mineral resources

2. soil resources

3. air and water resources

E. Understanding Global History:

On page 220 you read about three factors in global history. Which of these factors applies to each statement listed below? Fill in the number of the correct statement on page 220 in the space provided.

_____ **1.** The problems of the environment have an influence on people in all parts of the world.

_____ **2.** Failure to check pollution in one part of the world can cause that pollution to affect areas far from where the pollution began.

_____ **3.** Our economic goals are affected by the way we make use of the environment.

There are many things people can do to keep their environment clean and safe for the future. Can you name some?

Enrichment:
"Smog": The Fog That Kills

The poet Carl Sandburg wrote the following lines:

The fog comes
on little cat feet.
It sits looking
over harbor and city
on silent haunches
and then, moves on.

The fog that Sandburg saw was harmless, and, in many ways, beautiful. But there is another fog that can be deadly. When fog is mixed with smoke it becomes something known as "smog", and it can be deadly.

Almost all large cities face the problem of smog. It puts a haze around the sun, causes eyes to redden, and often causes sneezing and coughing. Sometimes it does more than annoy people. It kills them.

On October 27, 1948, the 12,000 people of Donora, Pennsylvania, awoke to a day of heavy fog. A local zinc plant in the city threw off its usual clouds of a gas called sulfur dioxide. The gas mixed with the fog and produced a smog. The smog settled over the city for a week. When the rains finally cleared the air, half of the people of Donora had been ill. Twenty people had actually died from the killer smog.

Killer smog hit in many other parts of the world. London, England, had long been known for its thick fogs. Those fogs were made worse by smoke from thousands of chimneys used by homes with fireplaces. The smoke and fog created smog that annoyed Londoners. Little was done to solve the problem, however.

In 1952 a thick white smog settled over London during Christmas week. Five days later the smog lifted, but 4,000 people had died in the city. As a result, officials in London passed laws forbidding the use of fireplaces that poured smoke out through chimneys.

Smog remains a problem in the many cities of the world. City smog is also beginning to affect many rural areas that were once known for their clean air. Environmental protection groups have led the effort to reduce air pollution and put an end to killer smogs. Their efforts have begun to take effect. In the United States, the Clean Air Act of 1971 has helped to clean the air in the environment. Its continued success is not certain, however. Political disputes about how the protection of the environment should be regulated and how it should be financed continue. Meanwhile, the threat of air pollution remains with us.

A coal mining area in India. Developing countries are becoming more aware of the serious problem created by industries through pollution.

227

Chapter 6

Traditional Ways of Life Change

Understanding Global History

Think about the following statements as you read about changing ways of life.

1. Contact among peoples and nations can lead to cultural changes.
2. Present culture is shaped by the past.
3. Providing for individual and group needs is a common goal of all peoples and cultures.

The traditional roles of men and women are changing in many societies. For example, many women hold jobs once only open to men.

Learning New Words and Terms

The following words are used in this chapter. Think about the meaning of each one.

extended family: a family made up of parents, children, grandparents, aunts, uncles, and cousins; a family whose members may often live in the same house or the same neighborhood

nuclear family: a family made up of only parents and their children

Think As You Read

1. How has the traditional role of women in society changed?
2. How have some traditional ideas about marriage changed?
3. How has the extended family changed in recent times?
4. How have some traditional ideas about class changed?

The world has changed in many ways since 1900. Much of the world has changed from an agricultural to an urban-industrial society. There have also been changes in transportation and communication. These changes have all affected older, traditional ways of life. Present-day customs and culture owe much to the past. Many of our beliefs are based upon past ideas, customs, and traditions.

New ideas have also taken hold in many parts of the world. Contacts with other peoples and societies have brought changes to traditional ways of life. Some changes are more evident today than in the past. In this chapter you will look at some changes that are happening, especially in the United States.

The Changing Roles of Women in Society

In most parts of the world, women have long been treated as less important than men. In the past, women had no chance of getting an education. Few jobs outside the home were open to them. They had few rights under the law. Women were not considered the equals of men.

In many societies, older beliefs about the place of women are changing. Some societies are trying to provide for the needs of women. Some are trying to make sure women have equal rights with men. Women have not yet gained full equality in many places, however.

In many societies, more women are attending schools. They hope to get jobs. There are growing numbers of jobs for women in industrial societies. In the United States, for example, only 18 percent of adult women were employed in 1900. That percentage rose to 28 percent in 1950. Today, it is more than 45 percent. More U.S. women are moving into professional and executive jobs. These jobs pay high salaries. The change is taking place at a slower rate in most parts of the world, however.

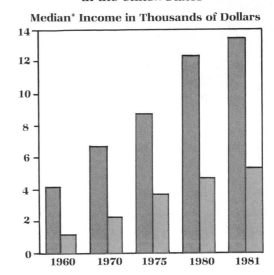

Income Levels of Men and Women in the United States

Median* Income in Thousands of Dollars

Legend: ■ Median Income of Men ■ Median Income of Women

*Median means the level at which half the total has more and half the total has less

Source: *U.S. Bureau of the Census*

Marriage and Divorce

Lifelong marriage to one person has long been part of life in many societies. Religion and traditional ideas about the family once made getting a divorce hard and rare. In some societies, this has changed over the past fifty years. For example, in the United States, the rate of divorce was 8 percent in 1900. The divorce rate rose to 20 percent in 1950. Today, it is about 50 percent.

Divorce rates in other countries, while not as high, have also risen. The increase in divorce has changed traditional family life in the United States. Today, large numbers of children are being raised by one parent. More women head households. These changes are linked to the changed role of women in the work force. Today, many women are replacing men as the breadwinners in their families.

The Extended Family

The **extended family** has been around for a long time in many parts of the world. It is a part of the traditional way of life. Extended families are very important in Asia and Africa. Parents, children, grandparents, uncles, aunts, and cousins are all part of the extended family. Members of an extended family often live in the same village, on the same street, or even under the same roof. The family members are very loyal to one another.

The extended family and its ways of life are strongest in rural, farming areas. Family members form a strong bond within the village. Members can call upon their family for help at all times.

Through the years, however, this close family relationship has been strained by the growing number of industries and cities. People have moved from the country to cities. They hoped to find work in the cities. The shift from village to city and from farming to industry has broken up many extended families. Family members are separated when they move from the village to cities in search of jobs or education.

The weakening of the extended family has caused many changes. People no longer have their families to be loyal to. They give their loyalty to larger political or economic groups. Many people now look for support from others. These may be employers, unions, local political leaders, or government groups. Modern urban-industrial societies are making the extended family less common. The **nuclear family** has become the standard family group in the urban-industrial society.

A farm family in Ethiopia. In most parts of the world children are expected to help in the work of the family.

Ideas of Class Change

The idea of classes in society has been in traditional societies for a long time. Many societies had a class of nobles. They believed that they were better than everyone else. They felt they were a superior class. This view was also shared by many large landowners. Belief in superior and inferior classes has carried over into many places.

The growth of industry has weakened the traditional view of classes in society. People began to move to cities. They worked in industry. Because of this, landowners lost much of their power. Rich factory owners, merchants, and bankers gained power. In some countries, royal rulers were overthrown. Nobles lost their power to other groups.

The traditional class system is now nearly gone in most industrial societies. In its place is a new type of class system. Today, we speak of an upper class, a middle class, and a lower class. It is hard to identify many people in terms of their class, however. Money, ways of behaving, education, and lifestyle are all involved. In the traditional class system, it was hard to move from one class to another. Today, there is much greater movement among classes. The traditional ideas of class have changed. There is no longer a clear idea of what they mean.

Technology Affects Our Lives

Technology has greatly changed people's lives. It has changed the way they use the environment. Feelings about people have also changed. Technology has helped change farmers into industrial workers. It has improved the standard of living in many parts of the world. The changes brought about by technology have brought people closer together. People have found out more about each other. It has sometimes led to better understanding. It has also led to more interdependence among countries. It has made the world seem like a smaller place.

The technological revolution has threatened to upset the balance of the world's system. At the same time, it has given the knowledge and ways to protect the system. It can help control the environment and improve our ways of life. We can make the world a better place. This is one of the most important challenges of our time.

A father and his daughter. Most families in urban-industrial countries are nuclear families. Some nuclear families may have just one parent, however.

Exercises

A. Finding the Main Idea:
Put a check next to the sentence that gives the main idea of what you have just read.

_____ **1.** Women have an important role in modern society.

_____ **2.** Family life has changed over the years.

_____ **3.** Changes in economic, political, and social life have changed traditional ways of life.

_____ **4.** There are still many classes in modern society as there were in past traditional societies.

B. What Did You Read?
Choose the answer that best completes each sentence. Write the letter of your answer in the space provided.

_____ **1.** In many industrial societies, the divorce rate is
  a. getting lower.
  b. remaining the same.
  c. rising.
  d. none of the above.

_____ **2.** The extended family is usually found in
  a. industrial societies.
  b. big cities.
  c. country villages.
  d. all of the above.

_____ **3.** In traditional societies, women had few
  a. legal rights.
  b. chances for getting an education.
  c. job opportunities.
  d. all of the above.

_____ **4.** The percentage of adult women employed in the United States in 1950 was
  a. lower than in 1900.
  b. lower than it is today.
  c. the same as in 1900.
  d. the same as it is today.

C. Checking For Details:

Read each statement. Put an F in the space next to each statement if it is a fact. Put an O in that space if it is an opinion. Remember that facts can be proved, but opinions cannot.

_____ **1.** Culture is a part of the environment.

_____ **2.** Past ideas are not as good as modern ideas.

_____ **3.** Women are happier today than in past years.

_____ **4.** In some societies, women have more high-paying jobs today than in past years.

_____ **5.** There is too much divorce in the United States.

_____ **6.** There are close loyalties in the extended family.

_____ **7.** Women are better breadwinners than men.

_____ **8.** Employers and government agencies have taken the place of extended family members in many places.

_____ **9.** There is no longer a clear idea of classes in our society.

D. Thinking It Over:

Select any two topics below. Write an essay of at least seven sentences for each topic you choose. Use a separate piece of paper. In your opinion, how have the changes brought about by technology affected

1. the traditional role of women in the workplace?

2. the traditional extended family?

3. the traditional ideas about classes in society?

E. Understanding Global History:

On page 228 you read about three factors in global history. Which of these factors applies to each statement listed below? Fill in the number of the correct statement on page 228 in the space provided.

_____ **1.** Customs and traditions of the past are the basis of many of our present-day beliefs.

_____ **2.** Traditional beliefs about the role of women are changing. This change has made it possible for women to have jobs that were once closed to them.

_____ **3.** Contact among people from different cultures have brought changes to the traditional ways of life.

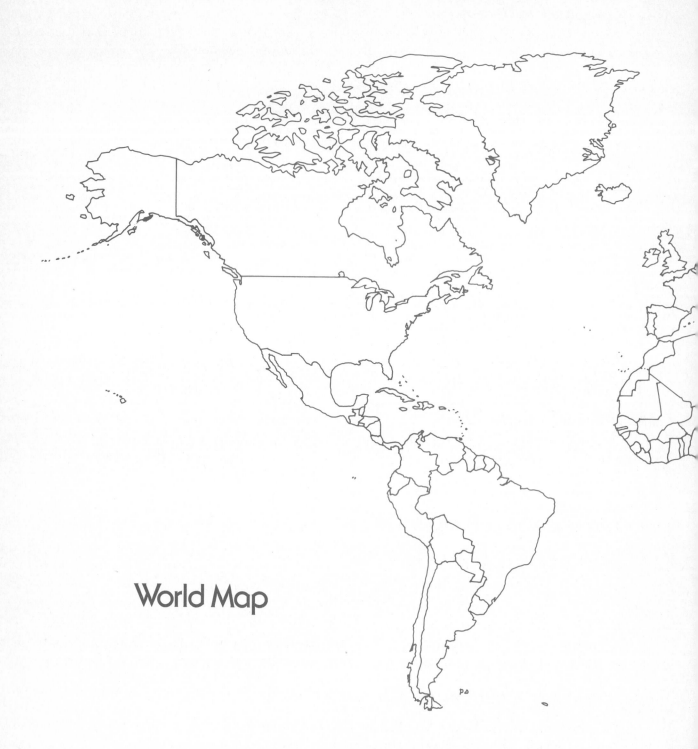

World Map

Use this map to locate and identify the continents, major bodies of water, and countries of the world. What other kinds of information can you show on the map?

GLOSSARY

alliances   (uh-LY-unts-sez) agreements between two or more nations to help each other **(103)**

anti-Semitism   (ant-eye-SEM-uh-tiz-um) a feeling of hatred toward Jews **(121)**

apartheid   (uh-PART-hayt) the Afrikaner word for separateness; in South Africa, a policy of separation of races **(175)**

aquifer   (AK-wuh-fur) an underground layer of rock and sand containing water **(222)**

arbitration   (are-buh-TRAY-shun) settling a fight by having someone who is not part of the fight listen to both sides and make a decision **(86)**

armistice   (ARE-muh-stis) an agreement to stop fighting **(107)**

assegais   (ASS-ih-guys) thin spears with iron tips; used by Zulu warriors in southern Africa **(77)**

balance of power   (BAL-uns uv POW-ur) a situation in which no one nation has more power than its neighbors or other nations **(103)**

barbarian   (bar-BER-ee-un) person who has no real culture and is not civilized **(36)**

blitzkrieg   (BLITS-kreeg) lightning war; a method of warfare used by the Germans involving a quick, all-out attack **(120)**

bloc   (BLAHK) a group of countries joined together to help one another or to take some action **(130)**

blockade   (blah-KAYD) stopping the passage of ships or troops into an area **(122)**

Boer   (BOHUR) a farmer from the Netherlands who settled in the area that is now South Africa **(77)**

British Commonwealth   (BRIT-ish KOM-un-welth) an association of more than 40 former British colonies and the United Kingdom; now known as the Commonwealth of Nations **(154)**

bushido   (BOO-she-DO) the code of honor for the samurai **(51)**

capital   (KAP-ut-ul) money used to start a business **(200)**

capitalism   (KAP-ut-ul-iz-um) an economic system in which private individuals own businesses; they hope to gain a profit after all the expenses of running the business have been met **(111)**

cartel   (kar-TEL) a group that tries to control the production of a good or item in order to drive up the price **(147)**

cash crops   (KASH KRAHPS) crops raised to be sold instead of to be eaten or used; single crops that are a country's main source of export income **(201)**

chauvinism   (SHOH-vih-niz-um) extreme patriotism **(103)**

civil disobedience   (SIV-ul dis-oh-BEED-ee-unts) disobeying laws believed to be wrong or unfair **(94)**

civil service   (SIV-ul SUR-vus) people who work for the government in most jobs except military jobs **(27)**

client-states   (KLY-unt-STAYTS) nations or states that are completely dependent on another nation or state **(192)**

cold war   (KOHLD WOR) a feeling of tension and bad feelings without real fighting; the state of relations between the Soviet Union and the United States after World War II **(132)**

collective farms   (kuh-LEK-tiv FARMZ) large farms run by the government; farms set up in the Soviet Union **(137)**

collective security   (kuh-LEK-tiv sih-KYUR-ut-ee) a plan of defense in which members agree to act together if any one is attacked **(113)**

command economy   (kuh-MAND ih-KAHN-uh-mee) an economy in which the government owns the means of production **(192)**

communes   (KAHM-yunz) organized groups of people working together for a common purpose **(160)**

communism   (KAHM-yuh-niz-um) a system of government in which the state owns all businesses, factories, and farms **(107)**

computer   (kum-PYOOT-ur) an electronic machine that solves problems with great speed **(215)**

conservation   (kahn-sur-VAY-shun) protecting resources from loss or waste **(222)**

cooperatives   (koh-OP-uh-rut-ivs) organized groups sharing in work and costs **(160)**

czar   (ZAHR) the title of the ruler of Russia **(107)**

daimyo (DI-myoh) a land-owning feudal lord in Japan; a noble **(50)**

Deccan (DEK-un) the southern part of India, especially the large plateau in the central part of the south of India **(11)**

demilitarized (dee-MIL-ih-tuh-ryzd) the removal of all military forces and equipment from an area **(119)**

détente (day-TAHNT) an easing of tensions or bad feelings between countries **(141)**

Diaspora (dy-AS-pur-uh) the scattering of Jews from Palestine into many other countries **(97)**

dictator (DIK-tayt-ur) a ruler who has all the power to make decisions and who treats the people of the country in a way that is not democratic **(83)**

dictatorship (dik-TAYT-ur-ship) a situation in which one person or one party rules the government **(111)**

direct rule (duh-REKT RUL) rule of a colony by the imperialist country **(19)**

discrimination (dis-krim-uh-NAY-shun) a difference in treatment of a person or group **(166)**

dissidents (DIS-ud-unts) people who disagree with the established view **(141)**

economic depression (ek-uh-NAHM-ik dih-PRESH-un) a time when many people are out of work and business is poor **(113)**

electronics (ih-lek-TRAHN-iks) the use of electrical energy in vacuum tubes and transistors **(215)**

embargo (em-BAR-goh) a government order that does not allow trade between countries **(174)**

extended family (ek-STEND-ed FAM-lee) a family made up of parents, children, grandparents, aunts, uncles, and cousins; a family whose members may often live in the same house or the same neighborhood **(230)**

extraterritoriality (ek-struh-ter-uh-tor-ee-AL-ut-ee) a special right the citizens of a foreign country may have. They are tried by the laws and courts of their own country. **(42)**

fascism (FASH-iz-um) a political idea that glorifies one nation; in a fascist state, the power is held by a dictator **(112)**

gross national product (GROHS NASH-uh-nul PRAHD-ukt) the total value of goods and services produced in a country in a year **(199)**

guerrillas (guh-RIL-uhs) military troops who carry out war on an irregular basis **(165)**

hadj (HAJ) a pilgrimage to Mecca required of all Muslims **(68)**

Holocaust (HAHL-uh-kost) a word used to describe the murder of Jews during World War II; the term also means "devastation by fire" **(122)**

imperialism (im-PIR-ee-uh-liz-um) the system in which one country takes over other countries and rules them as colonies **(3)**

indemnities (in-DEM-nut-ees) payments to make up for some harmful actions **(45)**

indirect rule (in-duh-REKT ROOL) rule of a land by taking charge of its leaders or institutions; the other land does not become a real colony of the imperialist country **(18)**

inflation (in-FLAY-shun) an increase in prices and a decline in the value of money **(113)**

interdependent (int-ur-dih-PEN-dunt) depending on one another; in global terms, the idea that nations are bound to one another **(191)**

internal-combustion engine (in-TURN-ul kum-BUS-chun) an engine that burns fuel in an enclosed area; this type of engine produces gases that provide mechanical power **(214)**

isolation (eye-suh-LAY-shun) keeping apart from other countries **(52)**

isolationism (eye-suh-LAY-shu-niz-um) a policy of avoiding relations with other nations **(114)**

jihad (jih-HAD) a Muslim holy war **(147)**

Kuomintang (KWO-MIN-DAHNG) Chinese national party **(95)**

literacy (LIT-uh-ruh-see) the percentage of the people in a country who can read and write **(199)**

majority (muh-JOR-ut-ee) more than half the people of a country or place **(35)**

mandates (MAN-dayts) former colonies whose governments are watched over by other nations **(131)**

market economy (MAR-kut ih-KAHN-uh-mee) an economy in which individuals own the means of production **(192)**

martial law (MAR-shul LAW) a law carried out by military officials in an emergency **(139)**

mediation (meed-ee-AY-shun) settlement of a dispute by use of another party; his or her proposals are not binding **(105)**

minority (muh-NOR-ut-ee) less than half the people of a country or place **(35)**

Mogul (MOH-gul) one of the Muslim rulers of India in the 1500s and 1600s A.D. **(12)**

monsoon (MAHN-soon) a wind in the region of Southeast Asia; it blows in one direction in the summer and in another direction in winter **(61)**

morale (muh-RAL) a sense of common purpose or common goals **(159)**

mutiny (MYUT-un-ee) a rebellion against the people in charge **(19)**

nationalism (NASH-nul-iz-um) a feeling of pride in and devotion to one's country **(103)**

neutral (NOO-trul) not taking sides in a dispute **(105)**

non-renewable resources (nahn-rih-NOO-uh-bul REE-sohrs-ez) resources that cannot be replaced once they are used up **(209)**

non-violence (non-VY-uh-lunts) dealing with problems in a peaceful way **(10)**

nuclear energy (NYOO-klee-ur EN-ur-jee) energy stored in the nucleus of an atom **(207)**

nuclear family (NYOO-klee-ur FAM-uh-lee) a family made up of only parents and their children **(230)**

nutrients (NYOO-tree-unts) substances that aid growth and life in humans, plants, and animals **(222)**

pagan (PAY-gun) a person who believes in many gods **(68)**

pan-African (pan-AF-rih-kun) having to do with all of Africa **(96)**

parent country (PAR-unt KUN-tree) a country that takes over another country and rules it as a colony **(4)**

partition (par-TISH-un) divided into two or more parts **(182)**

passive resistance (PAS-iv rih-ZIS-tunts) a form of civil disobedience using nonviolent methods **(153)**

peaceful coexistence (PEES-ful koh-ig-ZIS-tunts) a situation in which two or more nations exist in a state of peace **(140)**

per capita income (pur-KAP-ut-uh IN-kum) a number found by dividing the total amount of money earned in a year in a country by the number of people in that country **(199)**

protectorate (pruh-TEK-tuh-rut) a country that is controlled by a stronger country but is not a colony of the stronger country **(28)**

province (PRAHV-ints) a part of a country **(60)**

queue (KYU) a man's hair style; one long braid is worn at the back of the neck and most of the rest of the head is shaved **(35)**

racism (RAY-siz-um) the belief held by people of one race that they are better than people of other races **(4)**

radiation (rayd-ee-AY-shun) the particles released in a nuclear reaction **(208)**

radioactive fallout (rayd-ee-oh-AK-tiv) the deadly particles produced in a nuclear bomb blast **(208)**

rajah (RAJ-uh) an Indian prince or ruler **(17)**

recession (rih-SESH-un) a drop in business activity that lasts for a limited time **(202)**

reform (rih-FORM) to try to make things better by change **(159)**

refugees (ref-yoo-JEES) people forced to leave their homeland and find a new place to live **(70)**

regent (REE-junt) a person who rules in place of a ruler who is too young or is not able to rule for other reasons **(12)**

samurai (SAM-uh-ry) a Japanese feudal knight or warrior **(50)**

sanctions (SANK-shunz) actions taken by one country against another; limits placed on the trade or actions of another country **(174)**

satellites (SAT-ul-ytz) countries that are politically or economically controlled by another country **(130)**

segregated (SEG-rih-gayt-id) to be kept apart; when people of different races are separated from one another **(20)**

self-sufficient (self-suh-FISH-unt) able to take care of one's own needs **(154)**

sepoys (SEE-poys) Indians who fought as soldiers for the British **(18)**

shah (SHAH) the title of the ruler of Iran **(147)**

shogun (SHOH-gun) Japan's most important military leader; the military leader who acted as the ruler of Japan **(51)**

socialism (SOH-shuh-liz-um) a system in which society as a whole owns all property and runs all businesses **(112)**

sphere of influence (SFEER-uv-IN-floo-unts) an area in which one country gets the right to trade in another, weaker country and to keep out other trading countries. Usually the stronger country has some control of the government as well. **(41)**

stalemate (STAYL-mayt) a condition in which little or no action is taken **(185)**

Sudan (soo-DAN) a grassland area that lies south of the Sahara and Libyan deserts; the Sudan area **(67)**

suttee (suh-TEE) a custom in which a wife must die when her husband dies; the wife throws herself on her husband's funeral pile **(11)**

tariff (TAR-uf) a tax on goods coming into a country **(18)**

technology (tek-NAHL-uh-jee) the use of science and invention to improve people's lives in practical ways **(36)**; the use of science and machines in everyday life to solve practical problems **(213)**

totalitarian (toh-tal-uh-TER-ee-un) a system of government that has total power over the lives of the people **(112)**

trek (TREK) a long and hard journey on foot **(77)**

typhoon (ty-FOON) a very powerful storm with heavy winds and rain; a heavy storm found in the Pacific Ocean **(51)**

viceroy (VYS-roy) person who is in charge of a colony; the viceroy rules in the name of the imperialist country's ruler **(19)**

Western (WES-turn) connected with the ideas, customs, and ways of life of Europe and America **(4)**

Zionism (ZY-uh-niz-um) Jewish nationalism; the movement for Jews to return to Palestine **(97)**

Pronunciation Guide to Chinese Place Names

The following is a list of Chinese place names mentioned in this textbook. The first spelling is in *pinyin*. This is a way of spelling Chinese names in English. *Pinyin* was introduced by the Chinese in the 1950s. The spelling in *pinyin* is followed by its pronunciation. The second spelling is in Wade-Giles. This is the older way of spelling Chinese names.

Page where used	*Pinyin* spelling	Pronunciation	Wade-Giles spelling
25,27,35,43	Huang Ho	HWANG HUH	Hwang Ho, Yellow River
25,27,28,35,43	Chang Jiang	CHANG JYANG	Yangtze River
27	Xizang	SEE TSANG	Tibet
28	Huai	HWY	Hwai
27,28,35	Hangzhou	HAN JOO	Hangchow
32,34,35,42,43,161	Beijing	BAY GING	Peking
35,42,43,161	Guangzhou	GWAN JOO	Canton
40,161	Shanghai	SHANG HY	Shanghai
43	Shandong	SHAN DOONG	Shantung
43	Lushun	LOO SHOON	Port Arthur
43	Nanjing	NAN GING	Nanking
43	Qingdao	CHING DOU	Tsingtao
43	Ningbo	NING BAW	Ningpo
43	Chongqing	JOONG GING	Chungking
43	Amoy	AH MOIH	Amoy (Hsiamen)
114	Yanan	YEN AN	Yenan

Index

Index

A

Photo Acknowledgments:

Unit 1

vi: Peabody Museum of Salem/Mark Sexton. **2:** Historical Pictures Service, Chicago. **8:** Art Resource. **11.** Air India. **12:** The Granger Collection. **15:** Historical Pictures Service, Chicago. **16:** Leo de Wys. **18:** Historical Pictures Service, Chicago. **19, 24:** The Granger Collection. **26:** Brown Brothers. **28, 31:** The Granger Collection. **32:** Leo de Wys. **33:** Brown Brothers. **34:** The Granger Collection. **36:** Historical Pictures Service, Chicago. **40:** Leo de Wys. **42:** The Granger Collection. **44:** Brown Brothers. **45L:** The Granger Collection. **45R:** Brown Brothers. **48:** VU/T. Stuart © 1984. **50:** Japan Airlines. **51:** Culver Pictures. **53:** The Granger Collection. **58:** VU/T. Stuart © 1984. **60, 63:** Culver Pictures. **68:** Photo Researchers. **69:** The Metropolitan Museum of Art, the Michael C. Rockefeller Memorial Collection, Gift of Nelson A. Rockefeller, 1972. Photograph by Jerry L. Thompson. **70:** Brown Brothers. **74:** Art Resource. **76:** The Granger Collection. **78:** Library of Congress. **82:** The Granger Collection. **85, 86:** Culver Pictures. **87:** Brown Brothers. **92, 94:** Culver Pictures. **95:** Historical Pictures Service, Chicago.

Unit 2

100: U. S. Navy. **102:** Marine Corps Museum. **104R:** Library of Congress. **104L:** UPI. **105:** Austrian Information Service. **112, 113:** UPI. **114:** Culver Pictures. **118:** Frederic Lewis. **121:** The Bettmann Archive. **122, 124:** UPI. **128:** United Nations. **129:** Frederic Lewis. **131:** German Information Center. **133:** U. S. Army. **138:** Sovfoto. **139L:** United Nations. **139R:** UPI/Bettmann Archive. **140:** U. S. Army. **144:** UPI/Bettman Archive. **146:** Art Resource. **147, 148:** United Nations. **152:** Frederic Lewis. **153:** Wide World Photos. **154:** UPI. **155:** Sipa Press/Art Resource. **158:** Ries/Leo de Wys. **160:** Rodale Press. **166:** Vidler/Leo de Wys. **167:** UPI. **168:** Sipa Press/Art Resource. **172:** Frost Publishing Group. **174, 176:** United Nations. **177:** UPI/Bettmann Archive. **180:** Reininger/Leo de Wys. **182:** Brown Brothers. **184:** Frost Publishing Group. **184:** Maous/Gamma. **185:** Abbas/Gamma.

Unit 3

188: Courtesy of Apple Computer, Inc. **190:** Photo Researchers. **192:** N.Y. Convention and Visitors Bureau. **193:** Freelance Photographers Guild. **198:** Wide World. **202:** United Nations. **206:** Dept. of Energy. **208:** Portland General Electric Company. **212:** Photo Researchers. **214:** Esther C. Goddard Photo. **215:** Harold M. Lambert/Frederic Lewis. **216:** Dept. of HEW. **220:** Alexander M. Chabe. **221:** Salt River Project. **222, 223, 224, 227, 230:** United Nations. **226:** Reynolds Aluminum. **228:** Frederic Lewis. **231:** Art Resource.